# Buddha's Lions

# Buddha's Lions

## The Lives of the Eighty-Four Siddhas

*Caturaśīti-siddha-pravṛtti*
by Abhayadatta

Translated into Tibetan as
*Grub thob brgyad cu rtsa bzhi'i lo rgyus*
by sMon-grub Shes-rab

Translated into English by
James B. Robinson

DHARMA PUBLISHING

TIBETAN TRANSLATION SERIES

*Buddha's Lions*
*Calm and Clear*
*Dhammapada*
*Elegant Sayings*
*Golden Zephyr*
*Kindly Bent to Ease Us*
*Legend of the Great Stupa*
*The Life and Liberation of Padmasambhava*
*The Marvelous Companion*
*Mind in Buddhist Psychology*
*Mother of Knowledge*
*The Voice of the Buddha*


For information address: Dharma Publishing, 2425 Hillside Avenue,
Berkeley, California 94704 USA

Library of Congress Cataloging in Publication Data

Abhayadatta.
Buddha's lions = Caturaśīti-siddha-pravṛtti.

(Tibetan translation series ; 10)
Includes facsimile reproduction of the Tibetan text.
Bibliography: p. 289.
Includes index.
1. Siddhas—Biography. I. Title. II. Series.
BQ342.A2313 294.3'092'2 [B] 79-12397
ISBN 0-913546-60-7 casebound

The illustrations of the siddhas which appear throughout the translation have been drawn under the direction of Tarthang Tulku by Rosalyn White from various sets of thankas and wood-block prints, some of which were provided by John C. Huntington; the text has been verified with the Tibetan and edited by Debbie Black; design and production by Merrill Peterson.

Typeset in Fototronic Baskerville, printed and bound by
Dharma Press.

9 8 7 6 5 4 3

# Contents

Foreword . . . . . . . . . . xi
Preface . . . . . . . . . . xiv
Introduction . . . . . . . . . . 2

The Translation

1. Lūyipa . . . . . . . . . . 22
2. Līlapa . . . . . . . . . . 25
3. Virūpa . . . . . . . . . . 27
4. Ḍombipa . . . . . . . . . . 33
5. Śavaripa . . . . . . . . . . 37
6. Saraha . . . . . . . . . . 41
7. Kankaripa . . . . . . . . . . 44
8. Mīnapa . . . . . . . . . . 47
9. Goraksa . . . . . . . . . . 50
10. Caurāṅgi . . . . . . . . . . 54
11. Vīnapa . . . . . . . . . . 57
12. Śāntipa . . . . . . . . . . 60
13. Tantipa . . . . . . . . . . 65
14. Camaripa . . . . . . . . . . 69
15. Khaḍgapa . . . . . . . . . . 72
16. Nāgārjuna . . . . . . . . . . 75
17. Kāṇḥapa . . . . . . . . . . 81

18. Karṇaripa ........ 86
19. Thaganapa ........ 90
20. Nāropa ........ 93
21. Shalipa ........ 96
22. Tilopa ........ 98
23. Catrapa ........ 100
24. Bhadrapa ........ 103
25. Khandipa ........ 106
26. Ajokipa ........ 108
27. Kalapa ........ 110
28. Dhombipa ........ 112
29. Kaṅkana ........ 114
30. Kambala ........ 117
31. Ṭeṅgipa ........ 121
32. Bhandhepa ........ 124
33. Tandhepa ........ 126
34. Kukkuripa ........ 128
35. Kucipa ........ 131
36. Dharmapa ........ 134
37. Mahipa ........ 136
38. Acinta ........ 138
39. Babhahi ........ 141
40. Nalina ........ 143
41. Bhusuku ........ 145
42. Indrabhūti ........ 150
43. Mekopa ........ 153
44. Koṭali ........ 155
45. Kaṃparipa ........ 158
46. Jālandhari ........ 161
47. Rāhula ........ 163
48. Dharmapa ........ 166
49. Dhokaripa ........ 168
50. Medhina ........ 170
51. Paṅkaja ........ 172

52. Ghaṇḍhapa ........................ 174
53. Yogipa ........................ 180
54. Caluki ........................ 182
55. Gorura ........................ 184
56. Lucika ........................ 186
57. Niguṇa ........................ 188
58. Jayānanda ........................ 191
59. Pacari ........................ 193
60. Campaka ........................ 196
61. Bhikṣana ........................ 199
62. Telopa ........................ 201
63. Kumaripa ........................ 203
64. Caparipa ........................ 205
65. Maṇibhadrā ........................ 208
66. Mekhalā ........................ 211
67. Kanakhalā ........................ 213
68. Kalakala ........................ 214
69. Kantali ........................ 216
70. Dhahuli ........................ 218
71. Udheli ........................ 220
72. Kapalapa ........................ 222
73. Kirava ........................ 224
74. Sakara ........................ 227
75. Sarvabhakṣa ........................ 231
76. Nāgabodhi ........................ 233
77. Dārika ........................ 236
78. Putali ........................ 240
79. Panaha ........................ 242
80. Kokalipa ........................ 244
81. Anaṅga ........................ 247
82. Lakṣmīnkarā ........................ 250
83. Samudra ........................ 254
84. Vyali ........................ 256
Colophon ........................ 259

## Appendices

Iconography . . . . . . . . . . 262
Comparative Chart of the Siddhas . . . . . . . . . . 284
Bibliography . . . . . . . . . . 289
  Sanskrit Works . . . . . . . . . . 289
  Tibetan Works . . . . . . . . . . 307
  Modern Works . . . . . . . . . . 307
Tibetan Text . . . . . . . . . . 311
Notes . . . . . . . . . . 392
Index . . . . . . . . . . 399

# Foreword

The siddha tradition could, in many ways, be considered the foundation of Tibetan Buddhism, for the siddhas and their lives provide us with a central vision of the Vajrayāna teachings, the way to live in perfect freedom. The siddhas offer a special form of realization that cuts through confusion, like wind through clouds, to reveal clarity and confidence, inner health and well-being. More than simply life stories, these biographies embody profound teachings designed to contribute to our inner development. When we understand the siddhas' teachings, it is possible that we, here, today, can gain enlightenment. The way is truly simple, and open to us.

Because the enlightened mind is beyond duality, the yogin and his teachings can manifest in any form: they may even be 'hidden' within our ordinary reality. Yet before we can take full advantage of the Vajrayāna teachings, there must be preparation, which may take many years. Such preparation may manifest in different ways, perhaps through experiencing deeply the frustrations of life in the world, or even by living a monastic life. After such preparation there must then be the right juncture of well-prepared disciple and enlightened teacher; only then can the teacher transmit the Buddha's realization, so that enlightenment may be found within a single lifetime.

This text is perhaps the most comprehensive work in Tibetan to be found on the siddhas, and the one most representative of the various siddha traditions in Tibet. All of the siddhas in this text are Indian Masters who could be considered the founders of the siddha lineages that passed into Tibet during the eighth to the eleventh centuries. The list of siddhas, as well as some of the facts of their histories may differ, however, according to the various lineages. For example, some will recognize the siddha Sakara as Padmasambhava although many aspects of his history as found here and elsewhere are not the same.

The siddhas often appear under different names when they show themselves in different forms. Śāntideva, for example, reveals several different aspects in this text, appearing not only as scholar and siddha, but also as the monk Bhusuku. Each of these aspects is so unique, it may be difficult to see them all as expressions of the same person. Likewise, although other of the famous philosopher-siddhas such as Dharmakīrti, Dignāga, Candrakīrti, Candragomin, and Mar-me-mdzad are among the eighty-four, we may not know them in their different manifestations.

These and other siddhas are remembered for their writings which are expressed both in narrative and in the form of *dohas*, songs of enlightenment. Just as the siddhas inspired growth in all those whose lives they touched, their songs can uplift the quality of our lives as well. For the teachings of the *doha*, while directed toward ordinary people, are not in ordinary language, but in a language illumined by understanding. This inner lightness points the way through surface meanings to unfolding levels of realization, making each *doha* the actuality of perfect liberation.

The translation of poetry is difficult in any language, and translation of the *doha* presents unique problems. These days translators often try to solve their difficulties by turning to dictionaries as their gurus, depending on words to point out the meanings of the teachings. Yet the Buddha's teachings, in being directly a way of life, themselves point to the need for direct contact with the living meaning and embodiment of the Dharma.

The way this translation came into being reflects an understanding of the need for this process. As much as was possible with the limited resources of this age and time, the translator, James Robinson, undertook his task in the traditional manner, going to a learned lama, a living source of the teachings, to discover the meanings and to clarify those passages which were unclear. That he felt such a responsibility to the text is important, for this book is a symbol of the teachings passing to the West as they once passed from India to Tibet.

Dharma Publishing was created to make works such as this available in English. At first, in this pioneer scholarship, there is bound to be a certain roughness. In the future, here as in Tibet, there will certainly be many editions and revisions that will finally polish these works to a final form. Texts such as this provide a foundation, and are an important contribution to the knowledge of Buddhism in the West.

Tarthang Tulku
Padma Ling, 1979

# Preface

In India and Tibet, it is customary to begin a text with invocation and praise of one's teachers. It is most appropriate that I, also, begin in this way.

It was the late Richard H. Robinson, while we were sitting on the shore of Lake Mendota in Madison, Wisconsin, who suggested that I study the lives of the siddhas and translate their biography. Anyone who works in Buddhist Studies owes a great deal to him; for he was not only a fine scholar, he was a memorable presence.

It was my very good fortune that Geshe Lhundup Sopa consented to serve as resource and advisor to this work. He spent many hours going over the stories with me—often more at my convenience than his—and offered many corrections to my translations. He is truly the embodiment of patience (*bsod pa*). Being a scholar of Mādhyamika and a logician of note, he was able to bring a highly trained and critical mind to the translating problems this work presented. He explained the various ways in which thoughtful people within the tradition have seen the siddhas. This sort of information is obtainable in no other way. He is an inexhaustible source of insight, truly an 'auspicious friend' (*dge shes*).

I also wish to thank Dr. Stephan Beyer and Dr. Minoru Kiyota, who were both, in their own ways, encouraging and instructive. Credit must also be given to Mr. Elvin Jones, whose sharp and incisive comments have contributed greatly to my understanding of Buddhism in particular and religion in general.

I wish also to thank my wife Linda, who was spared the original process of translation, but with patience endured its revision.

James B. Robinson
Cedar Falls, Iowa

# Buddha's Lions

# Introduction

The Tibetan text which is here translated is itself a translation of the *Caturaśīti-siddha-pravṛtti*, a Sanskrit text written in the late eleventh or early twelfth century by Abhayadatta, 'the Great Guru of Campāra'.[1] The book is essentially a collection of short biographies, though these narratives, while clearly anchored to historical figures and traditions, could perhaps best be considered as 'hagiography', writings from within a living tradition honoring holy or exalted individuals.

The eighty-four siddhas, in general, represent all those throughout the ages who have, within a single lifetime, attained direct realization of the Buddha's teachings. In particular, these eighty-four siddhas brought about the flowering of the Tantric tradition during the later period of Indian Buddhism. While the exact dates for individual siddhas are by no means certain, we do know that this tradition was most prominent from the eighth to the twelfth centuries, particularly during the Pāla dynasty. When Buddhism took firm root in Tibet, the siddhas provided important links between Indian and Tibetan Buddhism, giving life to lineages which have continued in Tibet up to the present.

The eighty-four individuals represented here are thus honored both for what they accomplished for themselves—direct realization of the Buddha's teachings—and for what they did for others. The siddhas, after attaining success in the Vajrayāna practice, guided innumerable living beings to liberation before they themselves left the world. The siddhas and their lineages are therefore venerated in a two-fold way: first, because through the power of their own efforts, they successfully followed the Vajrayāna path and won the highest spiritual attainment. Secondly, their personal verification of the path guaranteed that those who followed their tradition were indeed following a path leading to success.

As Buddhism passed into Tibet, the criterion for a valid religious doctrine was considered to be its connection with the Indian doctrines of the Buddha as carried on by those whose understanding was like a Buddha. Living examples of what it meant to be successful in practice, the siddhas, like all of the great teachers of Buddhism, preserved the doctrine by embodying it in themselves; they transmitted a living lineage. By following such a lineage, one follows the teachings of the Buddha himself and travels a path that can lead to liberation within one's lifetime.

In order to reach this goal, the Buddha taught that one must develop the wisdom (Sanskrit *prajñā*, Tibetan *shes rab*) that comes from unifying both knowledge and practice. Traditionally, there are three progressive phases in the accumulation of this transforming wisdom: the knowledge gained by 'hearing' the doctrine (since learning in classical India relied strongly on an oral transmission); the knowledge gained by critical reflection (since one must not simply memorize the data, but also sift and absorb it); and the knowledge produced in meditation (this knowledge being the culminating achievement effecting the transformation that leads to liberation).

The Buddhist tradition has always held that the first two of these steps, study and the development of understanding, are essential to successful practice. However, doing justice to both knowledge and practice is not a simple matter, and throughout the history of Buddhism, a balance between the two has not always been maintained, either individually or collectively.

As early Buddhism developed, meditation practice gradually became overshadowed by the exposition of doctrine, and the tendency to substitute information *about* wisdom for the direct realization of wisdom had the result, over many years, of producing fewer and fewer spiritually realized beings. In response to this decline in practice, the teachings of the Mahāyāna emerged. The early Mahāyāna did not see itself as a repudiation of the early tradition of the Hīnayāna, but as simply putting into practice what had been preached. With the Mahāyāna's ideal of the Bodhisattva, 'the Being Striving for Enlightenment', a strong emphasis was again placed on winning the goal of Buddhahood.[2] Rather than basically reserving Buddhahood for those who chose the monastic life, the Bodhisattva path puts the goal within the reach of the layman as well.

The Mahāyāna schools of philosophy flowered in the second century A.D. with the development of the Mādhyamika doctrine of the great master Nāgārjuna, and again in the fourth century with the development of the Yogācāra doctrine introduced by the teachings of Asaṅga. These doctrines articulated the perfection of wisdom that was salvation, and with these schools, Buddhism reached its full philosophic flowering in India.

But the development of these schools also brought about

a reemphasis on the informational aspects of wisdom. Often attention was directed to the mastery of argument rather than to the direct realization of the wisdom in question. The ideal of the unity of wisdom and practice was never completely forgotten, however, and there was always a place within the tradition for those who, not content with mere rote learning, wished to transform the philosophical tenets into principles for action.

It is in this context that the Vajrayāna, the Buddhist Tantric system, became prominent. For just as the Mahāyāna emerged to balance the scholasticism of the Hīnayāna, so the tradition of the Vajrayāna came to the fore to balance the scholasticism of the Mahāyāna. The Vajrayāna did not reject the Mahāyāna; it simply insisted that the doctrine be supplemented by rigorous practice.

The siddhas—practitioners of the Vajrayāna—did not repudiate traditional Buddhist teachings, but put them into practice. The siddhas include in their ranks such scholars as Śāntarakṣita and Śāntideva, who are well-known for their mastery of philosophic Mahāyāna. The tradition also includes Nāgārjuna and Asaṅga, for there is no contradiction in being both a great scholar and a Tantric adept, with all the powers that this status implies.

Nevertheless, although the greatest of the siddhas, such as Nāgārjuna, combined great scholarship with the highest realization, most of the siddhas took a more unconventional approach to the gaining of wisdom. In contrast to the monastic tradition, many of the siddhas did not study the Buddhist texts in preparation for meditation, but immediately and wholeheartedly applied the instructions they received to their experience. In their reemphasis on the value of meditative practice and its successful consummation, the siddhas conveyed the profound optimism of the Buddhist tradition that one can take on all the power and freedom of divinity by one's own spiritual effort. All that is required is the guidance of the guru and the willingness to follow the teaching through. By transforming all experience into meditation, the siddhas realized ultimate truth.

Because the siddhas were able to speak from the wisdom gained in the highest meditations, they offered a different perspective than those who relied merely on the wisdom gained by study and reflection. The internal transformation of consciousness, which is the winning of *siddhi*—success in practice—freed the siddha to act in whatever way would be most efficacious to transmit the doctrine. Understanding that all activity can be an expression of Buddha-nature, the siddhas at times exhibited very unconventional behavior. Many of the siddhas adopted the path of the yogin, and traveled from place to place teaching whoever was ready to hear the holy Dharma; in many cases, the siddha emanated a great light from his body, and even rose in the air to preach to the multitudes.

Over the years, the word *siddhi*, meaning 'success', came to imply the extraordinary powers or accomplishments which result from success in meditational practice. Since a siddha was one who possessed the *siddhis*, or magical powers, the word *siddha* came to carry a connotation of magician or wonderworker. However, the Buddhist tradition distinguished carefully between the two meanings of siddhi. The highest siddhi is enlightenment, which is the 'transmundane' siddhi of transcendent success. These transmundane siddhis are the 'unique' or 'not shared' siddhis, obtainable only by the Buddhist path. In our stories, the highest is called the siddhi of Mahāmudrā or 'the Success of the Great Symbol'.[3]

The second type of siddhi refers to the worldly or 'magical' powers, the 'shared' siddhis that are a natural by-product of meditation and yogic practice, and which are obtainable in any yogic or shamanic tradition that cares to develop them. The Indian tradition, so fond of lists, has enumerated several sets of these siddhis, including control of the elements, knowledge of the elixir of immortality,[4] possessing the gem that grants whatever one desires, having the powers of clairvoyance, and so forth.

While both types of spiritual success are superior to the ordinary life, the transmundane is by far the highest. Yet the worldly siddhis (powers of success) generally come first, and there is some danger that the siddha-to-be may mistake these newly-won abilities for liberation. If he does so, instead of winning liberation, he may give himself over to a subtle kind of bondage, for by allowing himself to be beguiled by lesser powers, the siddha prevents himself from taking that one step further to total liberation.[5] In order to continue his development and to win complete success, the siddha, after obtaining siddhi, must work for the benefit of all living beings; only then does he gain the highest knowledge. Magical powers, although an inevitable part of the yogic practice, serve merely as a sign of incipient success.

Some early scholars of Buddhism, and some modern Buddhist spokesmen, have tried to treat the 'magic' of the siddhas as an anomaly or as evidence of a corrupting external influence on Buddhism, not part of 'pure' Buddhism. But magical abilities have been accepted in the mainstream of Buddhist thought from the beginning, and are even mentioned frequently in the Sūtras. The most obvious analogues to the siddhis or 'magic powers' in the early Buddhist tradition are the *abhijñās* or superknowledges mentioned in the Pali texts, in particular the first *abhijñā*—frequently called *ṛddhi* or *ṛddhipāda* (Pali, *iddhi*)—which was control of the elements.

In the *Sāmañña-phala-sutta* there is a list of the powers gained by the aspirant on the Āryan path:

> With his heart thus serene, made put, translucent, cultured, devoid of evil, supple, ready to act, firm and imperturbable, he (the *śrāmaṇa*) applies and bends down his mind to the modes of the wondrous gift (*iddhi/ṛddhi*). He enjoys the Wonderful Gift in its various modes—being one, he becomes many or having become many, becomes one again; he becomes visible or invisible; he goes feeling no obstruction to the further side of a wall or rampart or hill as if through air; he penetrates up and down through solid ground as if through water; he walks on water without breaking through as if on solid ground; he travels cross-legged in the sky like the birds on the wind; even the sun and moon, so potent, so mighty though they be, he touches and feels with his hand; he reaches in the very body even up to the heaven of Brahman.[6]

Having won success on the spiritual path, the siddhas merely manifest the natural results of meditation. The sanctity and the extraordinary powers of the siddhas go hand in hand, a linking of magic and spirituality that may seem strange to us in our so-called 'rationalistic' culture, but which is taken for granted in the yogic tradition. Many of the extraordinary episodes in the stories reveal the powers which the siddhas use for the benefit of others. Virūpa concludes the song in which he recollects a number of these episodes by saying: "If I did not do these miraculous deeds, why would people prefer even the outer Dharma?"

The siddhas can fly through the air, change iron into gold, survive fires unharmed, stop the sun, and are generally responsible for some rather unusual occurrences. At the same time, these men and women are holy personages, responsible for the propagation of the Vajrayāna; they are the highest examples of the successful practice of the Buddhist path, the very embodiment of the Dharma.

Each of the stories in the text deals with an individual who was successful in Buddhist Tantric practice. Although the accounts can be divided into two major types—the brief conventionalized stories, and the longer, more individualized accounts of the more important figures such as Virūpa, Nāgārjuna, and others—all of the narratives are essentially summaries of careers, not detailed life stories. Clearly the author of this text was primarily interested in presenting an overview of this set of Tantric heroes and heroines.[7]

Whether or not a story is individualized, the narrative follows a certain set pattern, which, with repetition, takes on an almost ritualistic quality. The central figure is first introduced by name, caste, and country; there then follows the precondition of transformation: a life crisis, a desire for instructions, etc. Into this opening in the individual's life, the guru enters, almost casually. Once the individual expresses a desire for the Dharma, the guru gives initiation and instruction (which is often in verse). This is followed by an account of the practice of the student, an indication of the time it takes for the individual to gain success, and the winning of siddhi. The activities of the siddha after his or her siddhi are then narrated, followed by the departure of the siddha to the heavenly realm, and an occasional final moral. Since each of these elements, although simply presented, is rich in meaning, it may be useful here to discuss each element in turn.

Each of the siddhas is introduced by a 'siddha-name', which is rarely the name by which the siddha was known in ordinary life. A name may derive from a siddha's personal idiosyncracies or incidents that occurred during the siddha's practice; other names derive from the objects of meditation. In some instances, there are variant names (which are included in the iconography section of this volume).

Following the name, the siddha's occupation and caste are given. While the most famous of the siddhas were Buddhist monks, the majority were laymen, an unusual circumstance in a religion that, in India at least, centered upon its monastic element. Furthermore, most of the siddhas had lowly origins and worked in rather menial positions. The fact that they elevated themselves to the highest human possibilities clearly reinforces the teaching that one can find and take up the Dharma from any walk of life.

Of course, Buddhism has always been known for its break with the caste system of the Hindus, for the Buddha never refused to preach the Dharma to anyone on the basis of social standing. But while the Buddhist doctrine (unlike the Vedic tradition, which is to be taught only to the three highest castes) was free of the rigid social structure attendant upon the caste system, Buddhism did function within Indian society. As the various divisions of caste and occupation became progressively stronger, many individual Buddhists could not help but be influenced by it to one degree or another.

Some of the stories suggest that the lower classes were discriminated against in religious teachings; perhaps it was thought that since their karma had put them in their lower position, they were not fit vessels for the Dharma. Camaripa, the shoemaker, tells a yogin that he has been unable to find a guru in spite of his desire for the Dharma. Kaṃparipa, the smith, expresses surprise and joy that a yogin is willing to instruct him.

Because Buddhist yogins were free of the idea of purity and impurity, and recognized the emptiness of distinctions based on birth (the very keystone of the caste system), they taught all castes and all levels of society. Since the religious mainstream appeared none too eager to teach the marginal members of society, the siddhas and yogins moved in to fill the void, teaching anyone who was spiritually mature enough to receive the teachings beneficially.

The siddhas, however, were not partial to the lower classes any more than to the upper classes; being 'anti-establishment' can be just as sterile as its opposite. The fact that many of the siddhas were low caste may simply indicate that the lower classes were more receptive to the types of Dharma preached by the siddhas than were the upper classes, who tended to be more content with the types of religious teachings that supported the *status quo*.

The story of Bhadrapa shows an encounter between a wandering yogin and a rather stuffy Brahman. The Brahman spares no pains to tell the yogin that he finds him disgusting and unclean. But the yogin asserts that it is the Brahman's pretensions, not the yogin's habits, that are unclean. When the Brahman seeks to become the yogin's disciple, he must first make offerings of pork and liquor, both anathema to the caste-conscious man. Once he has broken with the restrictions of his caste, the Brahman is initiated by the yogin, and becomes a siddha himself.

The story of Bhadrapa reinforces what is suggested in other stories, i.e. that the yogins (and many of the siddhas were yogins) seeking their inner perfection were often at odds with the more conservative members of society. But the story also points out that anyone can reach perfection, even an establishment Brahman, once he has freed himself of notions of propriety that do not correspond to reality. The key factor is not whether one conforms or does not conform to a particular set of social norms; rather it is the state of mind with which one acts. Hence, if the rigid holding to social conventions is a barrier to one's development, then this must be overcome.

While factors such as birth and occupation mean little for the siddha, one's psychological condition is crucial. Turning from the ordinary life is the necessary first step to transformation, for if one is content with the usual run of life, there is little desire to change it. Only when discontent arises does one begin to look for a different way of being.

Such internal discontent often manifests as a life-crisis; Kankaripa and Kapalapa have lost loved ones and are grieving in the cemetery when the guru arrives. Because they are painfully aware of the transitory nature of the world, they are receptive to a new way of life. Tantipa, the weaver, and Rāhula must deal with the problem of old age. Their gurus tell them that the Dharma can give them comfort now that everything else is gone. Yet the comfort they are offered is not just a pious hope for a future life but practices that can effect a dramatic change in that very life. The old men devote their total minds to practice because they know they have little time left; and by correct practice, they manage to conquer even old age.

Others of those who will become siddhas are at first concerned with their material well-being in some way. Neither Tandhepa, who has lost his fortune at dice, nor Acinta, who is obsessed with his poverty, see any hope in their present circumstances. Change is the only way out of dead-end lives. Still others of the siddhas have some affliction which makes their lives nearly unbearable; the malady is physical in the case of Kucipa, mental in the case of the lazy Ajokipa.

The guru almost always presents the Dharma as being the solution for the individual's immediate problems as well as for his more abstract spiritual situation. The teachers of the Dharma do not forget the very mundane way in which the misery of samsara expresses itself in personal affairs; they know that a man with a toothache is often more concerned with ending his immediate pain than he is with the state of his spiritual development.

Yet not all the shocks that turn the individual from his ordinary concerns are unpleasant. Bhandhepa sees an arhat walking through the sky and is inspired to gain this ability himself. Udheli longs to go where the wild goose goes and so works for the power that brings flight. Śavaripa is so impressed by a feat of magic that he wishes only to emulate it, and thus makes the necessary effort for attainment. The wandering yogin himself, the genuinely free man, points by his very presence to the higher possibilities in human existence. Many of the protagonists, just by seeing this possibility embodied before them, take interest in and request the teachings.

The central motif of the lives of the siddhas is the change that occurs when the preliminary discontent or life-crisis leads to the appearance of the guru. The encounter of the siddhas-to-be with a spiritual advisor is the pivotal factor; until then, their aspirations are unfocused, problems seem unsolvable, and they cannot consummate their desires.

Though the siddhas may meet their gurus anywhere, more often than not the meeting takes place in a cemetery. While the siddha-to-be is walking across the cemetery or is hiding there, or is in mourning for the loss of a loved one, there in the cemetery he finds his guru. Of course, cemeteries have always been believed to be the abode of spirits. The very awesomeness of a place of the dead—which makes most people avoid it—gives rise to the fear that the siddha-to-be must directly confront. The cemetery is symbolic of samsara, the realm of those who are caught in cycles of suffering. Only the guru can bring the seeker from samsara, which is characterized by impermanence and death, to the perfection of the highest life.[8]

The guru is most often portrayed as a yogin, a wandering religious ascetic who follows the standard yogic life-style, living on what he can beg, sleeping in cemeteries, wearing patched clothes, and so forth. But the stories of Līlapa and Kaṅkana make the point that one need not give up the worldly life to attain liberation. At the end of the story of Līlapa, we are told: If you are able to bring together the guru's teachings, your own effort, and the requisite previous karma, then you can be released without abandoning even the goods of the world.

Needless to say, this is a very attractive offer to those who are interested in religious practice, but who do not feel called to the life of the yogin. The story of King Kaṅkana reveals this in a particularly effective way. The king is willing to practice the Dharma, but unwilling to wear patched clothes and eat leftovers. The yogin protests that asceticism is the best way, but faced with the king's adamant refusal, tells him of a method which does not require such sacrifices.

Although the guru usually appears as a yogin, this is not always the case. The guru may also appear in superhuman form: Nāgārjuna's teachers are Bodhisattvas who come to guide him at crucial moments of his life. The guru may also be a ḍākinī,[9] the feminine embodiment of wisdom, who appears when she is needed to provoke insight. In one story, Virūpa becomes so disgusted with his meditation, no sign of success having come in many years, that he throws his rosary into a latrine. A ḍākinī then appears, gives him back the rosary, and instructs him on correct practice. The story of Dharmapa tells of a man who desires to complete in practice what he knows intellectually; a ḍākinī then appears in a dream to instruct him.

In several of the stories the ḍākinī-guru is clearly a human female adept. Lūyipa's breakthrough occurs in his confrontation with a barmaid who is actually a ḍākinī. She recognizes what the difficulty is that is blocking his practice, and causes him to deal with it. Kambala's mother, who also serves as his teacher, is a ḍākinī, and Kāṇḥapa's woman, Bandhe, has extraordinary powers, though she otherwise appears as a very human person. Kantali is instructed by the ḍākinī Veṭalī who "took the form of a girl."

Buddhism, in general, has given a better place to women than many other Indian traditions, and the Buddhist canon records the existence of female arhats. But the Vinaya reveals that many in the Buddhist traditions believed that women would make progress only if under the firm control of men. Many said that only men could win enlightenment; the best a woman could hope for was to build up enough merit to win a superior male birth in the next life. Of course, this view rests on the assumption that there is something inherent in being female that prevents women from reaching enlightenment. The doctrine of emptiness in its practical applications denies precisely such assumptions. In a famous episode in the *Vimalakīrti-nirdeśa-sūtra*, Śāriputra, a monk representing the conservative viewpoint, exchanges bodies with a goddess, and comes to recognize that the marks of sex are empty and have no bearing on one's capacity for spiritual attainment.

While all the great masters of the Mahāyāna were men, women had a much more prominent place in the Vajrayāna. It is not clear exactly why this was so; it may be that the Tantric tradition simply took seriously the implications of the doctrine of emptiness, and put the teachings of the Sūtras into practice.[10]

Whether appearing in human or superhuman, male or female form, the guru is absolutely essential for the transformation of the life of the siddha-to-be. While Theravada meditation manuals specify the importance of receiving instructions from a competent teacher of meditation, and the *kalyāṇa-mitra* or 'auspicious friend' of the Mahāyāna plays an important role in that vehicle, the Vajrayāna guru is considered to be the embodiment of his doctrine, and so must be looked upon in a special way. Since he is a link in a succession of gurus which began with the Buddha or some other high being such as Vajradhara, he is to be treated as a living Buddha by his students. The student must give a total commitment of faith to his teacher; he must surrender himself to the teaching, holding nothing back and offering no resistance. The knowledge that the guru imparts is much more than just simple information; it is actually a potent psychological force within the student himself. The instruction of the guru is the vital link to the highest attainment, the direct cognition of reality that is salvation.

The guru communicates two things: initiation and instruction. The concept of communicating some sort of force is inherent in the term 'initiation' (Sanskrit *abhiṣeka*, Tibetan *dbang skur*), for in the Vajrayāna context, this term refers to a ritual of coronation with the transmission of power; initiation is preparation for becoming a king of the spiritual realm.

After the initiation, the guru gives instructions to the student in terms that he can put to immediate use. The teachings are pragmatic, in that the student's worldly occupation is often used as a vehicle for transcending the world; the student's characteristic activities become the method of liberation. Engaging in meditation, and continuing one's worldly activities, are not mutually exclusive, so long as both are done in the proper way. For example, the instructions given to Kaṃparipa, a blacksmith who develops a disgust for samsara and, in particular, for his work, are to make his customary activity, the source of his depression, into the means of his transformation.

The instructions of Camaripa are another example of taking daily life as a spiritual exercise. Discontented with the ordinary life, Camaripa meets a yogin who gives him instructions that transform his work as a shoemaker into a spiritual activity. He is told to identify the mental distortions (Sanskrit *kleśas*, Tibetan *nyon mongs*) and his conceptualizations, the roots of his bondage, with the leather of his trade. This leather is sewn onto the boards of friendliness and compassion (two of the Four Immeasurables generated in traditional Buddhist practice) with the cords of non-attachment to worldly concerns. The drill to be used in the sewing is the instruction of the guru, the instrument by which the ordinary life is penetrated. The result is not an obliteration of his mental pattern, but a transformation of it, just as the leather is changed into a shoe.

The guru's instructions fall into several different but widely overlapping categories. Sometimes the instructions are based on interpretations of basic Buddhist tenets such as the Four Immeasurables and the Six Perfections. The guru's instructions usually also involve certain practices and visualizations that are to be accomplished in meditation. In other cases, the student is encouraged to meditate upon specific points of doctrine that are expressed in terms clearly derived from the great philosophical schools, Mādhyamika and Yogācāra. For example, Nāgārjuna tells Kucipa that he must free himself from notions of being and non-being—since how can there be pleasure and pain if existing things themselves are empty of inherent nature?

Once the siddha-to-be receives the instructions of the guru, he wholeheartedly applies them to his life. There is no hesitation or resistance to the teachings; each of the siddhas portrays a quality of complete willingness to practice the Dharma. Given the instructions of the guru and this willingness to put them into practice, it is only a matter of time before the siddha attains success.

The Vajrayāna prides itself on being the short path, and various times are given for winning enlightenment, ranging from a few weeks to twelve years. To reinforce this point, most of the stories conclude by saying that the siddha went to the paradise realm in this very life, and in this very body—but only after spending many years working for the sake of living beings until many others were also enlightened.

The teachings of many of the siddhas survive in part in the Tangyur; many of these teachings are songs in the various vernaculars of India, indicating that the audience would be the ordinary people, not the scholars and philosophers for whom Sanskrit was the only acceptable medium of expression. And the language and form of the songs make it clear that they are not meant to be philosophical tracts; they are more like mystical sermons, exhorting others to the way of freedom.

Like the songs of the siddhas, their stories are intended to inspire others to achieve liberation through understanding their own experience. On first reading, the formulaic structure of the stories creates an impression of simplicity. But as acquaintance with the stories deepens, their simple structure, reinforcing the message of the narrative, moves the reader into a state of more profound awareness. Like spokes moving in toward the hub of a wheel, the different individual accounts of attaining siddhi express the basic unity of the human experience. It becomes apparent that the teachings of the Dharma are applicable to any life situation, and the reader comes to realize more fully that liberation is possible for every human being.

These individuals, men and women, kings and beggars, young and old, not only represent those who have in the past attained direct realization of the Buddha's teaching, but stand for all humankind as well—demonstrating that anyone, no matter what his or her initial state, can reach the highest human condition within a single lifetime. Just as the experience of the siddha opened to these highest possibilities, so the reader may also experience an opening to the highest teachings of the Dharma.

# The Translation

*Homage to the sacred gurus*

Herein is written the true account of the eighty-four siddhas, Lūyipa and the others: eighty men who gained clear understanding and obtained siddhi, and four women who achieved clear understanding and won liberation. This assembly of eighty-four is indeed most welcome. (The yoginīs Maṇibhadrā, Mekhalā, Kanakhalā, and Lakṣmīnkarā were objects of devotion for five generations of King Kunji's descendents.

# Lūyipa

Guru Lūyipa received his name because he ate the innards of fish. This is his story. Once there was a king as wealthy as Kubera, the god of riches. He not only had a palace decorated with jewels, pearls, gold and silver, he also had three sons. When the king died, an astrologer was consulted as to which of the sons would inherit the kingdom. After the astrologer had made his calculations, he announced: "If the middle son inherits the kingdom, the realm will be stable and the people will be content." So the middle son was given the kingdom.

The older and younger brothers, together with all the subjects, crowned him as king, even though he himself did not wish this. He attempted to escape the throne, but his brothers and subjects prevented him, and put him in chains of gold.

The prince gave out gold and silver as a bribe to his guards and retainers. At night, having dressed in patched clothes and having given gold to an attendant to accompany him, the king fled to Rāmaneśvara, the city of King Rāmala. There he gave up his cushion of silk and took one of rough cloth; having abandoned the royal quarters, he now slept in ashes. He was, however, so handsome to look upon, that everyone gave him food and drink, and he never lacked for sustenance.

The prince then went to Bodhgaya where the ḍākinīs cared for him and gave him instructions; after that he went to Saliputra, the residence of the king.[11] He ate the food people gave him and took up his abode in a cemetery.

One day, while on his way to a market place, he visited a tavern. The tavern owner, who was actually a worldly ḍākinī, saw the prince and thought, "He has thoroughly purified the four cakras, but he still has a pea-sized impurity: his opinion of his social status." Thereupon she poured rotten food into a clay pot and gave it to him. When the prince threw it away, the ḍākinī became angry and said, "If you have not abandoned the conception of good and bad food, how can the Dharma come to you?"

The prince realized that categories and distinctions are

obstacles to enlightenment, so he rid himself of them. He took from the Ganges the intestines of fish discarded by the fishermen, and he ate these during his twelve years of practice. When the fish-market women saw him eating innards, they called him Lūyipa, 'Old Fish Guts'. He was famous everywhere as Lūyipa, and he obtained siddhi under this name. The rest of his story appears when telling of Ṭeṅgipa, and of Dārika, the man of the prostitutes.

# Līlapa

There was a king who sat upon a lion throne in south India. A yogin from another land came into his presence, and the king said to him: "You must be suffering greatly, wandering here and there in the kingdom." "I am not suffering," said the yogin. "It is you who are suffering." "Why do you say that?" asked the king. "You are afraid that you will lose your kingdom, and worried that your subjects may be discontented. That is why you suffer. Even if I were to jump into a fire, I would not burn. Even if I ate poison, I would not die. I will not suffer old age and death, because I have the instructions of the alchemists." The king took faith and said, "I cannot wander the kingdom like you can, but I can meditate while staying in my royal quarters. Would you give these instructions to me?" The yogin, hearing this, gave him the initiation of Hevajra and instructed him in the samādhi of a single-point.[12]

The king meditated on his lion-throne with its soft cushions of silk, surrounded by his wife, his ministers, and various kinds of musical entertainments. He meditated even during the night; but because of his sensuous enjoyments, he was known as Līlapa, 'the Sporting Man'.

Continuing to follow the instructions, he meditated unwaveringly on the ring on the finger of his right hand. Having done that, he visualized the divine hosts of Hevajra there. He then joined the Developing Stage and the Perfecting Stage and his perfect comprehension arose by its own power.[13] He obtained the siddhi of Mahāmudrā and then many qualities such as the superknowledges.

Therefore, if you collect these three together—the guru's teaching, your own effort, and the requisite previous karma—you can be released even without giving up the good things of the world. Līlapa aided innumerable sentient beings and then went to the realm of the Ḍākas.[14]

# Virūpa

Virūpa was born in the East, in Tṛipura, the city of King Devapāla.[15] There was, in south India, a vihāra called Somapurī,[16] 'the City of the Moon': a Dharma-circle with thousands of monks, a veritable ocean of them. Though he was only a novice, Virūpa asked for initiation. In twelve years, Virūpa twice-over recited the mantra of Vajravārāhī[17] a million times; but not one sign of siddhi came to him even in a dream. He became despondent at this, tore up his rosary, and threw it into the latrine. That evening, when he customarily gave worship, it occurred to him that he was without his rosary. A ḍākinī then appeared, put a rosary in his hand, and gave him these words of encouragement: "O worthy aspirant, do not despair for my blessing. Perform the practice that abandons all names and conceptions."

This place of the natural mind
is the essence of Vajravārāhī.
This is so for you as for everyone else;
you are inexperienced like a child.
The wishing gem of the mind
is not polished by conceptualizations.
To know the best of practice is sufficient.

Virūpa then practiced for twelve years, and obtained siddhi. His servant bought meat and wine and brought it to him; Virūpa then killed and ate the pigeons in the vihāra. When all the pigeons were gone, the monks asked, "Who among us would eat pigeons? Surely no monk would do such a thing." The monks then looked in all the cells, also going to Virūpa's room. As they looked in the window, they saw him drinking wine and eating pigeon meat. The monks then assembled and decided to expel Virūpa from the vihāra. So Virūpa offered his monk's robes and begging bowl in front of an image of the Buddha, did reverence, and left. As he was leaving, a monk said to him, "Where will you go now?" And Virūpa replied, "You expelled me; why should you care?"

Beside the vihāra there was a large lake. Virūpa cut off a

lotus flower floating on the water and offered it to the Buddha. Then, placing his foot on a lotus leaf at the edge of the lake, he walked across the water to the other shore. Those who were in Somapurī deeply repented; they grasped Virūpa's feet, did reverence to him, and asked him, "But why did you kill the pigeons?" "I did not kill them," Virūpa said, and he told his servant to bring him the pieces of the pigeon's wings. The master[18] snapped his fingers, and the feathers became pigeons again, which flew off bigger and better than before. This was seen by everyone. From then on, Virūpa put aside the habit of a monk and took on the ways of a yogin.

When Virūpa came to the bank of the Ganges, he begged food and drink from the Ganges goddess, but she did not give him any. The master became angry, parted the waters, and went to the other side.

In the city of Kanasati, Virūpa bought wine from a tavern girl; she gave him a glass of wine and a plate of rice which he greatly enjoyed. He continued eating and drinking. For the space of two days and a night, he prevented the sun from moving and the king, amazed, exclaimed: "Who is it who performs such a miracle?" In answer, the goddess of the sun appeared to the king in a dream and said, "A yogin has pledged me as payment to a tavern girl." The king and his subjects paid the price of the wine, which came to a million glasses, and Virūpa disappeared.

Virūpa then went to the land called Indra in the country of the idolators. In this place, there was an image, eighty-one cubits high, of Śiva as 'the Great Lord' Maheśvara. The inhabitants told Virūpa to do reverence to the image, whereupon Virūpa replied, "In no system does the older brother do reverence to the younger brother." The king and the others then said to him, "If you do not give reverence we will kill you." But the master replied, "It would be a sin to give reverence to it; so I will not bow down." "Then let the sin fall on me," said the king.

When the master brought his hands together and bowed down, the great statue of Śiva split in half. A voice coming from the sky called forth: "I vow to listen to you." After taking the oath, the statue was restored to its previous condition. The people made the offerings of the statue of Śiva to the master, and were then converted to Buddhism. It is said that the offerings still exist.

After that, the master went to the east of India to Devīkoṭa where the entire population of the country had become witches.[19] If anyone stayed in their castle, they put a spell on him.

The master, having arrived at this place of the witches, found food in the town, but no place could he find lodging. He met with a single Buddhist, a young Brahman, who told him that there were no humans left in the land, that all had become witches, and they were doing great harm to everyone. The master and the Brahman boy then proceeded to the temple where the master stayed. There the master initiated the Brahman boy and gave him mantras.

All the witches having gathered, they said among themselves, "What is to be offered: there are all kinds of meat here, but we have no human flesh." One of them spoke up and said, "I have two victims for you!" "Bring them here!" they all cried. But when the witch tried to bring them he was not able to do so, because of the power of the Brahman child. She tried over and over again, but to no avail.

The witches then saw Virūpa sitting on a fallen tree. They carried him away together with the tree; but although they planned to cook him, Virūpa drank up all the wine they were using as broth. They then thought to kill him another way: all the witches together made a hissing sound, but Virūpa just laughed twelve fearful laughs, and all the witches fainted dead away.

Later Virūpa bound the witches by oath: that from then on, they would take the Buddhist refuges and would not harm any who had faith in him. They were not to harm any living being, so they could only drink a handful of blood from the bodies of those who had not taken the refuges or who had not produced the thought of enlightenment. If they broke this oath, their necks would be cut off with his discus, and the Yakṣa of the North would drink their blood. Even now, the form of that discus and that yakṣa can be seen in the sky. He then bound the witches by oath and put them in the retinue of the Dharma-protectors.

Again Virūpa returned to Devīkoṭa. On the road, Śiva and the goddess Umā created for him a phantom city with 450,000 inhabitants, and the gods of the thirty-three heavens and all the divine realms made him extensive offerings of food. Virūpa spoke to them in verse:

As a novice and monk in Somapurī
I faithfully carried out the Vinaya,
and then, by power produced by previous karma,
I gained full initiation and teachings.
For twelve years I meditated with conceptions
and nothing occurred, even in a dream;
my weary mind cursing, I threw away my rosary.
After that, a ḍākinī appeared to advise me:
because of this, I strengthened myself
and rightly understood the character of samsara.
From then on I practiced without conceptions,
although the monks believed I was misbehaving.

So in order to destroy their misconceptions,
I walked on water without sinking.
I reversed the course of the Ganges, and while enjoying
myself,
I put up the sun as a pledge.
I split the idol of the idolators, breaking its pride,
and in Devīkoṭa, I controlled the witches.
When Śiva saw my many powers
he created a city to make me offerings.
Now, if I did not do these miraculous deeds,
why would people prefer even the outer Dharma?

Then he went to the realm of the Ḍākas.

# Ḍombipa

In the country of Magadha, there was a man of royal birth who had attained siddhi from Hevajra. He had been initiated by the guru Virūpa, and having been granted the instructions, he experienced their meaning. Though he regarded his subjects as a father thinks of his only son, the people did not know that their king had entered the door of the Dharma. But he was kindly by nature, so all the people unanimously affirmed: "This king is indeed a pious man."

One day, the king said to his minister: "The people are suffering in our country. Thieves and robbers are destroying property, and because of the people's little merit, there are increasing numbers of the poor and indigent. To deliver the land from fear and poverty, hang a great bell on the trunk of a tree. If anyone witnesses a crime or sees poverty, let him strike this bell." The minister did as he was told, and fear and poverty were brought to an end in Magadha.

A while later, a group of low-caste singers came to the capital, offering to sing and dance for the king. One of the singers had a twelve-year-old daughter who was very attractive. She had a lovely face and a good complexion; furthermore, she was unsullied by worldly thoughts and had all the qualities of a *padmaṇī*. So the king said to the low-caste singer, "Would you give your daughter to me?"

To this the singer replied, "Your majesty is a king of Magadha—you rule 800,000 cities. Because of your royal wealth, you do not have to work for a living. We are of low caste, denigrated and shunned by other classes of people. It is not fitting for you to make such a request."

The king made his request again, but in a more forceful way; he took the girl, after giving her father a sum equal to her value from the treasury. For twelve years, the people did not know that she was the king's Tantric consort; but eventually it was discovered. Soon it became known to everyone throughout Magadha: "The king consorts with a low-caste woman." So the king abdicated in favor of his son, and with his low-caste mistress, went into the forest. There he practiced for twelve years.

But the fortune of the land diminished by degrees, until finally the son and his people were no longer able to hold the country. The citizens assembled, and after conferring among themselves, sought the former king to offer him the kingdom once again.

A delegation went to the forest where the king was residing: there they saw him sitting at the base of a tree, while his woman went out to draw water. She stepped out on a lotus leaf on the surface of the lake and, without sinking, drew water from a depth of fifteen fathoms; she then brought it back to the king. The men were so amazed that they returned home to report what they had seen to the populace, who then sent an invitation to the king to call him back to the throne.

The king and his consort came riding out from the forest on a young tigress, using a poisonous snake as a whip. The people were astonished and said, "Surely if you rule the country everything will prosper. Will you please take the kingdom?" But the king replied, "If I am of low-caste, how am I fit to take the kingdom? After death, it no longer matters whether caste is good or bad; burn us in the fire, and when we are born again from it, I will do as you ask." So the people burned the two, king and consort, in a fire fueled with sandalwood: because there was so much wood, the fire burned for seven days. But within the fire they caught glimpses of the couple transformed into Hevajra and his consort, in a self-produced body, shining like dew. When they saw this, the people of Magadha took faith, and the king became known as the master Ḍombipa, 'He of the Low-caste Ḍombis'.

The king then spoke to all his ministers and subjects: "If you are able to do as I have done, I will rule you. If you cannot, I will not be king." All of the people were taken completely by surprise, and replied, "How could we do what you have done?" At this the king declared, "In this kingdom, there is little of benefit and much that is of fault; rather, I will rule a kingdom of the Dharma." From there he went to the realm of the Ḍākas for the sake of sentient beings.

# Śavaripa

On the mountain called Vikrama, in the mountains of Manda, there was a hunter named Śavaripa, who brought harm to many living beings by killing many animals and eating their flesh. This was the way he made his living.

Avalokiteśvara saw this hunter and became filled with compassion. In order to convert him, he transformed himself into a hunter like Śavaripa and went to where the hunter resided. The hunter asked him, "Who are you?" "I am also a *śavari*," Avalokiteśvara replied. "Where do you come from?" asked Śavaripa. "From far away," was the reply. "You have only one arrow. How many deer can you shoot with only one arrow?" "With it I can kill three hundred deer," the embodied Bodhisattva said. At this, Śavaripa exclaimed, "I would like to see a demonstration!"

On the next day, the manifestation took Śavaripa to a great plain and showed him five hundred deer, all of which had been produced by magic. As soon as Śavaripa saw them, he asked the embodiment, "How many of these deer will you kill with your arrow?" "I will kill all five hundred," was the reply. But Śavaripa said sarcastically, "Spare four hundred. It is enough to shoot one hundred deer." Thereupon the manifested Bodhisattva shot one hundred deer with the one arrow. He then asked Śavaripa to retrieve one of the dead deer; when Śavaripa was not able to lift it, the hunter's pride was broken. They returned home, and Śavaripa asked the Bodhisattva, "Teach me how to shoot an arrow like that." At this, the Bodhisattva replied, "For this teaching, you must give up eating meat for one month." So Śavaripa gave up his habit of harming and killing living beings.

The embodied Bodhisattva returned in seven days and asked Śavaripa, "What have you been eating?" "My wife and I have been eating fruit," Śavaripa replied. The manifestation then instructed, "Meditate kindliness and compassion for all living beings."

After a month, the Bodhisattva returned again. Śavaripa said, "Now you have taught me the Dharma of letting the deer escape." The Manifestation then produced a mandala, put flowers around it, and instructed Śavaripa and his wife to look into the mandala and to tell him what they saw there. They looked within the mandala and saw the eight great hells, with the two of them burning in it. They became afraid; they gasped, shuddered, and could not speak.

The embodied Bodhisattva asked them again what they saw, and Śavaripa finally replied, "I saw people just like us burning in hell." "Are you not afraid of being born there?" asked the Bodhisattva. "We are indeed afraid," they replied. "Is there any way we can be saved from such a fate?" "If there is a method, would you be willing to practice it?" "We are willing," they said. And so the Bodhisattva preached the Dharma to Śavaripa and his wife:

"When you take a life, there are various kinds of karma produced. You will be reborn in hell. Killing gives rise to a disposition to further taking of life, with the inherent result that your own life is short. The outer reflection of all this is that you will be very unattractive.

"But if you refrain from taking life, you may well obtain enlightenment. When you do not have the desire to kill, the inherent result will be a long life. The outer reflection of all this is that you will be born with considerable personal magnetism."

He preached to them the unpleasant results of the ten non-virtuous actions,[20] and the benefits of the ten virtues. And Śavaripa, now disgusted with samsara, obtained a firm and unwavering faith in the Dharma. Avalokiteśvara gave them further instructions, and then returned to the mountain Dodanti.

Having meditated great compassion without conceptualizing for twelve years, Śavaripa attained the superior siddhi of Mahāmudrā. He passed from the highest condition of great compassion, and went before the holy

Avalokiteśvara. The Holy One highly praised the qualities of Śavaripa: "O well-born son, the one-sided nirvana which is like a grass-fire going out is not the best kind. You should remain in the world for the sake of sentient beings, and benefit inconceivable numbers of beings."

So Śavaripa returned to his own land, where he remained. He is called Śrī Śavari. Because he clothes himself in peacock feathers, he is also called 'the Peacock-wing Wearer', and because he always stays in the mountains, he is called 'the Mountain-dwelling Hermit'. These are the three names by which he is known. He teaches the fortunate by song and symbol, and will remain on the continent of Jambudvīpa in this body until the coming of Maitreya the future Buddha.

# Saraha

Saraha, the son of a ḍākinī, was born a Brahman in a city called Roli in a particular part of Rajñī, in the east of India. Though he was a Brahman, he had faith in the Dharma of the Buddha, and because he had listened to the

Dharma from innumerable masters, he had trust in the Tantric doctrine. During the day, he practiced the Hindu system; at night, he practiced the Buddhist system. He also drank wine.

There came a time when this was discovered by the Brahmans, who then attempted to have him banished. They went to King Ratnapāla and said to him, "You are the king. Is it proper for you to allow a disreputable system of religion to be practiced in your country? Even though Saraha, 'the Arrow-shooter', is chief of fifteen thousand residences in Roli, he has lowered himself in caste by drinking wine, and therefore must be expelled."

The king, not wanting to expel a man who controlled fifteen thousand households, went to Saraha and said, "You are a Brahman; it is not fit that you drink wine." But Saraha replied, "I do not drink wine. Gather all the men and those Brahmans here, and I will take an oath to that effect." After they had gathered, Saraha stated, "If I have been drinking wine, let my hand burn. If I have not been drinking, may it not burn." He then put his hand in boiling oil, and it was not burnt. "In truth, he does not drink wine," the king said. But the Brahmans said, "But truly he does drink wine."

So Saraha spoke as before. He drank molten copper and was not burnt. "He still drinks," the Brahmans maintained. Saraha then said, "Whosoever sinks when entering the water, he is the one who drinks. If he does not sink, he does not drink." So he and another Brahman both entered the water. Saraha did not sink, but the other one did, so they finally said, "Saraha does not drink."

Similarly, Saraha was weighed on a scale: "Whoever is heavier does not drink," he said. They put three iron weights on the scale, each as heavy as a man, and still Saraha was heavier than the weights. He was heavier than even six of those weights. Finally the king said, "If anyone who has powers like these drinks wine, then let him drink."

The king and the Brahmans bowed to Saraha and asked for his instructions. Saraha then sang to the king, the queen, and all the subjects, of the three cycles of Doha.[21] The Brahmans all abandoned their own system and became Buddhists. The king with all his retinue attained siddhi.

Saraha married a fifteen-year-old house girl, left his home, and went into another land. He settled in a solitary place, where he practiced the Dharma while the girl went out begging for his food. One time, he asked her to prepare some radishes for him. She mixed some radishes in yogurt and took them to him, but he was sitting in meditation, so she went away without disturbing him.

Saraha remained uninterruptedly in meditation for twelve years. When he finally arose, he asked, "Where are my radishes?" The serving girl replied, "How could I keep them? You have not arisen from meditational trance for twelve years. It is now spring, and there are no radishes." Saraha then said to the girl, "I will go to the mountains to meditate." But the girl replied, "A solitary body does not mean solitude. The best solitude is the mind far away from names and conceptions. You have been meditating for twelve years, yet you have not cut off the idea of radishes. What good will it do to go to the mountains?" Saraha thought, "This is true." And so he abandoned names and conceptions.

By experiencing the essential meaning, he obtained the highest siddhi of Mahāmudrā, and furthered the aims of living beings. He, together with his woman, entered the realm of the Ḍākas.

# Kankaripa

There once was a low-caste householder of Maghahura who married a woman of the same caste. Experiencing the taste of domestic pleasures, he cared only for the things of this world, and did not direct his mind, even a little, to the virtues which are the path of liberation. Then karma ripened for his wife, and she died. He took his wife's body to the cemetery, and then was not able to leave the corpse. He just stayed beside it, weeping. A yogin of good understanding came up to him and asked, "Who are you and what are you doing in the cemetery?" The householder replied, "O yogin, do you not see my condition? I am a blind man whose eyes have been torn out. My good fortune is exhausted without my wife. Is there anyone in the world worse off than I?" The yogin then said to the householder:

"The end of birth is death. The end of composition is separation. All composite things are impermanent. Since everyone who lives in samsara suffers, do not grieve over the world's painful nature. What do you accomplish by guarding a corpse that is like a lump of clay? You can end your suffering only by means of the Dharma."

"If there is a method that would liberate me from the misery of birth and death in the world, please give it to me," said the householder. In reply the yogin said, "I have the guru's instructions which will bring about liberation." "Then I ask for them," said the householder. And the yogin proceeded to initiate him and to give him the instructions on the essence of egolessness.

The householder then asked, "How shall I meditate?" The yogin replied, "To get rid of the notion of your dead wife, meditate on your wife, devoid of self, as the nonduality of emptiness and bliss." Then he set the householder to meditating.

Finally, after six years, the householder shed the ordinary concept of his wife in emptiness and bliss. He cleared away the stains of the mind, and he experienced the inner experience of the pure light and great joy. He purged the poison of lethargy, and he awoke from ignorance. Having cleared away his error and delusions, he saw the unmistaken truth, and he obtained siddhi. He became famous in all directions as the yogin Kankaripa, and having preached the Dharma to many people in his own country of Maghahura, he went to the realm of the Ḍākas in this very body.

# Mīnapa

Mīnapa's country was in eastern India, and his caste was that of the fishermen. His guru was Mahādeva, and the siddhi which he obtained was worldly siddhi. In an ocean called Ita in Kāmarūpa,[22] every day the fishermen would fish and then sell their catch in the market. One day a certain fisherman fastened his hook with a cotton thread, and after baiting it with meat, threw it into the water. A huge fish took hold of it, tugged and jerked away, and pulled the fisherman into the water. The fish then swallowed the fisherman, but by the power of the man's karma, the fisherman did not die.

Now at that time, the goddess Umā was asking Mahādeva about the Dharma. Mahādeva said to her, "My Dharma is not to be expressed to just anyone. It is very secret, so let us erect a house under the ocean." Having thus spoken, it was done accordingly, and in the dwelling under the ocean, he preached the Dharma to the goddess Umā.

At this time, the fish who had swallowed the fisherman swam under the house. Now, during the explication of the Dharma, Umā had fallen asleep, so when Mahādeva asked her if she understood, the fisherman answered, "I understand." And so he heard the Dharma.

After the Dharma was preached, and when the Goddess had ended her sleep, she asked for the teaching, and Mahādeva said, "I have just spoken it." The Goddess replied, "I heard only up to the middle. I was then overcome by sleep, and I heard no more." "Then who was it who answered 'I understand'?" "I did not speak those words," said the Goddess.

Mahādeva then looked out with his superior sight and saw that the one who had heard the Dharma was a man in the stomach of a fish which had swum beneath his house. Since the fisherman had become his pupil, Mahādeva thought, "We are now of the same commitment." So he gave the fisherman initiation, and the fisherman meditated in the belly of the fish for twelve years.

At this time, a fisherman in the land of Śrītati caught the

fish and landed it. The fisherman thought, "How heavy! In the belly of this fish there must be gold, silver, and many other precious things." But when he cut open the belly of the fish, there appeared a man who told him, when asked, that he had been a fisherman at the time of king such-and-such. "This fish gulped me down and bore me off." When the people counted up the years and arrived at the figure of twelve years, they were extremely surprised, and the fisherman thus became famous as the yogin Mīnapa. Given offerings by everyone, Mīnapa danced all over the land, his feet never imprinting the ground. Once, however, he danced on a stone and his foot sank into it as if it were mud. Everyone was amazed. There he stood and sang from the stone:

> Now I am free of my previous karma;
> now I rejoice in the Dharma.
> The precious qualities arose in this way;
> O wonderful my precious mind!

Thus he sang for five hundred years for the welfare of all living beings. He held the name Mīnapa, and the name Vajrapāda, and the third name Acinta, 'Not Contained by Thought'. Having first obtained all the worldly powers of siddhi, he gradually progressed through the path and went bodily into the realm of the Ḍākas.

# Goraksa

In a country of eastern India, there lived a king named Devapāla who had only one son. When the prince was twelve years old, his mother became ill and was near death. Just before she died, the mother gave her last testament to her son: "All the happiness and misery of living beings arises from virtuous and nonvirtuous deeds. Even if it means you lose your life, do not do anything nonvirtuous." Then she died. The citizens of that land all advised the father, the king, to marry a queen from another country, and so he did. A few days after he married this queen, the king went into the forest to dispel his grief. The queen then went to the tower of the palace and looked out. Seeing the young prince, lust arose in her, and she sent him a message, which said: "Please come to me." But the prince refused.

The queen, embarrassed, thought to herself: "He holds me in contempt." She grew more bitter toward the prince than toward an enemy, and she thought to herself, "I must find some means to destroy him." She told her followers to kill him, but they refused, saying: "It would not be right to kill the prince, the son of a king, a holy person."

After they had refused, the queen carried out a deception: She cut herself all over her body until the blood flowed, and then she lay naked on her bed. When the king returned, he questioned her: "What terrible misfortune has befallen you?" "Your majesty's son has mistreated me in the way of a man," she replied, "and then left me in this fashion." The king, in anger, said to her, "If this has been done to you as you say, the prince will be killed." The king then gave orders to the two executioners: "Take the prince into the deep forest and cut off his hands and feet."

The executioners considered: "It is not right to kill the prince. We will save him by killing one of our own sons instead." The executioners then revealed their plan to the prince, saying, "We dare not kill Your Highness; we will kill one of our own sons for your sake." But the prince rejected this, saying, "That surely is not right. Kill me. In her last testament, my mother said, 'Do not do anything evil, even to save your body or your life.' Carry out the orders of my father." So the two executioners set the prince down at the foot of a tree, cut off his hands and feet, and then returned home.

Now, in that country there was a great yogin named Acinta who had initiated the prince and given him instructions. The yogin went among the herdsmen who were working about a kilometer distant from the prince, and the yogin said to them, "There is a man with his limbs cut off at the base of a tree above which the vultures are circling. Who is willing to go to him?" A small boy, the son of an incense seller, said, "I am willing to do it; but while I carry out your task, you must do mine."

And so he gave over the cattle he was watching to the yogin, and using the circling vultures as a landmark, he went to the tree. After seeing the man at the foot of it, he returned to the yogin and said, "It is as you say."

The yogin then asked the cowherd, "What do you have to eat and drink?" The boy replied, "I stay with the master of the herdsmen, and he gives me enough to eat and drink; I will take half to that man." "Good," said the yogin. "Now take care of him. His name is Caurāṅgi." So the boy made a roof of leaves around the tree, and after giving food to the prince, cleansed the impure things from the prince's wounds with his hands. He helped in this way for twelve years.

Then one day the boy arrived and saw the prince standing. Amazed, he asked how this could be, and the prince answered, "A holy guru, skilled in means, brought me to realize emptiness. How wondrous it is to know the one true nature of existing things and so to be without pleasure and pain! In accordance with reality, my hands and feet have grown again." Then he rose up in the air, saying to the cowherd, "You have been given instructions by me; now practice them."

But the herdsman replied, "I do not wish instructions. I have a master who asked me to make offerings to you, and I have acted accordingly." Having said this, he turned around and returned to guard his herd. When the yogin Acinta came again to the cowherd, the herdsman told of his experience, and the yogin rejoiced. Acinta then initiated the cowherd and gave him instructions. He then left for another land.

The cowherd meditated and obtained the siddhi of Mahāmudrā. When this happened, the guru returned, and said to him, "Do not depart from this world until you have awakened to enlightenment a hundred times a hundred living beings." Thereupon the herdsman initiated every living being who came to him.

Mahādeva chided him, saying, "You should not initiate everyone who comes to you. It is not fitting to teach those who lack discernment or faith. Give initiation only to those beings who make the proper request." The cowherd then did as he had been counseled.

Since he was a cowherd, he became famous everywhere as Goraksa. Even now, if you have pure karma, you may be initiated by him—you will then be able to hear the sound of his drum on special days though others will not hear it.

# Caurāṅgi

The story of how Caurāṅgi received his name 'Member of the Robber's Gang' is as follows: As was said before, the prince, whose limbs had been cut off, lay at the foot of a tree. Acinta had given him initiation and instructions concerning the vase-breathing technique, and had told him, "When you obtain siddhi, your body will become as it was before you were harmed." After Acinta had given these instructions, he left. Caurāṅgi then meditated as he had been told.

Twelve years later a group of royal merchants bearing gold, silver, glass, and other precious things, traveled through that particular area—which was known for its robbers and thieves. Night came, and the prince, having returned to the foot of his tree, heard the sounds of footsteps. "Who is it?" he asked, and the merchants, thinking him to be a thief or a robber, replied, "We are coal dealers." The prince replied simply, "So be it."

When the merchants arrived home they saw to their horror that their gold and other precious things had turned to coal. They tried to think how this could have happened; they were very confused. Then one of the more thoughtful of the merchants said, "When we were traveling at night, someone asked us: 'Who are you?' No doubt that person has the power to speak words that come true. Let us return to him and see if that is indeed the case."

The merchants returned to the woods, and seeing a man with his limbs cut off sitting underneath a tree, told their story to him. They then asked the prince to remove his words of truth. The prince replied, "What happened was not what I had intended. But since it occurred, let there be whatever precious things there were before."

The merchants returned home and saw that their precious things had indeed become as before. They wondered at this, and returned to the prince with gifts and to tell him what had occurred. The prince told them about the words of his guru, and then said, "Let my body resume its former state." And it was so.

Having attained all the powers of siddhi, the prince performed miraculous things. But holding his doctrines to be too important to give to men, he gave them instead to his tree. The tree became immortal, and it still exists, so it is said. This ends the story of the immortal Caurāṅgi.

# Vīnapa

Vīnapa, whose name means 'the Man Who Plays the Vīna',[23] came from the country of Ghahuri, and was born of royal family. His guru was Buddhapa, and he obtained his siddhis from Hevajra.

Vīnapa was the only son of the king of Ghahuri, and his parents and the people were very fond of him. He was brought up by eight nurses, but he preferred always to sit in the company of the music masters. When the prince played the vīna, he became totally involved with the sound of the music, and cognizance of the other things of the world simply did not enter his mind. His father and mother, the assembly of ministers, and the people discussed the matter: "The prince is the heir-apparent to the throne, and yet he is not interested in the affairs of the kingdom; he is interested only in the vīna. What should be done?"

While this discussion took place, a well-experienced yogin, Buddhapa, came before the prince. The prince took faith in him. Circumambulating and giving reverence to the yogin, he spoke sincerely with him. The yogin remained in the company of the prince for only a little while before he saw the time had come to train him. He then said to the prince, "O prince, would you not like to practice the Dharma?" The prince replied, "O yogin, I cannot give up my instrument. If there exists a method of accomplishing the Dharma without giving up the vīna, I will practice it." The yogin, upon being asked, then gave him the initiation which ripens the unripened causes, and the following instructions for meditation: "Give up distinguishing the sound of the vina from the hearing of it. Meditate so as to make the two—the experience of the sound and the idea of it—into one."

The prince meditated in that way for nine years, and purified the stains of the mind. Having produced the inner experience which is like the pure light of a lamp, he obtained the Mahāmudrā, and generated in himself the many auspicious abilities, such as clear understanding and others. Becoming known in all directions as the yogin Vīnapa, he taught countless doctrines to the assembled citizens in the cities of Ghahuri. Finally, having narrated his experiences, he went in that very body to the realm of the Ḍākas.

# Śāntipa

During the time when King Devapāla held dominion over the cities of Magadha, there was a great monk and teacher of Brahman caste in Vikramaśīla named Ratnākaraśānti. He had mastered the five fields of learning and had become a great and very highly respected scholar, his fame spreading in all directions.

There was also at that time a king of Ceylon, Kabina by name, who by his merit did not lack any desirable quality. Though the teachings of the Buddha had not been previously known in Ceylon, he had heard good things about the Buddha Dharma from men who had come from India. As of that time, he had not met with anyone who could teach the Dharma, but he heard that there lived in Magadha a great master, a teacher named Śāntipa. So king Kabina and the people of Ceylon sent out a messenger to invite the master to come to their country.

When the messenger arrived at Vikramaśīla, he bowed down to Śāntipa and payed homage from the king of Ceylon. He delivered gifts of gold, silver, pearls, and silk, saying, "We are people at the edge of the world. We have been dimmed by the darkness of ignorance; we burn in the fires of the passions; we are tormented by the weapons of anger. The vision of knowledge has been covered by the stains of wrong views. The liberating path, the Dharma of the Great Vehicle of the Mahāyāna, has been dispersed. If you have any compassion at all for us, it would be fitting to consider coming to the land of Siṇhāla. I ask this for the sake of living beings."

The master, reflecting on these sentiments, announced that he would go. Thereupon Śāntipa, together with an assembly of students two thousand strong, set forth, carrying the Scriptures on horses and elephants. They wandered progressively to the cities of Nālandā, Odantapurī, Rājagṛha, Bodhgaya, and others, and then came to the shore of the Siṇhāla ocean. There they sent a messenger ahead, and the master with his company boarded a boat and departed for Ceylon.

When the messenger arrived in Ceylon and announced

that Śāntipa was coming, King Kabina, his ministers, and all the people were as happy as if they had attained the first level of Bodhisattvahood. They turned their minds away from worldly activities and directed their thoughts to the shore of the ocean. When a week had passed, the people saw signs: parasols and elephants—and they rejoiced. They swept the road clean from their city up to the ocean, covering the road with cloth for the master to walk upon. King Kabina and his people honored the master with flowers and incense, with flags, and the other various instruments of honor.

For three years, from the honored place on a high seat, the master preached many doctrines from the Scriptures. Then Śāntipa and his students prepared to return to central India. King Kabina and all the people gave them horses and elephants, gold, silver, and pearls, in immeasurable quantities. The company then set out on the longest route to return to Vikramaśīla.

Now, when King Rāmanapolaka of Rāmeśvara was searching for a wife, he had built a great temple and installed in it an image of Maheśvara, the 'Great Lord' Śiva. This is how the city of Rāmeśvara got its name. The master had his company take provisions for a week, for they were to travel towards that city along a road where they would meet no man for seven days. They had traveled along the road for only four days, when they met with the fortunate Togcepa, whose story of initiation is told in another place.

Finally, Śāntipa and his circle arrived at Vikramaśīla. The master had become very old and blind, and his body could no longer function properly. His disciples fed him with yogurt and sugar, for he had to give up rough food and could eat only small quantities. The master was now already a hundred years old.

For twelve years, Togcepa had meditated without conceptions, while Śāntipa had remained in the realm of conceptualization. In that twelve years, Togcepa had perfected the highest Dharma-nature. Because of this, while Śāntipa had to be cared for by his disciples, all the gods and ḍākinīs gave reverence to Togcepa, pouring ambrosia over his head—which contented him greatly. The gods and ḍākinīs reverenced him as the actual Vajrasattva, and through his spiritual efficacy, the auspicious objects which constitute the wealth of the gods began to increase. Togcepa said: "Until obtaining the instructions of the guru, I dug only in the outer mountain. After I obtained them, I dug in the mountain of the mind and obtained siddhi."

Indra and the gods of the thirty-three heavens then invited Togcepa to the divine abodes, but Togcepa refused, saying to them, "I will give reverence to my teacher, for my guru is kinder than even a Buddha." Then Togcepa arrived at Vikramaśīla in a moment, though looking with the eye of knowledge, one could see it was a six months' journey between cities. In his mental body, Togcepa bowed down to his guru, though he was unseen by his teacher's retinue. Togcepa then revealed himself in his actual physical body and did measureless reverences.

When Togcepa put his head to the master's feet, Śāntipa asked, "Who are you?" "I am a student of yours," Togcepa replied. "But I have had numberless students," said Śāntipa, "and I do not recognize you." "I am Togcepa," was the reply, and the two masters recognized one another and joyfully set to conversing.

Śāntipa said to his student, "What abilities and qualities have you obtained?" And Togcepa answered, "Having experienced the instructions of my teachers, I have truly obtained the most excellent Dharma-body of Mahāmudrā." The guru Śāntipa then said, "Though I have spoken much, I have not practiced very much and have not met with the actual meaning. Since you have chiefly practiced and have not spoken, you have encountered the meaning directly. I have forgotten that I gave instructions to you; now you must instruct me. Whatever factors and qualities there are, teach them to me."

So, in a quiet place, Togcepa revealed the many qualities of the Dharma-body to his guru. And the guru, Ratnākaraśānti, carried out his own previous instructions, and in twelve years attained the highest siddhi of Mahāmudrā. Having aided the aims of living beings, he went to the realm of the Ḍākas.

# Tantipa

In the city of Sandhonāgara, there lived a weaver with many sons. Through his weaving, he became possessed of immeasurable wealth, and married wives of good family to all his sons. He continued to live with them, and the entire family of this weaver prospered without measure. The wife of the weaver died when the weaver himself was eighty-nine years old and had become aged, decrepit, and infirm in body. He would eat successively with each of his daughters-in-law, but everyone laughed and made fun of the behavior caused by his age.

The daughters all met together, for they saw that people were turning away from seeing their old father-in-law, and they were accumulating evil. "Let us build a thatched hut in the garden," they said, "and feed him there." They all agreed to this, and acted accordingly.

By chance, the guru Jālandharapa came to that area and went to the house of the weaver's eldest son, asking for food. They invited him to sit down, and when the wife had completed the cooking preparations, she invited him in. The guru went inside and ate the food prepared for him. As the guru Jālandhari was preparing to leave, the wife of the weaver said to him, "Guru, sleep here. Do not go to another place." But he replied, "I do not sleep among men." To this the wife said, "Then please sleep in our garden." And they led him out to the garden and set a lamp there.

The old weaver heard the sound of a man, and wondering to himself who it might be, asked, "Who is that making the noise?" "I am a guest, a man of the Dharma," the master answered. "Who are you?" "I am a weaver," was the reply, "the father of the house. When I was a young man, I was the real owner of this place and its property. Now all my sons and daughters-in-law ridicule me, so I have been put here in this garden. Indeed, the things of the world are insubstantial."

Then Jālandharapa said to the weaver, "All composite things are impermanent. All the world is painful. All existing things are without substance. Only nirvana is peaceful and happy. Do you want the Dharma which is provision for death?" And the weaver said, "I want it." Jālandharapa then gave the weaver initiation in the mandala of Hevajra, gave him secret instructions, and started him meditating. The guru then went elsewhere.

The weaver committed the guru's instructions to memory, but he did not tell these instructions to any of his family. He practiced for twclvc years and obtained many qualities which were not observed by men. At this time, the eldest son had just finished weaving a fine cloth of silk, and was giving a party to celebrate, so he forgot to bring food to his father. That night, the daughter-in-law remembered, and unseen by her husband and the guests, went to take food to the old man.

Inside the hut, there was a great brilliance. The old weaver was surrounded by fifteen maidens, and there were many kinds of food in view. The woman, seeing ornaments and clothing not belonging to the world of men, hastily returned to the house. She said to her husband, "Go and see your old father!" The husband began weeping, thinking that his father was dead, but the other men went into the garden to look. All of them saw these things and were amazed.

After returning indoors, they said among themselves, "This is not human—it must be the work of a demon." But by the next morning, the news had spread, and all the people of Sandhonāgara came and gave reverence to the weaver. He then came forth, transforming his body into that of a sixteen-year-old youth. Measureless rays of light arose from his body, and none could bear to look upon him. His body was like a polished mirror, and everything appeared as light.

The old weaver became famous everywhere as Tantipa, and he did measureless deeds for the benefit of living beings.

Finally, he went bodily to the realm of the Ḍākas, together with an uncounted number of living beings from Sandhonāgara. By having faith and devotion and listening to the instructions of the guru, this old man was able to gain the success of Mahāmudrā in this very life.

# Camaripa

The name Camaripa means 'the Shoemaker'. In the city of Viṣṇunagara there were eighteen different artisan castes, and Camaripa's caste was that of the shoemakers. He practiced his trade on old and new shoes, and his time was completely taken up in working. One day, a yogin happened by. Camaripa broke off immediately from his work, put his hands to the feet of the monk, and spoke to him saying, "I am disgusted with samsara and would like to practice the Dharma. But since I have not met with a spiritual friend, I have not even entered the door of the Dharma. I ask you to tell me the Dharma for the benefit of both this life and the next." The yogin answered, "If you are able to practice the Dharma, I will give it to you." The cobbler then asked the yogin if he would eat food in his low-caste home, and the yogin replied, "When I return tonight, I will do so." After this, the cobbler announced the arrival of the yogin to his wife and her helpers.

When the yogin returned that night, the shoemaker laid out a seat, washed the yogin's feet, and offered him various nourishment. The wife and daughter offered him all the necessities, and massaged him with oil. Then the yogin, being pleased, initiated the cobbler and his wife and gave them these instructions:

> Let the mental distortions and conceptions be the leather.
> On the board of friendliness and compassion,
> with the drill of the guru's instructions,
> sew properly with the cords
> of giving up the eight worldly concerns.[24]
> Then a shoe, a miraculous result, will appear.
> This wondrous shoe of the Dharma-body
> will not be understood if you hold to wrong views.

"Give up the pleasant and the unpleasant by the thread of non-grasping. Let all the marks and conceptions become the leather. Meditate on making the marvelous shoe of the Dharma-body by sewing the leather with the thread of your own experience and the guru's instructions."

"What experiences will arise when I meditate in this way?" asked the shoemaker. The yogin replied: "First a feeling of disgust with samsara will arise. Then gradually the elements will merge into the Dharma-nature." After saying these words, the yogin disappeared.

The shoemaker then left his old house and went to a quiet place, where he meditated. Later, the signs arose progressively just as the guru had said. Through the analogies of his craft, the shoemaker came to understand the six root distortions and the ignorance that underlies them; he produced a clear understanding, and made the shoe of the guru's instructions. He practiced for twelve years, traversing the entire realm of ignorance.

When Camaripa cleared away all the stains of ignorance, he obtained the siddhi of Mahāmudrā. During those twelve years, he meditated without distinguishing the words of his guru and the making of shoes, and took no notice of day and night. All the shoe craft was done by Viśvakarman,[25] so it was not known in Viṣṇunagara that he had attained success in meditation and in the accumulation of qualities. One day, however, one of the men of his guild came to visit him, and was amazed when he saw the shoemaker meditating and Viśvakarman working. One by one, others came to see, until everyone had seen this. They then gathered together and asked the shoemaker for instruction.

He taught the benefits of relying on the guru. Then, after having preached many doctrines to living beings in Viṣṇunagara, he became known everywhere as the yogin Camaripa. Having worked for the benefit of immeasurable living beings, he went in that very body to the realm of the Ḍākas.

# Khaḍgapa

Khaḍgapa, 'the Man with a Sword', came from the country of Magadha. He was of low caste, his guru was the yogin Carpati, and he obtained the sword siddhi which is one of the eight shared powers. Khaḍgapa's father had been a farmer, but Khaḍgapa gave up this work to become a thief. Day and night, his thoughts were directed toward only one thing—stealing. At one time, this thief went into a city of Magadha in order to steal, but he returned empty-handed. On his way home, he passed through a cemetery and came upon Carpati. He asked him what he was doing there, sitting like that, and Carpati replied, "I am practicing meditation, for I fear birth and death in samsara." "What good will come of practicing meditation?" asked the thief. To which the yogin replied, "Since the yogin attains high birth as the result of his meditation and can even attain that happiness which is the fruit of the final good, would not even you like to practice the Dharma?"

"Admirable though the Dharma may be, since I must continually be robbing, I do not have the leisure to sit meditating in a cemetery. What do you think I am, a king's minister? I ask for a power by which I can take what I want when I am robbing a house, and not get caught by anyone, even if there is a struggle."

So the yogin gave the robber initiation and instructions: "In the land of Magadha, in the city of Gorisamakra, there is a structure with the outer form of a stūpa. Within it there is a chapel; within the chapel there is a statue of Avalokiteśvara, filled with spiritual power. Circumambulate the statue for three weeks without sitting down either day or night. Even eat while standing. Then, when you see a snake come out from under the foot of the figure, fearlessly grab its head. Then you will obtain power." With these words, the yogin set him to practicing. The robber took the instructions to heart, and practiced accordingly.

In twenty-one days, a great black snake came out from under the foot of Avalokiteśvara. The robber grabbed its head, and the snake changed into a sword: thus he held the shining sword of knowledge in his hands. He then purified himself of the mental stains of stealing, and obtained the siddhi of the sword. He became famous under the name of the yogin Khaḍgapa, and having purified himself of all delusions of body, speech, and mind, preached the Dharma to everyone in Magadha for twenty-one days. Having explained his clear understanding, he went bodily into the realm of the Ḍākas.

# Nāgārjuna

Nāgārjuna lived in a place called Kahora, a section of Kañci in eastern India. He was of Brahman caste, and he obtained siddhi from Tārā. There were 1,500 cities in Kahora, and all of them had been plundered and despoiled.

The Brahmans gathered together and decided to leave the strife-torn land and go to another country. The master heard this and sent a messenger to these Brahmans, counseling them not to go to another land, for they would find suffering in those places as well. Then he gave them all his property and wealth. After this, the master left Kahora, and having come to Nālandā, on the other side of the Śītavana, he became a monk.

Mastering the five sciences, Nāgārjuna arrived at the pinnacle of knowledge. Then, becoming disgusted with just preaching, he set himself to practicing, and saw Tārā face to face. He then abandoned the home and sustenance of Nālandā—where abide the hundred assemblies of the Dharma-circle—and begged alms in another city. When again he returned to his home, he thought to himself: "With such a mental attitude as I now have, I will not be able to accomplish the benefit of living beings."

In order to obtain the qualities to benefit living beings, Nāgārjuna went to Rājagṛha. On the first day of reciting mantras, twelve demonesses of the principal order of demons shook the earth. On the second day, they caused water to flood. Fire appeared on the third day, and on the fourth, a great wind. On the fifth day, a rain of weapons fell, and on the sixth, a rain of stones. On the seventh day, all the demonesses appeared in their own form and threw things around, but they did not frighten the master out of his meditation.

Then these demonesses of the North came to him and said, "What can we do to serve you?" "Serve me enough to sustain me; I need nothing more," Nāgārjuna said to them. So every day from then on, they gave him four handfuls of rice and five vegetables. The master ate these and practiced for twelve years. During this time, one hundred and eight demonesses gathered under his power, and his thoughts were on doing benefit for living beings.

Nāgārjuna then went to the mountain Ghadhaśīla and considered transforming that mountain into gold for the benefit of living beings. He made the mountain first into iron, and then into copper. But then the holy Mañjuśrī counseled him that the gold would bring about a great quarrel among the people, and evil would accumulate. Hearing this, Nāgārjuna abandoned further effort. Yet to the dull-witted Ghadhaśīla still appears as a copper-colored lump.

After this, Nāgārjuna traveled south toward Śrīparvata.[26] Along the way, he came to the shores of the Brahmapūtra where he met a group of cowherds. He asked them about a passage across the river, and they showed him an inauspicious way which was filled with ravines and crocodiles. But another cowherd came along who cautioned him about the river and showed him a better place to cross. And the cowherd set out across the river carrying the master on his back.

In the middle of the river, Nāgārjuna caused crocodiles and other fearful things to appear, but the herdsman continued on, saying, "You need not be afraid while I am still alive." The master then did away with the apparitions. When they came to the shore, the master said, "I am the Ārya Nāgārjuna. Do you know me?" "I have indeed heard talk of you," said the herdsman, "but I did not recognize you." "Yet you have saved me from the river. What can I give you as a reward?" The herdsman was elated. "I would like a method to become king," he said. So the master cleared away some ground, sprinkled water on the trunk of a sala tree, and it immediately turned into an elephant. "That will be your vehicle," said Nāgārjuna. When the herdsman asked him if he would need an army, the master replied, "If the elephant trumpets, an army will appear." It occurred exactly as was said: the cowherd became King Śalabhaṇḍa, his queen was called Sindhi, and he ruled over the extraordinary city of Bhahitana. Under this king there were eight hundred tax-paying cities of 100,000 people.

The master went south to Śrīparvata, and he remained there practicing meditation. But King Śalabhaṇḍa missed his guru. He went to Śrīparvata, gave reverence to Nāgārjuna, and circumambulated him. "Since my kingdom has small value and large problems, my unhappiness is increasing. I do not need a kingdom. I ask only to sit before the eyes of the master."

"Do not desert your kingdom," replied Nāgārjuna. "Let the precious rosary be your master. Rule the kingdom, and I will give you the elixir which removes fear of death." The king was chagrined. "If it is necessary to rule the kingdom at the same time as I obtain the elixir, then I will do so. But I hope it is not necessary."

Although the king did not want to return to his kingdom, but only wished to remain in that place, the master gave him instructions to practice in his own country. The king then accomplished the alchemical art, and for one hundred years he ruled the kingdom. During that time, the people became wealthy, and even the birds and wild animals in the mountains lived happily.

After one hundred years, the king had reason to go again to Nāgārjuna, who was working to extend the teachings of the Buddha. The evil spirit Sunandeśvara had grown jealous and was producing various misfortunes and disruptive omens. The moon and the sun had become dim and without luster; all the fruit was rotting spontaneously; the rain did not fall at the right time; and famine was afflicting the people. Sickness and war increased. The trees and forests were drying up, and various other unfortunate signs were appearing.

King Śalabhaṇḍa reflected on this, thinking that these portents were a sign that harm had come to his guru. He gave the kingdom to his son Candhikumara and together with only a few of his followers, he went to Śrīparvata to the presence of the master, who asked him, "My son, why have you come?" The king replied:

Either I and the people have exhausted our fortune,
or the Conqueror's teachings have decayed.
Or the darker half has become the victor;
or the great compassion white like the moon,
has been covered by demons like rainclouds.
Will the holy guru who is like a diamond
follow the nature of compounded things?
I have come because these signs have occurred—
out of your compassion, please remain in the world.

The master replied, "All that is born must die. All compounded things must disintegrate. All accumulations are spent. Since all compound things are impermanent, why are you unhappy? Take the elixir for yourself and go."

"The elixir is there in front of the guru. If the guru will not remain in the world, what need I of the elixir?" And so the king remained. Then the holy master made gifts of all his property. When the god Brahma appeared as a Brahman and begged for his head, Nāgārjuna agreed to give it to him. The king, Śalabhaṇḍa, could not bear suffering the death of his teacher, and laying his forehead to the foot of the master, he died. Everyone turned on the Brahman and blamed him for this.

The master then gave his head. However, no one could sever it; so he finally had to cut off his own head, which he did with a stalk of kusha grass. When he then gave his head to the Brahman, all the trees withered, and the people's merit degenerated. Eight of his yakṣīs were set to guarding the master's body; they are still there.

A light then entered Nāgabodhi, the guru's successor, and emanated for about a month during the year in which light emanates. It is said that the body of the master will rise in the future, and will aid living beings when the Buddha Maitreya appears.

# Kāṇhapa

The master Kāṇhapa is also known as the master Kṛṣṇācāri. He lived in Somapurī, his guru was Jālandhari, and he was of the scribe's caste. Kāṇhapa was a monk of the vihāra of Somapurī, which had been built by King

Devapāla. Having been initiated and given the instructions of Hevajra by the guru Jālandhari, Kāṇhapa practiced for twelve years. One day, the earth shook, and he saw the divine hosts of Hevajra. At this he became very happy. But a ḍākinī said to him, "O well-born son, since these signs do not have any special value, you should not feel boastful; you have not realized the truth."

Yet when Kāṇhapa stepped up onto a stone and sank his footprint into it, he became very proud. He ignored what the ḍākinī had said, thinking that he had obtained every power of siddhi. And when he was able to raise himself so that his foot did not touch ground by a cubit's height, his pride grew even greater than before. Soon seven umbrellas and seven drums came down from the sky to accompany him; when he heard the characteristic sounds of the elements, he considered that he had obtained the powers of siddhi by his own means.

Then he said to his students: "Since I have obtained such powers of siddhi, let us go to the demonic realm of Laṅkā, the land of rākṣasas, to work for the sake of living beings." He set out at once with an entourage of three thousand students. When they came to the ocean, Kāṇhapa went on without sinking into the water, thinking in his heart: "Even my guru does not have the abilities I have." His pride grew greater, whereupon his powers left him, and he sank into the water. As the waves showed him his end, he looked up and saw his guru Jālandhari appear in the sky. "Where are you going, Kāṇhapa," asked Jālandhari, "and what are you doing?" Kāṇhapa became ashamed. "I was setting out to the demon's realm of Laṅkā. Believing my powers to be greater than my guru's, my powers left me. Because of my pride, I sank into the water." "This will not do," said his guru. "In my country of Saliputra, where a righteous king named

Dharmapāla resides, there lives a disciple of mine, a weaver. Go to him and do whatever he says."

When Kāṇhapa decided he must act according to his guru's instructions, he regained all his former abilities. His feet did not touch the ground; umbrellas and drums appeared in the sky; he left his footprints in stone. Together with his circle of three thousand disciples, he went to Saliputra.

Leaving his disciples in one place, the master went in search of the weaver. He met many weavers on the road and examined them closely, but they all needed tools to splice together yarn that had been cut. Finally Kāṇhapa came to a place at the outskirts of town where a weaver lived. He tested him, and saw that he, of all the weavers, was able to splice cut yarn. Having determined that he was certainly the right weaver, Kāṇhapa circumambulated him and did reverence.

"Will you listen to what I tell you?" the weaver asked. Kāṇhapa agreed to do so. They then went to a cemetery. Coming upon a corpse, the weaver said to Kāṇhapa, "If you are able to eat that meat, then eat it." Kāṇhapa took out his knife, and began to trim the flesh. "Just eat it!" said the weaver, and so Kāṇhapa transformed himself into a wolf and ate the flesh.

"You can only tolerate eating flesh when you take another shape," said the weaver. Then the weaver made three pellets of great odor and offered one to Kāṇhapa, saying: "Eat it!" Kāṇhapa refused, saying, "People would scorn me." Then the weaver ate one pellet; the gods of heaven carried away one, and the nāgas from below carried away the other.

After that, both Kāṇhapa and the weaver returned to town. The weaver bought food and wine with five pennies, saying: "Go summon all your followers, and assemble them in a circle." Kāṇhapa thought, "This food will not satisfy even one man; how can it feed three thousand?" But he assembled his students.

By the miraculous power of the weaver-yogin, the vessels became filled with rice-paste and other delicious things. The followers could not consume the abundance of good things even in seven days. "Your food and drink are like an ocean which cannot be exhausted," said Kāṇhapa. Then, when Kāṇhapa and his followers were about to leave, the weaver spoke:

Listen. Those yogins
who separate wisdom and means
bring themselves down
like childish people.
It will do you no good
to go to another place.

"The parasols and drums are trivial achievements. You have not realized the Dharma-nature, so continue to practice."

Kāṇhapa did not like to hear this, so he went to a place called Bhandokora, a city a hundred miles from the vihāra of Somapurī in the East. As he was approaching the city, he saw a girl at the foot of a tree, whose fruit is called lychee. "Give me a fruit," Kāṇhapa ordered the girl. She did not want to give him one, so the master, by his manner of gazing, caused a fruit to drop. However, the girl, by *her* manner of gazing, caused the fruit to be refastened to the tree. Kāṇhapa became enraged, and began to utter mantras against the girl. Blood dripped from all the girl's limbs, and she fell to the ground. The people became indignant. "Those who call themselves Buddhists have great compassion. Yogins do not kill!" they said.

So Kāṇhapa calmed his mind, extended his thoughts of compassion to the girl, and withdrew the spell. But in doing so, he dropped his own protection, and the girl cast a spell on him. Kāṇhapa became very sick, vomiting blood and also losing it from below. He said to a ḍākinī named Bandhe: "In the South, on the mountain Śrīparvata, there is a medicine which is good for this vomiting of mine. Get it and give it to me." In one day Bandhe arrived in Śrīparvata, although the road she took ordinarily takes six months to travel; and she obtained the medicine.

Seven days along the return road, Bandhe came upon the same girl as before, who had now transformed herself into an old woman and was sitting beside the road, crying. "Why are you crying?" asked Bandhe. "Why shouldn't I cry?" the woman replied. "The yogin Kāṇhapa is dead and I am destitute." Bandhe thought, "The medicine is of no use now." So she threw it on the ground, and the old woman carried it off. The ḍākinī then hurried to the house where Kāṇhapa was staying, and she saw that he was not dead. "Where is the medicine?" asked Kāṇhapa. Bandhe told her story: Alas, she was without it.

Then, for seven days Kāṇhapa explained the Dharma to his assembly of students and gave them the instructions of Vārāhī 'with the cut-off head'. The master then dropped off this body of ripened karma and went to the realm of the Ḍākas.

The ḍākinī Bandhe grew angry and went looking for the girl. She could not find her in the realms of the gods above, or in the lower realms of the nāgas, or in the middle realm of men—because the girl was hiding within a tree called the Shimbhila. The ḍākinī found her, cast a spell, and killed the tree.

One should know that pride and jealousy are hindrances.

# Karṇaripa

Karṇaripa was born of a miraculous birth from among the four possible modes of birth.[27] He went to the monastery of Śrī Nālandā, where he was made master of all the monks and where he had a hundred thousand pupils. But though he sought instructions from many masters, realization did not come forth. One day he heard that the great master Nāgārjuna was residing in the South, and with considerable faith and joy, he set out on the southern road.

On the shore of a great ocean, the holy Mañjuśrī appeared in the form of a fisherman. Karṇaripa saw him, gave reverence to him, and presented a mandala to him. "I am going to the southern lands where the master Nāgārjuna abides. Please show me the way," he said. "Nāgārjuna lives within the thick forest over there, practicing alchemy," said the fisherman.

Karṇaripa went to the forest and he saw that the master, having collected the necessary materials for alchemical operations, was preparing them. Doing reverence, Karṇaripa made his request. Nāgārjuna cared for him and gave him encouragement. Karṇaripa was initiated into the mandala of Guhyasamāja, and having been given instructions, he sat down to meditate in front of the master.

Not far from this thick forest, there was a city where the two masters would go to beg alms. Karṇaripa received sweets as his alms, but the master Nāgārjuna did not. "Because these alms of yours were given by a lustful woman, they are not sweet," said Nāgārjuna. "It is not auspicious for you to obtain sweet food. Next time, do not put it on the top of the large leaf[28] you use to collect food, but take it up on the point of a needle." Karṇaripa then accepted a little rice gruel, which he ate instead.

The next day, the women made wheatcakes and put all sorts of sweets on top of them. Karṇaripa took them up on the point of a needle and, in turn, served them to his guru. Nāgārjuna then asked him, "How did you obtain this?" "I took it just as my guru had said I should do," Karṇaripa replied. "From now on," said Nāgārjuna, "you are not to go into town. Stay inside the house."

Karṇaripa obeyed and remained there, but while he was there, a tree goddess appeared in her true form and served him many sweet foods. She gave him reverence and praised him. He took these alms and served them to his guru, who asked, "From whom did you get these?" "A tree-goddess brought them," Karṇaripa replied.

The holy master went out to the tree goddess to discover the truth. He looked for her, but he did not see her in her true form; he saw only an arm up to the shoulder. "You showed your true form to my student," the master said. "Why is it that you do not show it to me?" "You have not abandoned a portion of your mental distortions," said a voice from the tree. "Your disciple has abandoned such mental distortions without remainder and so he saw me."

Both the master and the student considered these words. "It is necessary to take the elixir of the alchemists," Nāgārjuna said. He gave it to Āryadeva (as Karṇaripa was now called) and he himself also took some. Then Karṇaripa smeared the elixir on a barren tree and the tree grew leaves. When the master saw this, he smiled. "If you smear my alchemical elixir on a tree, come bring some of the elixir to me." "I will serve it as you wish," said Karṇaripa. He then put his own water into a full water-vessel and stirred the water with a stick. It became as the essence of the alchemists. Then he picked up the elixir and offered it to his master. Nāgārjuna discarded the elixir on a barren tree, and the tree grew. In this way, the master determined whether or not his student's realization had grown.

Seeing that Karṇaripa's experience of realization had arisen, Nāgārjuna spoke: "Do not stay in samsara." Immediately upon hearing this, Karṇaripa prepared to go into the sky, but suddenly a woman who had followed him, did reverence to him. "Why do you want to do reverence to me?" Karṇaripa asked. "I must have your eye," the woman answered. "I am bound by attachment to your eye; nothing else is necessary for me." The master took out his right eye and gave it to her. And he became known as Āryadeva, 'With One Eye'.

Āryadeva (Karṇaripa) then mastered the instructions of Nāgārjuna. He purified the stains of his mind and was completely freed from all bonds. He praised the words of his guru, and rising seven talas into the air, he preached the Dharma to many living beings, causing them to be free of bonds. With his hands folded, but with his feet up in the air and his head below, he did reverence to his guru sitting beneath him.

Then Āryadeva went to the top of the heavens where the gods of the height caused a rain of flowers. After that he became invisible. This ends the story of the master Āryadeva, who has the second name, the guru Karṇaripa.

# Thaganapa

Thaganapa means 'the Man Who Always Tells Lies'; this is his story. Thaganapa lived in the east of India, and as a result of his karma, he made his living as a man of low caste. One day, while sitting on a tree trunk, he entered into thought, considering in what ways he could tell lies to others. A well-disciplined monk came near him and asked, "What are you doing here?" "Your reverence, I do not want to say," he said. "Tell me without lying," said the monk. "If you lie, there are various kinds of karma produced. You may be reborn in hell. You will want to lie and others will not trust you. The result reflecting the cause is that a bad smell will come from your mouth and you will speak deviously. The predominant result will be that in the future state, your tongue will be like a plow in a rocky field, producing fruit of little vigor."

Thaganapa had never realized what results would come from his lying. Having heard these words, he became very afraid, and spoke truthfully to the monk: "Your reverence, I am called Thaganapa. I am always lying and have not spoken even a hundredth part of a hair of the truth. What can I do about my lying?"

"Will you practice the Dharma?" asked the monk. "If your reverence will preach the Dharma to me. But since I have been accustomed to lying from early on, I may not be able to give it up so easily." "There are instructions which do not require giving up lying," said the monk. Upon hearing this, Thaganapa became happy and said, "Would you kindly grant me that Dharma?"

The monk initiated him in a way appropriate to his bodily constituents, mind, and dispositions. He instructed him that just as one uses water to remove water from the ear, so lying can be the antidote to lying. He told Thaganapa to meditate on things being false from the very beginning; and his mental stream became fully mature. The essence of the teachings is as follows:

"All existing things which are objects of knowledge are from the beginning, false. Everything experienced by the six sense faculties and the six objects—your seeing and hearing and so forth—is false. So meditate on everything as only falsehood."

As for the existing things of this world of appearances,
what is not known to be true is seen as false.
Indeed, knowing and the objects of knowing are all false;
so if the six senses and their objects are false,
where do you find the truth?
And so you remain in the misery of samsara.
O child, if you do not recognize the false as false,
you take it as true; and like a waterwheel,
you are lost again and again in samsara.
Therefore you should actually meditate on the falseness
of all existing things.
Just as words are false,
so also are the physical forms and such.
So grasping this, meditate on the false.

Having been instructed in this way, Thaganapa meditated on all the data of consciousness as false. In seven years, the realization arose that this world of appearances indeed appears falsely; and he realized that all existing things are false. Because of this, he turned away from holding them as real. Again the guru came and explained: "The existing things are not efficacious, even as falsehoods. Since their very nature is empty, these existing things are neither created nor destroyed. Meditate now in this way."

Thaganapa came to realization in that way. He took conceptualization as his path, and he obtained siddhi. In all directions, he was known as the guru Thaganapa. He gave instructions to many fortunate ones, and in this very body, he went to the realm of the Ḍākas.

# Nāropa

Nāropa came from a family of wine-sellers, but he himself gave up this family profession. In Saliputra, in eastern India, he earned his living by gathering wood. Now, Nāropa heard it told that there lived, in Viṣṇunagara, a very wise man named Tilopa. Thereupon Nāropa exchanged his load of wood for a black antelope's pelt, took up the habit of a yogin, and finally set out in search of the yogin Tilopa.

He came to Viṣṇunagara and asked for the yogin, but the master had gone off, leaving everyone bereft. Nāropa wandered through the land, but did not find him. Finally, after a long search, he met Tilopa on the road. Nāropa did reverence, and circumambulated Tilopa saying, "O guru, are you in good health?" "I am not your guru and you are not my student," said Tilopa. And in anger he began to thrash Nāropa, but Nāropa's faith only increased.

Nāropa then gathered alms in a clay pot and presented them in front of his guru—who became angry and beat him as before. Nāropa's faith increased even more. He ate the remaining food and made circumambulation. Nāropa brought alms again in the evening, and the next morning he went out for more. In this way, for twelve years, he did reverence before the guru without despairing, although the guru did not speak any words to him except in anger.

One day, Nāropa was begging alms where a wedding was taking place. He received great amounts of food of many different kinds and a quantity of a very tasty dish called 'green patasa' which had eighty-four different ingredients. He gave this dish to his guru. The guru ate it and was so pleased that he said: "My son, where did you get such food? Who gave it to you?"

Nāropa felt the extraordinary joy that is obtained in the first Bodhisattva stage. He thought to himself: "For twelve years I stayed near my guru and he did not even say 'Who are you?' Now he has said 'My son'." As he reflected on this, Nāropa became very happy. "Son," said Tilopa, "go get me some more of this delicious dish." Four times Nāropa went to get the food, and everyone in the house was glad to give it to him. The fifth time, Nāropa was ashamed to ask again, but felt that if he did not get it, the guru would be displeased. So he went to ask once more; seeing that all the guests of the householder were distracted, he stole the pot full of food and carried it away. When he presented it to his guru, the guru was most pleased. Nāropa was initiated with blessings and given the instructions of Vajravārāhī. After meditating for six months, he obtained siddhi and became famous everywhere under the name Nāropa. From every direction, people came to make offerings to him, and a light arose from his heart that was visible for the distance of a month's travel. After working for the benefit of countless beings, he finally went to the realm of the Ḍākas.

# Shalipa

The name Shalipa means 'the Wolf-man'. Shalipa, who was of low caste, lived in the city of Vighāsura near a cemetery where packs of wolves howled at night. Day and night, without ceasing, Shalipa lived with the fear of wolves on his mind. One day, a monk came to his home and asked for food. Shalipa brought him food and drink, and the monk preached the Dharma in compensation for what he was given. Shalipa then bowed to the feet of the monk and spoke openly: "Your Reverence, the Dharma which you give as payment is very wonderful indeed. But if you have a doctrine which gives rise to fearlessness as well, please give it to me."

"Do you fear the misery of samsara?" asked the yogin. "What other than that could you be afraid of?" "Fear of the misery of samsara is universal," said Shalipa. "Everybody has that. But I live near the cemetery, and I am afraid of the howling of wolves. My fear is always with me, day or night. It applies to me alone. If there is a teaching which will be of benefit, please give it to me."

"There is a mantra which will help cure fear," said the yogin, "But first of all, there must be an initiation." Shalipa requested the initiation and presented many things, as well as gold and silver, as an initiation fee. He received these instructions: "To rid yourself of fear, meditate unceasingly on the fact that all the various sounds of the world are identical to the howl of a wolf. Build a little dwelling in the cemetery and live there."

Shalipa acted accordingly and meditated in this way. And he overcame his fear of wolf-howls when he realized that all sounds were inseparable from emptiness. Freed from his own fears, he produced an unbroken state of great joy; after meditating for nine years, he purified the stains of mind and body, and he obtained the siddhi of Mahāmudrā. He carried a dead wolf on his shoulders, and because of that practice, he was known everywhere as the yogin Shalipa. He gave many instructions about the inseparability of emptiness and appearances to those ready for such teachings, and finally, in that very body, he went to the realm of the Ḍākas.

# Tilopa

In the land of Bhigunagara, there lived a very learned master named Tilopa. He was the object of the king's devotion and worship and was given a subsidy of five hundred gold coins every day. One day he became disturbed while preaching the Dharma to the measureless circle of students that surrounded him. He reflected on the meaninglessness of his life, and filled with this thought, desired to slip away. His followers tried to prevent him from doing so, but when he was alone, the master put aside his monastic garb and dressed himself in patched clothing. He wrote a letter and left it in his house: "I will not return again. Do not come after me." During the night, he left.

Tilopa settled down in a cemetery in the city of Kañci, where he took food and provender and practiced. Nāropa came to him and offered food, and while living like this, Tilopa purified the stains without remainder. After practicing for ten years, he obtained the success of Mahāmudrā.

Having gone to the realm of the gods, Tilopa was given food offerings by the deities. Having obtained the successful powers of body, speech, and mind, he became famous in all directions as Tilopa. He set measureless numbers of persons on the path, and worked for the benefit of living beings. Finally, in this very body, he went to the realm of the Ḍākas.

# Catrapa

Catrapa, 'the Beggar Who Carries a Book', lived in Sandhonāgara, and though he was a beggar, he carried a small dictionary in his hand. One day he met with a well-disciplined yogin who asked him, "What are you doing?" "I am begging for my livelihood," Catrapa replied. The yogin then asked him, "Do you not need the path for your next life?" But the beggar asked the yogin, "How should I regard such a path?" The yogin then initiated him into Hevajra and gave him these instructions:

Confess all your sins;
meditate joy all day and night.
Look to your body for what you have done before;
what will happen later depends on your mind.
When you have meditated this way for a long time,
the signs will arise progressively,
and you will obtain Buddhahood
in this very life.

But Catrapa did not understand the meaning of this. The guru explained: " 'Sin' means ignorance, and from it all sorts of delusions arise. But if you hold to the view that realizes that the world of appearances is Mahāmudrā, your sins will be purified.

" 'Meditate joy, day and night' means that if you meditate compassion continuously, the bliss of the Dharma-nature will arise by itself. If one does not hold the deeds of past and future as absolute, the mode of living which arises from inner power will be perfect.

" 'What will occur later' means all your happiness and misery arise from your mind. It depends on whether or not you are still clinging to your attachments.

" 'In this way for a long time' means you should cultivate vigor and examine the mind undistractedly. If you meditate in this way, you will turn away from the mind's delusions —and as a result, you will obtain Buddhahood in this very life."

After the guru had given his instructions in this way, Catrapa meditated in Sandhonāgara. In six years, he obtained the siddhi of Mahāmudrā. And being famous in all directions as the guru Catrapa, together with a circle of five hundred, he went to the realm of the Ḍākas.

# Bhadrapa

In a place called Maṇidhara, there lived a Brahman who was accustomed to diverting himself with a wealth of amusements and companions. One day, after taking leave of his friends, he was taking a bath when a well-disciplined yogin came to his house, asking for food. The Brahman said to him, "Get out of here. You are impure. By coming here, you pollute my home. My household and my friends will see me here with you and will gossip. Get out." But the yogin said, "What do you mean 'impure'?"

"I'll tell you what I mean," the Brahman replied. "You don't bathe. You go around without clothes. You carry a skull as a cup. You eat polluted food. You are of low caste. So get out."

"That is not impurity," said the yogin. "When the body, speech, and mind contain unvirtuous qualities, that is impurity. By washing the body, you do not purify the defilements of the mind. That which cleans the stains of the mind are the guru's instructions–which are pure from the very beginning." And he continued:

Those of the Mahāyāna family are the highest,
Kṣatriya or Brahman are not as good.
While it is not good to have a dirty body,
merely bathing with water will not make you pure.
Only the instructions of a well-qualified guru
can wash you completely clean.
The highest food and drink are without attributions;
rice and milk cannot accomplish that.

When the yogin had spoken this and more, the Brahman took faith, and asked the yogin to give him instructions. The yogin answered, "Well, I will do as you ask if you give me food."

"If you teach me the Dharma here in my home," said the Brahman, "my household and friends will be suspicious. I will go to where you live. Where are you staying?" "I live in a cemetery," the yogin replied. "Come there, bringing wine and pork." "If it is improper for a Brahman even to pronounce the words 'wine' and 'pork', how can it be proper to carry them with me?" But the yogin replied, "Bring them if you want the instructions." "I cannot ask for these things by day," said the Brahman, "so I will come to you at night."

The Brahman, disguising himself, went to the market and bought the wine and pork, after which he went to the cemetery and presented them to the yogin. The yogin ate some himself and gave some to the Brahman. He then gave the Brahman the initiation which transfers spiritual power, and the Brahman offered a mandala.

The yogin then made the Brahman sweep the house to break his pride in caste, after which he explained the symbols of right understanding. He had the Brahman plaster the walls, and then he explained the symbols of proper activity: "The color of the plaster is the symbol of meditation. The conjunction of the three—the wall, the plaster, and the act of applying it—is the symbol of the result."

The Brahman, realizing the meaning of these symbols, understood that the world of appearances is the projection of illusion. He abandoned all conception of caste, and he became a yogin. In six years of meditating, he obtained the siddhi of Mahāmudrā, and became famous everywhere as the yogin Bhadrapa. He worked for the benefit of living beings, and finally, with a circle of five hundred followers, he went to the realm of the Ḍākas in this very life.

# Khandipa

Khandipa or Dhukandi, if translated, means 'He Who Makes Two into One'. He was of the sweepers caste, and was a beggar in the city of Ghaṇḍapura. He made his clothes by collecting scraps from the garbage piles and skillfully patching them together. One day, a well-disciplined yogin came along and asked him how he could live in such misery and poverty. "Wouldn't you rather practice the Dharma?" The beggar replied, "Who would teach the Dharma to me?" "I will teach you," said the yogin, and initiated the beggar into Cakrasamvara. He gave him instructions on the Developing Stage, the Perfecting Stage, and their Total Integration.

The beggar tried to meditate, but found himself thinking about sewing clothes, and did not want to continue. "I do not want to meditate this morning," he said to the yogin, "because I have distracting thoughts." The yogin then gave instructions which would take these thoughts as path:

> Existing things are in suchness;
> there is no sewing or things to be sewn.
> The gods and mantras are like that;
> and the realization of this is the Dharmadhātu.

When the beggar meditated accordingly, he lost the thoughts of sewing clothes, even losing the gods and mantras in the realm of the Dharma-nature. He realized the Developing Stage, the Perfecting Stage, and their Total Integration. In twelve years, he obtained the siddhi of Mahāmudrā. He worked for the benefit of countless living beings and went to the realm of the Ḍākas.

# Ajokipa

The name Ajokipa means 'the Lazy Bum'. In the city of Saliputra, there was a son of a householder, who was very fat. Of the four modes of action—lying down, sitting, standing, and walking—his most common mode was the first. His parents and relatives chased him out, saying, "What good is a son like this?" He came to a cemetery, and there he lay down. A yogin happened along, and upon seeing the boy, compassion arose in him.

Now, the yogin had obtained food and drink in the city, which he then gave to the young man. But the boy did not even get up to eat the food. "If you will not get up to eat," said the yogin, "what in the world can you do?" "My parents got rid of me because I could do nothing," Ajokipa replied. "Could you not use the Dharma while you are lying there?" asked the yogin. "I could indeed," said Ajokipa, "but who would teach the Dharma to one like me?" "I will give it to you," replied the yogin, and he gave him the initiation of Hevajra. He gave instructions on the stages of the Lesser Consummation:

"In the meditation of the Upper Door, meditate condensing the three world systems into a drop, the size of a white mustard seed, on the tip of your nose." Ajokipa then asked, "What signs will occur during this meditation?" "Meditate and you will know them," was the yogin's reply.

Ajokipa meditated in this way, and having dissolved the image of the three world systems and the mustard seed into emptiness, he produced the realization of Mahāmudrā. He meditated for nine years, and he obtained the siddhi of Mahāmudrā. After working for the benefit of living beings, he went in this very body to the land of the Ḍākas.

# Kalapa

Kalapa's country was Rājapura, and his guru was a yogin with a well-disciplined mind-stream. As a result of meditating on patience in a previous life, Kalapa had a very handsome appearance, which caused the people of Rājapura to gaze at him and follow him around. Kalapa became so upset at this that he went to a cemetery where he remained.

A well-disciplined yogin came by and asked him, "What are you doing, staying here in the cemetery?" The man replied, "I am staying here because people will not leave me alone." "Now then," said the yogin, "don't you need the Dharma?" "I do indeed need the Dharma, but who will give it?" The yogin replied, "If you need the Dharma, I will give it to you." And he initiated him into Cakrasamvara, setting him meditating on the goals of the Developing and the Perfecting Stages. After the man dissolved the dualistic idea of self and other into the realization of the Developing Stage, the Perfecting Stage, and the Integration of the two, he acted according to the spontaneous behavior arising from inner power. The people of Rājapura all called him a crazy man, but he said:

Some things are held as self, some appear as other:
These two appear to have an absolute nature.
If the wise understand these correctly,
the divine hosts of conceptualizations
within the letter A
dissipate like the rainbow in the sky.
Arising, duration, and cessation
no longer pertain to me, the Crazy One.
My behavior arising from non-dual power is bliss!
The clear unceasing realization is bliss!
Meditating unceasingly on the six assemblies is bliss!
The effortless result is bliss!

He then rose seven talas in the sky and displayed various miracles. From then on, he was called the guru Kalapa. Later he went to the realm of the Ḍākas.

# Dhombipa

In the city of Saliputra, there lived two men of the washerman caste, father and son, who made their living by washing clothes. A well-disciplined yogin came along and begged food from them. They gave alms to him, and they also asked if they could wash his clothes. The yogin then took in his hand a piece of coal: "If you wash this coal, can you clean it?" he asked. "It is the nature of coal to be black; not even washing it will make it white," replied the son. "Yet you wash only the outside," said the yogin. "If I do not purify the stains of the three inner poisons, it will do me no good to wear clothes cleansed only by an external washing. You must wash things many times to keep them clean, yet there are instructions that make washing once sufficient. I have these instructions; do you not need them?" "We do indeed," they replied.

The yogin then initiated the two men into Cakrasamvara. He gave them the instructions, and blessed them with mantras, mudrās and samādhis. They meditated for twelve years, purifying their bodies by mudrās, their speech by mantras, and the stains of their minds by samādhi. This is the essence of their instructions:

By the scalding water of mudrās,
the stains of the body are cleansed;
by the water of vowels and consonants,
the stains of speech are purified.
Joining the hero and heroic lady,
the stains of the mind are wiped away.

They accordingly performed the mudrās and recited the mantras. Having meditated on the mind as inseparable from the Developing and Perfecting Stages, they purified the stains of body, speech, and mind. When they obtained the siddhi of Mahāmudrā, the clothes were cleansed by themselves without the men having to wash them. The people saw this, and realized that the washermen had perfected these qualities. They became famous in all directions as Dhombipa; they worked for the benefit of sentient beings, and after a hundred years, went to the realm of the Ḍākas.

# Kaṅkana

In a place called Viṣṇunagara, there was a king who, having fully developed his kingdom, did not lack for any desirable qualities. One day, a well-developed yogin came to that place asking for alms. The yogin said to the king, "Your

Majesty, the kingdom is without substance. Samsara is like a watermill of birth, old age, and death; every worldly realm is painful. There is no end to the various kinds of pain, for even in paradise, there is the pain of transformation. Even the grand monarch of a world-system can fall into a bad destiny. Desirable things are deceiving, and they evaporate like dew. Your Majesty should be without attachment, and practice the Dharma."

"If there is a method of practicing the Dharma which does not force me to give up the things I like, then give it to me. If there is none, well, I cannot live by eating alms and wearing patched clothes," said the king.

"Patched clothes and alms for food are the very best way," said the yogin. "It is important for Your Majesty to take up such a life."

"Patched clothes disgust me, and the idea of eating leftovers in a skull cup disgusts me even more. I cannot do it.

At that, the yogin said, "Ruling the kingdom with such pride as yours, you will surely experience the misery of a bad destiny in a later life. There is, however, a method which brings joy as its result which does not mean patched clothes, leftovers, or a skull cup." And he told the king that there was indeed a method of practicing the Dharma which does not mean giving up desirable things.

The king responded, "Well then, I will practice that Dharma. Please show it to me."

The yogin then instructed the king: "Your Majesty, give up your pride and attachment to that shining bracelet on your arm. Combine the unattached mind and the light of the jewels into one, and meditate." The yogin then gave the king the following instructions:

The light of the bracelet radiates everywhere.
Look at it. It is the joy of your own mind.

The many sorts of outer ornaments
produce many kinds of color,
but their own nature does not change.
In the same way, the various appearances
give rise to many memories and ponderings,
but the mind itself is radiant like a jewel.

The king then directed his mind to the bracelet on his left arm and meditated. Having experienced the mind itself through these objects of desire, he obtained siddhi in six months. When his retinue looked through the door they were amazed at the sight of a circle of countless divine maidens. They requested instructions from the king and he said:

The experience of the mind itself is king;
Great Bliss is the kingdom.
The integration of the two is the highest enjoyment.
If you need a king, do likewise.

He preached to his court and to all the various peoples of Viṣṇunagara, and he became known as Kaṅkanapa, 'the Man with the Bracelet'. After five hundred years, he went to the realm of the Ḍākas in this very body.

# Kambala

In the land of Kankarāma, there was a king who ruled some 8,400,000 cities. He had two sons. When this king died, the eldest son, due to his pleasing nature, was consecrated as king by the subjects. Because of the king's virtues, the inhabitants all prospered; they lived in luxury, eating from plates of gold.

After becoming king, the prince, who had not seen his mother for many months, asked, "Where has my mother gone? Why does she not come to see me anymore?" "She is grieving for your father," was the answer.

After a year had passed, his mother came to him crying. "Why is my mother crying?" he asked. "I am crying because I am not happy that you are sitting on the jeweled throne, ruling the kingdom." So the prince said to his mother, "What if I were to set my younger brother to ruling the kingdom and entered the monastic order? Would my mother then be happy?" "That would be the right thing to do," she said. So he gave the kingdom to his younger brother, entered the order, and remained in a vihāra together with a circle of three hundred monks. But again his mother came to him weeping.

He greeted her and said, "Mother, why are you crying?" "I am still not happy," she said. "Though you are in the monastic order, you are just like a king in the midst of a bustling crowd." "What then should I do?" asked the prince. "Abandon this bustle for an isolated place," she replied. So he gave up the vihāra, and he sat at the foot of a tree in an isolated place, getting his provisions by begging alms.

Again his mother came to him and wept. The son greeted her, and said, "What should I do now?" And his mother said, "Why are you holding on to those senseless monastic implements of livelihood?" So he discarded his monk's robe and bowl and such and took up the habit of a yogin. He went into another country and, on the way, his mother, who was a ḍākinī, initiated him into Cakrasamvara and explained the Dharma.

The son slept in the ashes of the cemetery and practiced for twelve years. He obtained the siddhi of Mahāmudrā, and went to the heavens. His mother, together with many ḍākinīs, followed him to the heavens and said to her son, "Of what use is this great wonder, this walking in the skies, if you do not work for the benefit of sentient beings? If you are able to do so, work for the benefit of living beings."

So the master set out for the west to Malapura in Uḍḍiyāna, a city of 250,000 inhabitants. In a place called Karbira, in an isolated place in Banava, he sat in a cave called 'The Opening at the Top of the Talas'.

The witches of the area noticed his presence. One witch informed another, and the queen of the witches, Padmadevī, together with her entourage, went to obstruct him.

The master, wearing a black wool cloak, went to beg alms in the town. On the road, he met with a witchgirl, who came up to him saying, "We have prepared food for you; please come into our house." "I do not eat inside houses," the master replied. "I go about begging." He departed, but he entrusted his wool garment to Padmadevī and the others. The witches then ran away with it, saying: "If we are to diminish his power, we must eat this woolen garment." So they ate it, and burnt what was left over.

When the master returned, he said to the witches, "Give me the woolen cloak I entrusted to you." But the witches gave him another woolen cloak instead of his own. "I want my own garment," the master said. They offered him gold in exchange, but he would not take it.

The master then went before the king, saying, "If you are the king, why do you not protect me against robbers?" "What robbers?" asked the king. "Your witches who took my woolen garment," the master replied.

The king then summoned the witches and ordered them to return the woolen robe to the yogin. But they claimed they did not have it, and they did not give it up.

The master went to the cave of the Top of the Talas, and

there he practiced. He offered torma to the ḍākinīs, and when the witches dried up the water in the cave, the master told the earth-goddess to give forth water, and the water arose again.

The master then summoned all the witches from all four continents to Mount Meru, at which time he turned them all, including the queen, into sheep. The queen, taken by surprise, pleaded with the master to change them back to their original form, but to no avail. He sheared the fleece off the head of all the sheep, and when he turned them back into women, they all had shaven heads.

Also while staying in that place, the gods of the Desire Realm split a rock so that it would fall on him—but the master pointed his forefinger up, and the rock went back into the sky and remained there.

The king then advised the witches, "What is the matter with you? So many witches cannot control him! You should submit to him." But the witches would not listen.

The guru then bound all the witches, after saying to them, "Shall I give you over to Yāma, the King of the Dharma? Or will you remain in my teachings, and be true to your oath?" Fearful of the master's power, the witches took the refuges, and remained true to their oath. The witches then disgorged every bit of the wool robe which they had eaten. The master collected all the pieces, and putting them in order, found the robe was only a little shorter than before. Then, taking the robe with him, he departed.

He became famous under the name Kambala or Lva-pa. For countless years he worked for the benefit of living beings, and in that very body, he went to the realm of the Ḍākas.

# Ṭeṅgipa

Ṭeṅgipa was a Brahman, a minister of King Indrapāla of Saliputra. He and the king became disgusted with samsara, so they both went to the cemetery where Lūyipa lived, and knocked on the door of his hut. "Who is there?" asked the master. "The king and his minister," they replied. Lūyipa then welcomed them in, and after they had first submitted their bodies as an initiation fee, initiated them into the mandala of Cakrasamvara.

They went into a foreign land, Odissa, and there the three, master and students, begged alms. It was there that the king was sold, as is told in the story of Dārika.

The two, the master Lūyipa and the Brahman minister, arrived a week later at Jintapura, the place of a Buddhist king. They went to the residence of a wine-selling woman, and finding the chief wine-seller at home, Lūyipa said to her, "O Lady, will you please buy him?" From the inside, she replied, "I will buy him. How much do you want?" "Three hundred gold coins will do," he said. She paid the price, and took the Brahman away. As the master was leaving, he said, "For such a price, may he sleep alone; and let him go when your money is regained."

The Brahman was very happy carrying out his duties as a wine-seller, and eventually he became the chief of the woman's whole household. Then one day, although he had finished his day's work at the inn, he was not brought his food. When night came, he went to sleep in the garden, but still the wine-selling woman had not sent food. When finally she remembered and sent food to him, those who brought him his food saw five-hundred divine maidens making offerings to the Brahman, whose body was shining. They reported this to the woman, and she repented of what she had done.

She said to the minister, "I have sinned for making you work these twelve years. Please, to make up for this, would you consent to be my object of reverence for twelve years? I will make offerings to you and honor you."

He did not accept the offer, but instead, after preaching the Dharma to the wine-selling woman and the people of

Jintapura, he gave them instructions for practice. He then went to the realm of the Ḍākas with a retinue of seven hundred.

Because he performed the work of a rice-husker, he became known as Ṭeṅgipa, and so it is said in this verse:

Ṭeṅgipa who recited the Vedas
took up the idea of husking rice.
He always husked the rice carefully,
gathering it into piles by hand.
He beat the rice grains by the guru's instructions;
the dark rice grains he beat.
At first, he pounded sin with virtue,
by the pestle of vajra knowledge.
He shone like the sun and the moon,
in the emptiness of the mortar.
He pounded acquiring and renouncing into non-duality,
and churned his conceptions with the sound of HŪM.
The pure butter of great joy arose,
and he tasted the flavor of non-duality.

Ṭeṅgipa was sold to the wine-selling woman because of his considerable attachment to his being a Brahman; the wine-selling woman, having taken him in, cut down his pride in caste.

# Bhandhepa

Bhandhepa means 'He Who Holds the God of Wealth'. His land was Śrāvastī; his occupation was icon-painter; his guru was the master Kṛṣṇācāri. One day, when Bhandhepa was abiding in the sky, he saw a holy arhat walking through the sky dressed as a monk, carrying a bowl, a walking staff, and parasol. The arhat was radiant and majestic. Bhandhepa, amazed at this sight, asked Viśvakarman: "O Noble One, who is this wondrous man who goes through the sky in such a manner?"

Viśvakarman answered, "That is a holy arhat who has abandoned the defilements." Bhandhepa, desiring to become comparable, returned to Jambudvīpa. He requested the Dharma from the master Kṛṣṇācāri, who initiated him in the Guhyasamāja and gave him instructions on the Four Immeasurables as methods of yogic protection.

Having produced the fruits of compassion, happiness, friendliness, and equanimity in meditation, he purified all the poisons of delusions and wrong views. He obtained the Mahāmudrā siddhi, and became famous in all directions as the yogin Bhandhepa. When Viśvakarman inquired of him, he replied:

> Vision without perceptions,
> meditation without cutting the flow,
> deeds like mother and father,
> and results like the sky.
> These are the four I see without distinction.
> How can one succeed by holding things wrongly?
> Behold, one should always rely on a guru
> who is a master of wonders.

For four hundred years Bhandhepa spoke in this way and worked for the welfare of measureless living beings in the six great realms of Śrāvastī. Then, together with four hundred followers, he went to the realm of the Ḍākas in this very body.

# Tandhepa

Tandhepa, 'the Dice-player', was a person of low caste in the land of Kausāmbī. Having exhausted all of his wealth by continuously playing dice, he was soon penniless. He continued to compulsively play dice, but since he had lost all of his money, everyone avoided him. He became so dejected that he went to a cemetery and remained there.

A yogin came along and said to him, "What are you doing here?" Tandhepa replied, "I love to play dice, but I have lost my entire fortune. Both my body and mind are tormented, and so I am staying here." The yogin then asked him, "Would the Dharma be of use to you?" To which Tandhepa replied, "I cannot give up dice-playing. But if there is a teaching which would not make me give it up, then I could use it." "There is such a one," said the yogin, and he gave him initiations and instructions:

"Meditate on the three worlds being emptied just as your purse is emptied when you play dice. Meditate on the mind itself being empty, as empty as the three worlds."

Just as you can get rid of a fortune at dice,
you can get rid of conceptions by the dice of knowledge.
You should pound the conceptions
into the Dharma-body
just as you are now pounding on yourself.
Just as surely as you sleep in this cemetery,
you will rest in great joy.

Tandhepa meditated according to the way he was taught, dissolving the conceptualizations of the three worlds into the Dharma-nature. In this way, he acquired the knowledge arising from the clear understanding that everything is without self-nature. Having obtained the fruit of Mahāmudrā, he said:

If at first distress did not arise,
then how could I enter the path of liberation?
If I had not taken recourse to my guru with faith,
how would I have entered the highest siddhi?

After he had spoken, he rose in the sky, and in that very body, he went to the realm of the Ḍākas.

# Kukkuripa

Once there was a Brahman from Kapilaśakru who took faith in the mantra vehicle. Taking up the practices of a yogin, he went about begging for provisions. One day, he came across a starving female puppy on the road that leads to the city of Lumbinī. Feeling compassion for her, he intended to take her with him to the city. After looking all around, he found an empty cave where he left the puppy while he obtained provisions. He then decided to practice in that place.

After twelve years, he obtained the worldly siddhis such as clairvoyance and other powers; he therefore was invited to the heavens of the thirty-three gods. And so he went there, leaving the dog in the cave by herself. Left without the man, she dug into the earth; water and food arose, and so she remained in the cave.

The gods made offerings to the yogin, but then he remembered his dog of former times. When he started to return, the gods tried to prevent him, saying, "Having obtained your abilities, it is not right to hold ideas such as that of a dog. You should remain here." They repeated this again and again, holding him back.

However one day, he did not listen to them, and returned to the cave with its stream. When he patted the dog, she became a ḍākinī, who said:

> Well done, well done, you are a son of good family!
> You did not remain in those powers that hinder.
> You will attain the higher siddhi.
> The previous powers can deceive—
> you have purified your wrong views.
> Having these abilities is not such a wonder.
> The mother will bestow the holy siddhis,
> the highest of great joys without impurity.

Speaking in this way, she gave him the teachings of the symbols which unite wisdom and method, and he obtained the highest siddhi. The mental outlook which is pure and unchanging arose, and from then on, everyone in Lumbinī called him the guru Kukkuripa. He worked for the benefit of living beings, and together with an assembly of people from the city of Kapilaśakru, he went to the realm of the Ḍākas in that very body.

# Kucipa

Kucipa, 'the Man with a Neck Tumor', was a man of low caste in Kari who made his living by working in the fields. One day, as a result of his previous karma, a tumor began to grow on his neck. As it grew larger and more painful, he went to a lonely place so that no one could see him. While he was living there, the holy Nāgārjuna came along. Kucipa took faith in him and greeted him saying, "Your Reverence, how wonderful that you have come! I am being tormented by previous karma; I can hardly endure this pain. Please give me a method of freeing myself from this hardship."

The Holy One replied, "There is a method of liberation from this. Would you be able to practice it diligently? If you are able, you can free yourself from pain, using it as a method of going to great joy." "Your Reverence," said Kucipa, "why would I not be able to practice diligently? I will do it!" So Nāgārjuna initiated him into the Guhyasamāja and gave him the instructions on the Developing and the Perfecting Stages. He gave the teachings which take pain as path in this way: "Meditate that the tumor on your neck is growing larger. That is the objective of the Developing Stage."

Kucipa meditated in that way, and the tumor became larger than before and was still painful. Again the Holy One came and asked, "Are you happy?" And Kucipa replied, "No, I am in great pain."

Nāgārjuna then said, "Meditate as the objective of the Perfecting Stage that all existing things are contained in your tumor."

When Kucipa meditated in this way, the tumor disappeared, and he was happy. Again the Holy One came and asked, "Are you happy?" "I am happy," was the answer, and so Nāgārjuna gave these instructions:

> Pain and pleasure arise from being and non-being.
> When free from the notions of these two extremes,
> How can there be pain and pleasure?
> Existing things themselves are empty of inherent nature.

Kucipa came to an excellent realization of these things, and he obtained the siddhi of Mahāmudrā without mental constructions. For seven hundred years he worked for the benefit of the living beings in Kahira. He became famous as the guru Kucipa, and together with seven hundred followers, he went to the realm of the Ḍākas.

# Dharmapa

Dharmapa means 'the Man Who Has the Wisdom Gained by Study'. In a place called Vikramāsura, there lived a Brahman who studied diligently but was without the wisdom of critical reflection or meditation. One day, a yogin came along and said to him, "Since you have done so much studying, there must be much Dharma in your mind."

"Yogin," the man answered, "I have studied a great deal of Dharma, but I am not able to practice what I have learned. Please tell me, are there instructions that will help me to retain what I learn?"

The yogin said there were and gave him the initiation which transfers spiritual power. He then gave him instructions on how to integrate the many themes of the Dharma:

> Just as the particles of precious metal
> become well-fused by the smith,
> so the various things you have studied
> must melt together in your mind.

As this was said to him, Dharmapa understood it, as well as what it signified. As he realized in his mind the unified wholeness of the many doctrines he had heard, he obtained the siddhi of Mahāmudrā. He became famous under the name of Dharmapa, because he explicated the way of liberation to those to be subdued. He then went to the realm of the Ḍākas in this very body.

# Mahipa

Mahipa, 'the Braggart', was a man of low caste who lived in the land of Magadha. He had great bodily strength, but was always under the power of his pride, for he thought he could subdue any man or indeed any living being. One day a yogin came by and seeing him, said, "What are you thinking about?" "I am not thinking of anything," Mahipa replied. "Well then, what about 'there is nothing I cannot overpower'? What do you consider that?" Thereupon Mahipa became a believer and did reverence to the yogin, saying, "I give you most respectful greetings." The yogin, in reply, told him to purify the stains of his arrogance. "Please teach me how," said Mahipa. The yogin said he would teach him, and gave him the initiation which transfers spiritual power:

> You should know that appearances are in the mind,
> but the mind is empty—not produced, not destroyed.
> Meditation is holding to that without distraction—
> as a result, the mind becomes the vast expanse.

But Mahipa answered, "I do not understand this." So the yogin then continued:

> Since you are powerful,
> there is nothing you cannot subdue.
> These three—appearances, breath, and wisdom—
> you must hold to be like the sky's expanse.

Mahipa was taught the instructions which take contradictions as path. Thinking, "What is the difficulty in that?" he held to the path and persevered. Since he could not find an object, he was no longer conscious of being the subject. By the emptiness which is like the expanse of sky, he obtained siddhi.

For three hundred years, he gave powerful instructions to countless beings to be converted in the country of Magadha, and with a circle of 250 followers, he entered the realm of the Ḍākas in this very body.

# Acinta

In the city of Dhanarūpa, there lived a man of the wood-seller caste whose name was Acinta, which means 'He Who Is Beyond Thought'. He was very poor and longed day and night for wealth; he had no other interest in the world than how he could obtain money and fortune. But since these were only daydreams, he became discouraged and went off to a deserted place to brood.

The yogin Kambala came along, saw this woodseller, and said, "You are alone and silent in this lonely spot. What is it that you are thinking about, sitting here?" "I am depressed, yogin, for my heart dwells on money and worldly fortunes. I cannot think about anything else." "If there were instructions to find wealth and fortune, could you practice them?" asked the yogin. "Without a method, I cannot practice anything," the man said. And he requested instruction. The yogin then initiated him into Cakrasamvara and gave him these instructions on the profound Perfecting Stage:

How can you obtain wealth by just wishful
thinking?
Give up these daydreams,
which are like the son of a barren woman.
The best body has the nature of the sky.
Contemplate that your mind is as bright as the
many stars,
and you will become like the god of wealth himself.
When these things become evident,
then everything you desire will arise.

The wood-seller meditated accordingly. He fused his ideas about wealth and fortune with the stars, and dissolved these stars into the nature of the sky. And in this way, he became devoid of conceptions.

Then his guru came again and said, "Having spoken with no conceptions whatsoever, you have become free of them."

Since your nature has become like the sky,
did you use it as an object, or what?

If you meditate free of color and shape,
in what way can you desire things?

Having realized the meaning of this, the wood-seller obtained the siddhi of Mahāmudrā. He became famous as the guru Acinta, and instructed others on the real nature of things, working for the benefit of living beings for three hundred years. Then with a circle of followers measureless in extent, he went in that very body to the realm of the Ḍākas.

# Babhahi

The meaning of Babhahi is 'the Man Who Gets Milk from Water'. In the land of Dhanjura, there lived a man of kṣatriya caste, who was attracted to all the advantages of kingship. A well-disciplined yogin came to him asking for food and provisions. The kṣatriya offered him food and drink, and then took faith and asked for the Dharma.

The yogin said, "Faith is the root of the entire Dharma. The guru is the root of all siddhi." Then he gave him the initiation which transfers spiritual power and gave instructions on the *nāḍis*, *prāṇa*, and *bindu*, in this way:[29]

With that special body possessing method,
mix the semen with the great ocean of blood,
and hold it in the mandala of the vulva.
When you have carried it to its proper place,
it will spread within, causing unbroken joy.
When you have overcome joy with joy,
Meditate that it is inseparable from emptiness.

Taking this into his mind, he purified the stains obstructing his vision, and in twelve years, he obtained siddhi. He performed many benefits for those to be trained, saying:

As the king of geese
separates milk from water,
the instructions of a revered guru
draw out the elixir of enlightenment.

And in that very body, he went to the realm of the Ḍākas.

# Nalina

In the city of Saliputra, there lived a very poor man, by the name of Nalina, 'the Lotus-root', who made his living by gathering lotus roots from the lakes. One day, he met a yogin who preached the ills of samsara and the qualities of nirvana. The man experienced a revulsion against samsara and said, "O guru, please give me a method of gaining liberation." Saying, "I will do it," the yogin initiated him into Guhyasamāja and gave instructions which use one's own body as method:

> In the place of great joy at the top of your head,
> visualize that there is a pure white HAM.
> Cause the letter AM to appear at your navel,
> and let the HAM drip down in blazing light.
> When the joy, absence of joy, greatest joy,
> and the inherent joy arise in order,
> you will cast away the ills of samsara,
> and will take the great joy of liberation.

Nalina meditated accordingly. Just as the lotus grows from the mud but is not covered with the mud from which it arises, the four joys of meditation manifested themselves in the four cakras. Meditating, he was no longer enmeshed in the ills or conceptions of samsara.

In nine years, realizing the meaning of his meditations, he purified the stains of his delusions. Obtaining the siddhi of Mahāmudrā, for four hundred years he worked for the benefit of living beings in Saliputra. Together with 550 of his followers, he went in this very body to the realm of the Ḍākas.

# Bhusuku

Because Bhusuku, who was of the kṣatriya caste, appeared to have an auspicious character, he was accepted as a monk in the monastery of Nālandā. At this time, Devapāla was king, and he provided food and drink for the group of seven hundred monks in the Dharma-circle of Nālandā; the abbot of the ordinary section of the four sections of the Sangha had about three hundred students. By their diligence, they had all become skillful in the five sciences, except for this kṣatriya monk, who was very lethargic in his studies. Moreover, each morning he ate five full bowls of rice because his appetite was like a raging fire. King Devapāla said of him, "This person is a *bhusuku*, a lazy bum." And so the monk became known by the name of Bhusuku because he did only three things: eat, sleep, and wander around.

It was the general practice in Nālandā to have those in the Dharma-circle recite the Sūtras in turn. The abbot, speaking for the entire place, said to Bhusuku, "Since you will not take your turn reciting the Sūtras, please go elsewhere!" But Bhusuku replied, "I have not broken any of the rules. It is not right to throw me out. It is just that I have no luck in learning academic subjects." So he was permitted to stay.

But when it was again time for Bhusuku to recite the Sūtras, the monks told him to prepare well, because this time he would have to take his turn. He accepted that he would have to do it, and all the monks of Nālandā planned to come to hear him and laugh at him.

The abbot said to Bhusuku, "When you should have been studying, you were eating or sleeping instead of preparing the Sūtras for the master of Nālandā." Bhusuku replied, "I will recite the Sūtras."

The abbot then said to him, "If you cannot recite the Sūtras, you will be expelled." Bhusuku said he understood. But he still could not do it, so the abbot taught him the mantra of the holy Mañjuśrī—A-RA-BA-TSA-NA—and told him to recite the mantra during the night without sleeping. He set Bhusuku to reciting the mantra with a meditation cord around his neck and knee to prevent his dozing.

As Bhusuku was reciting the mantra, the holy Mañjuśrī appeared to him and said, "How are you doing, Bhusuku?" Bhusuku replied, "In the morning, it will be my turn to recite the Sūtras. It is about this that I am making a request to the holy Mañjuśrī." The holy one said, "Do you not recognize me?" "No, sir, I do not," he answered. "I am Mañjuśrī." "Oh!" said Bhusuku. "Mañjuśrī, please, I want the siddhi of the most excellent wisdom." "Prepare your Sūtra in the morning," said Mañjuśrī. "I will give you the knowledge." Then Mañjuśrī disappeared.

On the morning of the Sūtra-recitation, the monks, the mass of people, and the king arrived at the assembly hall, all telling each other how they had come to look at Bhusuku. The implements of offering, the flowers, and so forth were then carried in, and the assembly settled down, ready to have a good laugh.

Bhusuku, having requested the monk's parasol, went to the throne of the vihāra without apprehension; when he sat down, he became extraordinarily radiant. Even though there was a curtain in front of Bhusuku, everyone was wondering what was happening.

"Should I recite the Sūtras in the way they have been done before, or should I explain them in a way that has not been done before?" asked Bhusuku.

The scholars all looked at each other while the king and the people laughed. The king said, "You have developed a method of eating that has never been seen before, and a method of sleeping and strolling about that has never been seen before. Now preach us the Dharma in a way that has not been done before."

Bhusuku proceeded to explain the essence of the ten divisions of the *Bodhicaryāvatāra*,[30] and then rose up into the air. The five hundred scholars of Nālandā, King Devapāla, and the crowds of people all took faith and threw flowers that nearly covered Bhusuku up to his knees. "You are not a *bhusuku*," they said. "You are a master."

The king and all the scholars called him Śāntideva, 'Peaceful Deity', because he quieted the pride of the king and scholars. The assembled scholars requested him to make a commentary. When that was done, they asked him to become the abbot. But he did not agree to that.

He placed in the temple his most precious belongings as a monk, the monk's robes and the begging bowl, and to the surprise of the abbot and the monks, he left the vihāra. Eventually he came to the city of fifty-thousand inhabitants called Dekira. Holding a gilt-handled wooden sword in his hand, he went to the king and said: "It is seemly that I be your swordsman." And so he made his living in this way, and was given ten times ten gold coins a day. For twelve years he was a swordsman, yet he never deviated from his noble aim.

Then one day in autumn, the swordsmen, including Śāntideva, made offerings to an image of the Goddess Umā. While they were all washing their swords, one of the men saw that Śāntideva's sword appeared to be of wood, and he reported this to the king.

The king said to Śāntideva, "Show me your sword." But Śāntideva replied, "If I showed it to you, it might bring you harm." "Even if it were to harm me, so be it," said the king. "Then cover your eyes," said Śāntideva. He then drew the sword from its scabbard; its light was so bright the people could not endure it. They begged him to put the sword away, for even their covered eyes were blinded. Śāntideva then anointed them with his tears, and their sight was restored. Amazed, they asked him to remain and be an object of veneration, but he would not stay.

Śāntideva went up onto a rocky mountain, where he was seen killing wild animals by his magic power. He was also seen eating their flesh, and this was reported to the king. The king and his court went to the mountain and questioned Śāntideva: "Once you were an ascetic, chief of those at Nālandā. There you explained the Dharma; here you demonstrated that you could cure blindness. With such abilities, how can you bear to do an injury, let alone take life?"

But Śāntideva said, "I have not killed anything." He then opened the door of his hut. They all looked out upon the mountain and saw that the wild animals had been restored to life, and had even doubled in number. Soon the animals extended over mountain and valley. When the animals finally disappeared in the distance, and the king and the fortunate others were again alone, they realized that all existing things are illusory, only a dream. Then, realizing that things are not real from the very beginning, they set out upon the spiritual path. Śāntideva spoke:

These animals which I killed
in the beginning did not come from anywhere.
In the duration, they did not stay anywhere.
In the end, they were not destroyed into anything.
From the outset, existing things are not real,
so how can the killing and the killed be real?
Behold, still having compassion for living beings,
Bhusuku has said this.

Reciting this, manifesting his abilities to all, he humbled the king and all the others and instructed them in the Dharma. He obtained the siddhi of Mahāmudrā, realizing the unity of body, speech, and mind. The qualities of the Dharma arose in him instantly; finally, after a hundred years, he went in that very body to the realm of the Ḍākas.

# Indrabhūti

There were 500,000 cities in Uḍḍiyāna, and these cities were ruled by two kings. Indrabhūti ruled the 250,000 cities in Sambola, and King Jalendra ruled the 250,000 cities of Laṅkāpura.

Indrabhūti, the king of Sambola, had a seven-year-old sister named Lakṣmīnkarā. He offered her in marriage to the young son of Jalendra, king of Laṅkāpura. But when King Indrabhūti met with his ministers, they counseled him that since Jalendra did not practice the Dharma, he should consider someone else. So Indrabhūti ended the agreement, telling Jalendra's messenger that since those who practice the Dharma and those who do not have little in common, the couple should not marry.

But a year later, Jalendra's son came to Sambola and met with Lakṣmīnkarā. They seemed to be compatible, so when the prince set out for his own country, Indrabhūti sent with him horses, elephants, and many men bearing gold and silver as presents. When the son returned to his own land, his father asked him about his young wife, and the prince replied, "I did not bring her with me because she is too young. But all is well."

Now Indrabhūti had many wives, and all of them had faith in the Dharma. The guru Kambala had initiated and given instructions to all those noble ladies as well as to the princess, and they all endeavored toward accomplishment.

The princess was sixteen years old when King Jalendra sent a messenger for her; but when she was sixteen years old she had already turned her mind from samsara. (As is explained in the story about the princess herself, she finally accomplished her aim and, along with a sweeper, she flew up into the sky.) King Jalendra sent a messenger to Indrabhūti concerning the life-style of the princess: "That the lady has attained a high level of accomplishment is a good thing, but it has not brought about my own peace of mind—and that is not good."

Then it occurred to King Indrabhūti: "My sister is working for the benefit of living beings. My kingdom gives me little benefit and great concern: I should give it up and practice the Dharma." So the king gave his kingdom to his son, and having practiced in the palace for twelve years, he obtained the siddhi of Mahāmudrā. His entourage, however, did not know this. One day, the son and the courtiers were looking for the king and they were about to open his door, when a voice from the sky said: "Do not open the door, I am here."

When they heard this, they looked up and saw King Indrabhūti sitting in the sky. Upon seeing this, they were as happy as if they had obtained the first Bodhisattva-level. The royal father remained sitting there for seven days, preaching from the sky to those who honored him in their faith. To the son and the courtiers, he told of the great, profound, and inconceivable Dharma, and then, with seven hundred followers, in that very body, he went to the realm of the Ḍākas.

# Mekopa

In the land of Bengal, there was a person of the food-seller's caste who always gave provisions to a certain yogin. One day, the yogin asked him, "Why are you giving reverence to me?" "Because I need provisions for the path to my future life," the food-seller replied. "Well then, are you able to accomplish such provisions?" The man said he could, so the yogin gave him the initiation which transfers spiritual power; he also gave him instructions which introduced him to the nature of the mind itself.

To the ordinary mind,
even though it is jewel-like,
samsara and nirvana
appear to be different.
It depends on whether or not
you have clear understanding.
For this, you should look
to the unchanging nature of the mind itself.
How can the idea of duality arise,
since there is no such absolute nature?
None of the existing things
have any reality whatsoever.
If you do not realize this,
you will be bound by illusory desires.

The food-seller understood by this that appearances were in his own mind. Having understood that, in reality, the mind does not move, and concentrating on the meaning that the mind itself does not change, he destroyed his delusions in six months; he realized the primal nature of the mind itself.

Prowling the cemetery like a wild beast, he went from town to town looking like a madman and gazing about with wide-open eyes in a fearsome manner. The people said: "The guru has the gaze of a wrathful deity."

Everywhere he became famous as Mekopa. He guided many beings to be trained in the profound Dharma, and finally, having narrated his experiences, he went in that very body to the realm of the Ḍākas.

# Koṭali

Koṭali, who was also known as Togcepa, lived in the land of Rāmeśvara until he went to live in a land four days journey distant, where he hoed the mountain fields for a living. The master Śāntipa, who had been invited to Siṇhāla by the king, happened by the mountain field on his way to Madhyadeśa, and asked Koṭali, "What are you doing?" Koṭali respectfully greeted him, and said that he was hoeing the mountain. He went on to say, "Evil kings have destroyed the land, and everyone is suffering. I cannot get land in Rāmeśvara, and so I have come to this mountain area to work." Śāntipa then asked him, "If I had Mantric instructions for plowing the mountain, could you use them?" "I could," Koṭali answered, and so Śāntipa said:

Deeds like those you are doing
will tire the body
and so those deeds are very bad.
These are the six mistaken deeds.
But truly, plowing the land is charity,
and morality, such as not harming others.
It is the patience which endures pain,
and the vigor which accomplishes.
It is the unwavering mindfulness,
and the wisdom which knows these.
By the six true deeds,
one abandons the mistaken deeds.
Venerating the guru is charity;
morality is guarding your own mental stream.
Patience is the endurance of the mind itself.
Vigor is meditation;
mindfulness is unwavering,
and wisdom is that which knows these things.
Meditate always on these.

But Togcepa said, "Please explain the meaning of this." The master replied, "Venerate the guru, since all pleasure and pain arise from one's own mind. Meditate on the primal nature of one's own mind, for the primal nature of the mind is unchanging like the mountain. By luminous knowledge which cannot perish, dig as if you were hoeing. These two efforts, meditating and hoeing, are like the right and left hand. You should hoe without separating them."

When he understood what the verses actually meant, Togcepa said:

> Pleasure and pain arise from the mind;
> I will hoe the mountain of the mind with these teachings.
> When one only hoes the physical mountain,
> One cannot realize the great bliss of the primal nature.

Meditating accordingly, he obtained siddhi in twelve years. He performed many benefits for living beings, and in that very body, he went to the realm of the Ḍākas.

# Kaṃparipa

In the land of Saliputra, Kaṃparipa, 'the Smith', worked hard at the profession of his caste. Then one day, a yogin came to the place where he was working. "What are you doing?" the yogin asked. "I am simply doing the work of my caste," Kaṃparipa responded. "Do you enjoy your work?" asked the yogin. "Do I look happy?" asked the smith. "The fire, sparks, and heat all torment me. I must suffer just to make a living."

The yogin then asked for food, and as he ate, the smith and his wife said to him, "We offered you alms, and it is amazing that you take food from the hands of low-caste people. We are most happy at this." The yogin then asked them, "Don't you practice the Dharma?" "We are of such low caste—who would instruct us?" they replied. "If you have faith in the Dharma," said the yogin, "and are able to practice, I will give you instructions." They were elated. They pleased the yogin with their veneration and many offerings, and then asked for the instructions. The yogin, having given the initiation which transfers spiritual power, also gave them instructions on the visualizations of the three mystic veins in this way:

"Meditate within yourself that you see the bellows, fuel, fire, and the hammering of iron, just as you do in the external world. Make the two veins, *lalanā* and *rasanā*, the bellows. Consider the central vein, the *avadhūtī*, as the anvil.[31] Let the consciousness be the smith. Ignite the fire of knowledge and make conceptualizations the coal; then hammer the iron of the three poisons. When the great joy and the non-dual Dharma-body ripen as a result, there will be light."

Let your inner acts of meditation
be like those deeds you do outwardly.
The *lalanā* and *rasanā*, right and left,
let those two be the bellows.
Let the *avadhūtī* be the anvil;
let the consciousness be the smith.
Let the conceptions be the fuel,
and investigation and knowledge be the shining fire.

Hammer the iron of misery and the three poisons:
the result will be the stainless Dharma-body.

The smith, having generated faith within himself, meditated, and in six years he obtained the siddhi of Mahāmudrā. Without exertion he accomplished all sorts of things in their proper manner. The smith then said to the inhabitants of Saliputra that he had obtained all the qualities of the Dharma, and they were amazed. Everywhere he was known as the guru Kaṃpari, and he accomplished benefits for living beings. After narrating his experiences, he went to the realm of the Ḍākas.

# Jālandhari

Jālandhari, 'the Man Who Holds a Net', was a Brahman who lived in the city of Thod-tha. He had become disgusted with the things of the world, and so he went to a cemetery. While sitting at the base of a tree, he experienced the bliss of knowledge. A ḍākinī appeared in the sky, and a voice said: "O noble son, you should know that your mind is the nature of reality itself." In his joy, the Brahman prayed over and over again. The ḍākinī of knowledge then showed herself in her true form, bestowed upon him the initiation of Hevajra, and gave him instructions on the Perfecting Stage in this way:

"Include all the living and nonliving things of the three worlds into the three veins, and join the two veins into the *dhūtī*. When various concepts and memories have gone out from the place of Brahma at the top of the head, meditate in that central vein on the inseparability of emptiness and appearance."

Gather without remainder,
existing things, inner and outer.
Join them into the three:
body, speech, and mind.
Join the right and left veins into the *avadhūtī*,
and all of this to the place of Brahma—
then emptiness and the highest joy will arise
from the nature of pure yoga.
Understand in your meditation
the total integration of joy and emptiness.

Having been granted the Perfecting Stage in this way, he meditated, and in seven years, he obtained the siddhi of Mahāmudrā. He then narrated his experiences, and worked for the benefit of countless living beings. Together with a circle of three hundred, he went to the realm of the Ḍākas.

# Rāhula

Rāhula, 'He Who Has Grasped Rāhu', was born of low caste in Kāmarūpa. When he became an old man and unable to control his bodily functions, all his relatives abused him. He was very unhappy at being despised–so, thinking of his next birth, he went to a cemetery. A yogin came along and asked him: "What are you doing here in this cemetery?" And the old man answered:

The moon of my youth has been eclipsed
by the Rāhu-dragon of old age.
My sons and others abuse me,
so I remain here, happy to die.

The yogin replied:

Your karma is ripening:
The rivers of childhood,
youth, and old age
have all flowed past.
The river of death
has now arrived.
Shouldn't you practice the Dharma
as provision for death?

The old man replied, "O guru, give the Dharma to me. Even though I am old and without wealth, please give me the Dharma."

The yogin said in reply:

The natural mind is without old age.
Your nature is not dependent on wealth–
if, with devotion, you are able to practice
the holy Dharma, I will take care of you.

He gave him initiation which transfers spiritual power, and he gave him instructions on the seed-point in this way: "Meditate the circle of the moon[32] arising from the letter A on the top of your head. Meditate all the concepts of the visible world entering into it."

Eclipse the concepts of which you have taken hold
by the Rāhu of non-dual experience.

At the great bliss at the top of your head,
the profound seed-point will arise.
By the continuous integration of emptiness and bliss,
you will overcome the enemies, the skandhas.[33]
The qualities of the Buddhas will arise
and lo, there will be unceasing wonders.

The old man received these instructions, and as he meditated in the way he was told, the moon of holding to duality was entirely devoured by the Rāhu of non-duality. The nectar of non-duality entered the fire at the Brahma opening at the top of his head, and the nectar expanded throughout his entire body. He practiced for sixteen years, and then he won the siddhi of Mahāmudrā. He trained living beings in Kāmarūpa, and having narrated his experiences, he went to the realm of the Ḍākas in this very body.

# Dharmapa

Dharmapa, 'the Man of the Dharma', was a scholar in the land of Bodhinagara who mainly preached without practicing. Later, as he grew older and was losing his sight, a thought occurred to him: "Would it not be fitting that I meet with a guru?" A ḍākinī spoke to him in a dream, giving him encouragement and saying, "I am your spiritual friend." Then she revealed herself in her true form and initiated him, giving him these instructions:

> Meditate all existing things as a vessel;
> meditate all conceptualizations as butter.
> Meditate your consciousness as fuel;
> then meditate the flashing fire of knowledge.
> Into the vessel—all existing things without exception—
> pour the butter of conceptualizations.
> Let the fire burn the fuel of thoughts,
> and the jewel of the mind itself will appear.

For five years he recited mantras and practiced the precepts which develop into realized knowledge. When the realized knowledge occurred, to the astonishment of the people, his body became like that of an eight-year-old. Then he said:

> How can the collection of causes and conditions,
> being empty, give rise to any result?
> But until you possess an enlightened mind,
> you must exert effort.

He worked for the benefit of living beings until finally, having narrated his experiences, he went to the realm of the Ḍākas.

# Dhokaripa

Dhokaripa, 'the Man Who Carries a Pot', was a man of low caste in Saliputra who always carried a pot. Whatever he could beg as alms, he would put into the pot. One day, unable to find sustenance, he sat down at the foot of a tree. A yogin came up to him, and Dhokaripa said to him, "I have nothing for you today." "Well then," said the yogin, "couldn't you use the Dharma?" "Indeed I could, but I have not met with a spiritual friend," said Dhokaripa. "Would you be able to practice it?" asked the yogin. "I would be able to do it," Dhokaripa replied.

Then having initiated Dhokaripa into Hevajra, the yogin gave him instructions on the Developing Stage and the Perfecting Stage in this manner:

> O Dhokaripa, you who carry a pot:
> Put all the sustenance of realization
> inside the vessel of the Dharma
> and meditate these two as inseparable.

He meditated in this way; he understood the meaning, and in three years he obtained siddhi. After this, when he was seen carrying his pot around, the people would ask him, "O guru, what do you carry there?" And he would answer:

> I carry the vessel of the Great Emptiness:
> I am collecting the fruit of the Great Bliss;
> Dhokaripa has what he desires.
> Is this not known by the fortunate?

He worked for the benefit of many beings and finally, having narrated his experiences, he became famous as Dhokaripa, and went in this very body to the realm of the Ḍākas.

# Medhina

Medhina, 'the Man of the Field', was a low-caste man of Saliputra. One day, while laboring in the fields, he just stopped and stood there. A yogin came along and asked him, "What are you doing, just standing there?" "I have stopped doing field work," he replied. "Wouldn't you like to get away from this pain and suffering?" asked the yogin. "The Dharma can accomplish that." "But who would give me the Dharma?" "I will give it to you if you are able to practice it," replied the yogin, and Medhina indicated he was able.

The yogin then gave him instructions on the Developing Stage and the Perfecting Stage, and then set him to meditating. But the thoughts of his field work continually interrupted him, and Medhina lost his desire to meditate. He went back to his guru, who gave him instructions that were more consistent with his thoughts:

> Make your thoughts into a plow,
> and make pleasure and pain into oxen.
> Contemplate your body as the field,
> and contemplate the fruit, the bliss of the Dharma-
> nature,
> coming forth night and day.
> Make your concepts into a plow,
> your feelings of pleasure and pain into oxen.
> Sow the seeds of the elements
> to ripen on the field of your body.
> Exerting yourself on that field,
> work day and night!
> The fruit, the bliss of the Dharma-nature
> will never end.

He meditated accordingly for twelve years, and having stopped the various kinds of worldly conceptions, he obtained siddhi. He ascended a tree which grew seven talas up into the sky, and from there he narrated his experiences.

He worked for the benefit of countless beings in the city of Saliputra, and then went to the realm of the Ḍākas in this very body.

# Paṅkaja

Paṅkaja, the son of a Brahman, was called Paṅkaja because he was born from a lotus in his parents' peaceful garden of lotuses. His siddhi came from Avalokiteśvara. A short while after his birth, an image of Avalokiteśvara was placed near the pond of lotuses. Now, it was customary in that area to reverence Mahādeva, and for twelve years, Paṅkaja made offerings to the image, believing it to be Mahādeva. In accordance with local custom, he made offerings of flowers three times a day, placing them on top of the head of the image.

One day, while Paṅkaja was making an offering, the master Nāgārjuna came and offered a flower. The image accepted it and placed it upon its own head. Paṅkaja became angry at this, and thought to himself, "For twelve years, I made offerings and the image did not accept them. He made only one offering, and the image received it and responded." Then out of the mouth of the image came these words: "Your thoughts were not pure. I was not pleased with your actions."

At this, remorse arose in Paṅkaja, and he prostrated himself before the master Nāgārjuna and respectfully asked to become his pupil. Nāgārjuna initiated him and instructed him in the integration of vision and activity:

You cannot be successful with faith alone
or with just the bliss of compassion.
You must see truly without distinctions
just as do the Āryans themselves.

Understanding this, Paṅkaja practiced, and in seven days he obtained siddhi. He brought many blessings to living beings by his compassionate gaze and by his instructions on method. Finally in this very body, he went to the realm of the Ḍākas.

# Ghaṇḍhapa

Ghaṇḍhapa, who took the vows of a monk at Śrī Nālandā, did not transgress them. When he mastered the five sciences, his fame spread in every direction; as a master, he worked for the benefit of sentient beings in every land.

There was a king, Devapāla by name, who by the power of his merit brought great prosperity to his country. The wealth of his kingdom was immeasurable: his own cities numbered 1,800,000; there were 900,000 in Kamari, 400,000 in Bengal, and in addition, over 3,100,000 pledged fealty to him. One day, the master came to Saliputra, the seat of King Devapāla, begging alms. He took his place at the foot of a tree and lived there.

Now King Devapāla, being a religious man, had countless objects of devotion. One night, the king took counsel with his wife: "All compound things are impermanent. All worldly things are painful. Existing things have no substance. If I am to rule a kingdom, both now and in the future, and if we are to remain husband and wife, we must accumulate merit as provision for the future life by making worthy men our objects of reverence. That indeed would be the right thing to do."

"You have revered countless men before," the queen answered, "but there now lives at the edge of the city an Āryan who is superior to all the others. He is truly an object of reverence. He holds to the monastic rule; he collects alms, wears monk's robes, and lives on meager provisions. You should take food and drink to him—the eighty-four vegetables, and the five drinks such as grape-juice and so on. You should offer the light of jewels instead of the light of a lamp; give him all the desirable things of the kingdom." "That is certainly the right thing to do," said the king. So the next day he sent several of his circle to bring the master to him; but they returned without the monk. The king and his retinue then went themselves and bowed to the master, who asked them. "Why have you come here?" "I have come out of faith, to invite the master to be my object of reverence," the king replied. "I will not go with you," said Ghaṇḍhapa, "for the kingdom of a king is an evil thing." At this, the king said, "Even if you do not stay permanently, come for at least one year." The king insisted, but still the master refused.

In the same way, the king asked again and again: "For six months?" "For three months?" "For one month?" "For two weeks?" Finally, he asked, "For just one day?" To all of this the master replied, "I will not come, for your nature is wholly evil. You practice harmful modes of action."

For forty days the king urgently pleaded, over and again, but the master still would not come. The king and his people became angry, and the fire of hatred flamed in their hearts. The king made a general proclamation: "Whoever is able to cause this monk to abandon his purity, I will give him half the kingdom and a ton of gold."

There was a woman in that land, a most clever prostitute, who told the king that she could accomplish what he desired. "Well then, do it!" exclaimed the king. "Do it with skill and energy!"

Now, the prostitute had a twelve-year-old daughter, so beautiful she did not even appear to belong to this world. She had a lovely face, a voluptuous body, a pleasant voice, and a charming way of walking. If the sun could see her, he would not be able to move. The prostitute thought: "If I send her to that monk, she will be able to separate him from the virtuous conduct which frees him from the things of samsara." She then instructed her daughter to do reverence to the monk, circumambulate him, and then return. After the girl had done this for ten days, she said to the monk, "I will be your patron for the three summer months." But he refused this.

For an entire month, over and over, the girl made this offer; finally the master assented. The girl was elated, and performed a ceremony to celebrate. "A beguiling girl," she thought, "if she desires eighty things, can gain a hundred."

And she thought further: "If I am clever, I could seduce the four continents. What need I say for this monk? However pure his mind may be, I can beguile him." But at the time food was being brought, the master said to her, "Send men to bring food to me. A girl should not do it." And she replied, "I will do as you wish."

During the first two months, only men brought the master sugar-water and rice dishes. Then the clever prostitute, decorating her daughter with all sorts of ornaments, sent her with five hundred maidens carrying many vessels with all sorts of food and drink. Near the place of the master, the girl told the others to return home. Then she went inside the monk's hut, recollecting the beguiling ways she had been taught by her mother.

The monk, seeing that those who usually brought him food had not come, went inside. There he saw the young maiden decorated with ornaments. "Where is everyone?" he asked. "They do not have the time," the girl replied. "But truly we do." And she stayed a long time. Finally he said, "Now go!" But by now five-colored clouds had gathered in the sky, and it began to rain. Saying that she would go when it stopped, she stayed a while longer. Finally the sun went down.

"I have no traveling companion," she said. "If the wrong people see these clothes and ornaments, they may take my life." He said he did not think that would happen. But she then asked to sleep there because she was afraid of the night, and so he let her sleep near him. By the power of being so close, the two joined bodies together. Uniting together, they experienced the four joys and began to travel the path.

The next day, the girl did not want to return to her mother; instead, she went out to get food and drink for both herself and the monk. They lived together for a year, and a son was born to them.

The king was always pestering the prostitute about how things were progressing, but she was not able to give the desired answer. Then, after three years had passed, the prostitute said to the king: "O great king, the intent of your Majesty's decree has been fulfilled. Now may your heart be happy." The king answered, "Well then, in three days, bring this monk here and call your daughter." And the king and the people of Saliputra prepared to examine the monk.

The monk asked the girl, "Should we stay here, or should we go somewhere else?" "If we stay," the girl said, "all these people will revile us for doing sinful deeds. We can be happy even if we wander away from the habitations of men." The girl took up the child and a bottle of wine, and the two companion-lovers left. They then met with the king in the middle of the road. He dismounted from the back of his elephant, saying, "What is that inside your monk's clothes? Who is this woman with you?" "Inside these clothes are a child and a bottle. The woman is my wife," said Ghaṇḍhapa. "I remember once you said you would not go into the presence of a sinner. Now, what about your wife and child? You yourself are a sinner." "There has been no wrong-doing here, so do not slander me," the master said.

When the king repeated what he had said, the master threw the child and the bottle to the ground. The earth-goddess was frightened, the earth split, and water gushed out. In the water, the child turned into a vajra, and the bottle into a bell. The master became Cakrasamvara, and his woman became Vajravārāhī. In the sky above the king and his entourage, Cakrasamvara and Vajravārāhī, in yab-yum position, appeared holding a vajra and bell.

The king and the rest looked up and made reverence to the master as a protector, but the monk would not end his samādhi of vajra-anger. The king and his retinue were sinking in the water which was gushing from the split ground, and were nearing death. In an instant, the holy Avalokiteśvara appeared and, with his foot, blocked the water from the split ground. King Devapāla and the others, having been saved, again made apologies to the guru. The master spoke the syllable HŪṀ and all the water disappeared. An image of the holy one was formed out of the rock itself, and it is said that a little stream still flows out from under the foot. Then the master gave instructions to the king and the others in this way:

> Just as medicine and poison
> can be identical in themselves
> and yet give rise to two different effects,
> so one is avoided and the other is readily taken,
> although they have one nature;
> there is no difference.
> The masters who realize this do not renounce things.
> Those who are not masters must do so,
> for lacking realization, they wander in samsara.

The king and the people ceased to slander the monk. In one accord, they took faith, and numberless living beings were set on the path. The master became known as Ghaṇḍhapa, and he grew famous in all directions.

Despite the fact that in this life she was an impediment to morality, the woman had been prepared in six previous lives by the master. The master, removing all conceptualizations of holding to duality in the nature of Dharmahood, consummated the path by the power of maturing his stream of consciousness. Both the son, Vajrapāṇi, and the woman purified their stains by the benefits of veneration. Then, being endowed with the holy qualities, the master Ghaṇḍhapa and his partner both, in that very body, went to the realm of the Ḍākas.

# Yogipa

Yogipa, who lived in Odantapuri, was of the caṇḍala caste, and his guru was Śavaripa. Yet though Yogipa made great effort, it led to little wisdom. One day, the guru Śavaripa came to him and initiated him into Hevajra. After giving him instructions for the Developing Stage and the Perfecting Stage, he set him to meditating. But Yogipa still was not able to understand the meaning of the instructions. He said to the guru, "I cannot meditate effectively," and made a request to perform meritorious acts by just body and speech.

So the guru taught him the recitation of Vajra-Heruka and told him to consummate his practice by going to the twenty-four great places. Yogipa practiced accordingly, and in twelve years, he purified the stains and obtained the siddhi of Mahāmudrā. He told of his understanding, and for five years he aided the various purposes of living beings. Then, in that very body, he went to the realm of the Ḍākas.

# Caluki

Caluki lived in Maṅgalapura; he was of low caste, and his guru was Maitripa. Caluki was a great sleeper: always under the power of sleep. He was not even able to begin effort. Now at one time, he conceived the notion that samsara was evil, and he took his place at the foot of a tree. A yogin came to that spot and asked him, "What are you doing here?"

Caluki replied, "I had thought to practice the Dharma to free myself from the world, but I have not met with a master who would teach the doctrine to me. My nature is lethargic; I am a great sleeper, and I am not able to begin the effort. You may be able to give the Dharma to me, but if you do not give me a method to diminish my need for sleep, the instructions will not work."

"If I initiate you," said Maitripa, "you will be able to free yourself from the world by diminishing your need for sleep." The yogin then initiated Caluki into Cakrasamvara. He gave him the instructions of the vital breath and the mystic veins, and of the elementary Perfecting Stage in this way:

"Assimilate all appearances into your own body, speech, and mind. Bind the *lalanā*, the left vein, and the *rasanā*, the right vein, to the middle vein, the *avadhūtī*. Contemplate the bodily *avadhūtī* as an ocean; then contemplate your knowledge as a goose. After that, contemplate the goose flying over the ocean of essence. As your need for sleep also diminishes, the vital breath will be joined to the *avadhūtī* and the condition of being without conceptions will arise by its own power."

Caluki meditated in that way for nine years and, clearing away the stains, he successfully attained the siddhi of Mahāmudrā. He collected all appearances of the world into his body, speech, and mind, and then these three were collected into subject and object and the flower—and the two veins were then collected into the center. By attaining discriminating knowledge, he won siddhi which was like the goose extracting the essence from the ocean. He told of his experiences, and he went in that very body to the realm of the Ḍākas.

# Gorura

Gorura, the 'Bird-man', was of the bird-catcher caste —that is to say, he carried a net and captured birds. Now, at one time a yogin came along and asked him: "You there, sir, what are you doing?" Gorura replied, "I accumulated evil in a former life, so I was born into the caste of the bird-catchers. In this life I make my living at taking life, and so I am despondent." And the yogin replied:

Because karma is piling on karma here,
you will suffer in this life and in the next.
The holy Dharma is always joyful.
Why not practice it?

"What guru would have compassion and give instruction to a man of such low caste?" asked the bird-catcher. "As a result, I am unable to practice."

So the yogin gave Gorura the initiation which transfers spiritual power, and instructions which would conform to his own character: "Contemplate that all the sounds of the world are like the sounds of birds. Join the two—your conscious thought and the sounds of birds—into one. Then again, free the mind of sound.

Listen for the song of the cuckoo:
The many sounds become one sound.
Then grasp the sound itself as sound,
and contemplate the Dharma-nature
spreading everywhere.

Gorura meditated accordingly and experienced the emptiness of sound without differentiation. For nine years he purified his mind and he obtained the siddhi of Mahāmudrā. He remained in the world a hundred years, narrating his experiences and working for the immeasurable benefit of living beings. Then, together with three hundred followers, in this very body, he went to the realm of the Ḍākas.

# Lucika

Lucika, 'the Man Who Stood Up after Sitting', was a Brahman who lived in the eastern part of Bengal. When he came to realize the universality of death, his mind had a revulsion against samsara, and so he went to a quiet place, intending to practice the Dharma. But he was without instruction and did nothing but think sadly that he had not met with a guru who could instruct him in the Dharma.

Now one day, a yogin came there—which made him very happy. He gave reverence to him, and the yogin said, "What do you want that you give reverence to me?" "I have a revulsion against samsara," Lucika replied, "and have intended to practice the Dharma. Yet I have not met a guru who could give me instructions. Now that I have finally met with a guru, I ask for instructions." And so the yogin gave him initiation into Cakrasamvara and gave him instructions on the Developing Stage and the Perfecting Stage.

Lucika exerted himself and meditated. In twelve years, he was able to join the Developing and the Perfecting Stages and thus attained siddhi. He became famous as Lucika and spoke thus:

I see no distinction
between samsara and nirvana.
Yet liberation is great bliss,
for when you hold to low things,
it is difficult to cross over.

In this very body, he went to the realm of the Ḍākas. From the sky he narrated his experiences and then disappeared.

# Niguṇa

Niguṇa, 'the Man without Qualities', was the son of a low-caste householder in the country of Pūrvadeśa. While he was being brought up, he was very lazy, and did not think at all of the affairs of the world, being indifferent to what others considered good or evil. If he saw a fruit he liked, he would think it good; but if he could not reach it without effort, he would curse it as evil. In such a state of mind, he went to a quiet place.

A yogin came along and said to him, "Come, let us get alms in the city." But Niguṇa replied, "But what if we don't get anything?" And he did not even get up from the ground. The yogin, out of compassion, gave food to him and said, "Don't you have any good qualities?" "Yogin," Niguṇa replied, "if someone has been given the name 'Niguṇa' then he is without good qualities."

As Niguṇa ate the rest of the food, the yogin asked him, "Doesn't death frighten you?" "Indeed it does," Niguṇa replied, "but I have no way to deal with it." "If you can practice it, I will give you a method," said the yogin. "Then I will practice during the time I sleep," said Niguṇa. And so the yogin gave him initiation. He then gave him instructions on conjoining emptiness and appearances:

Subject and object have no reality whatsoever,
yet beings are not enlightened.
Suffering, they are pitiful in their torment,
which from the beginning, has no reality.
Appearances are inseparable from emptiness;
the pure light is continually present.
And though you act like a crazy man,
you will enter into the pure city.

The yogin spoke in this way and Niguṇa, gathering alms, practiced. When he produced the realization of Total Integration and the clear light, he attained siddhi. He wandered in all directions, asking: "Who are these men?" Whenever he saw people, he would say, "O pity men such as these!" and weep. For those to be trained, he demonstrated the path which does not split appearance and emptiness.

Then, like a ship on the ocean, he wiped out all the marks of delusion. Attaining the siddhi of Mahāmudrā in this very body, he went to the realm of the Ḍākas.

# Jayānanda

Jayānanda was a Brahman minister to the king of Bengal. He followed the religion of the Brahmans but then, secretly, he began to practice the Dharma of the secret mantras, and though blessings arose, no one witnessed them.

In the course of time, however, he began to make many torma offerings.[34] The other ministers, finding this unendurable, reported it to the king. So the king had him clasped in irons. Jayānanda pleaded with the king, "Set me free from these chains. I have not allowed even half a handful of your Majesty's wealth to be wasted." But the king would not listen.

Later, at the time the Brahman was accustomed to give torma offerings, many birds appeared—not finding the offerings, the birds gathered on the king's palace. While the soldiers tried to remove them, the people watched and wondered. As the gathering of the birds increased, a man who had the ability to understand the voices of birds heard them say: "That Brahman, who was like a mother and father to us, has been condemned by the king."

He related this to the king, and the king replied, "If that is so, I will pardon him if he agrees to remain in a lonely place. Ask the birds to leave." The man gave the message to the birds, and they left. The king took faith, and every day he gave the Brahman twenty bushels of rice as materials for torma offerings. From then on, the minister was known as the guru Jayānanda. He spoke in this way:

> The knowledge of the Inborn has been truly realized
> through the kindness of the guru.
> I have become the minister of greatest bliss,
> and I remain no more in the whirl of samsara.
> The King, the clear and natural state,
> has conquered the enemies of subject and object
> and does not lust after the delights of the world.
> Behold, O unenlightened beings.
> I cry out and say: 'Jaya! Victory!'

And so he worked for the benefit of beings, and after seven hundred years, he went to the realm of the Ḍākas.

# Pacari

Pacari was from the land of Campaka and his caste was that of the pastry-sellers. He was so poor he did not even have clothes of cheap cotton. He would obtain pastries from a rich householder, cook them in butter, and sell them. He then repaid the householder and lived on the profits. One day, as he had not yet sold them, he took half of the pastries to eat himself. Avalokiteśvara, taking the form of a monk, went to him. Pacari, taking faith, did him reverence and gave the monk the other half of the pastries. The monk then asked, "Where did you get these?" When Pacari answered truthfully, the monk said, "Well now, we both must offer payment. I will give something to my donor." And so he made a mandala offering and offered flowers. The manifestation then gave Pacari the spiritual power which produces the thought of taking the refuges, and also gave him the instructions of the Six Syllables.[35] Out of devotion, Pacari gave his life over as an offering.

At the time Pacari attained siddhi, the pastry-master of before came along and asked for his money. "But I do not have any," Pacari replied. Upon hearing this, the pastry-master beat him. Pacari then said, "I did not eat them alone. The master and I both ate them—but you are only beating me." Then, to both of their amazement, a voice spoke out from the walls, saying the same thing. The pastry-maker said, "So take my pastries and go," and then released him. Pacari went to a temple where there was an image of his patron deity. He then gave a hundred gold coins to the householder as a price of the pastries, thus purifying his former sin, even though it was trifling.

It then occurred to Pacari that his guru was the Holy One, and so he set off for the Potala mountain. Along the way, while traveling through a forest, a thorn entered his foot and he suffered great pain from it. He cried out the Great Mantra to the Holy One, who then appeared to him in his true form. He said, "I am your guru. You should not be interested in securing only your own benefit. Turn back and work to guide those to be trained."

Becoming very happy, Pacari ascended into the sky and

descended again in Campaka. Everyone who saw him was amazed. He gave instructions on the inseparability of emptiness and appearances, and in that very body, he went to the realm of the Ḍākas.

# Campaka

There is a land called Campaka which received its name from the flower. Living in that land was a prince who did not lack for any of the enjoyments or any of the wealth of the kingdom. He was so captivated by his pleasures and his pride in these things that he did not think about the future. The prince had a flower-house skillfully built in his pleasure garden of campakas. In the garden there were seats and cushions made of campakas—flowers of a golden color with sweet perfume—and he lived there in the garden.

One day, a yogin came to the garden, begging alms. The king washed the yogin's feet, brought him a seat, and made him comfortablc. He then gave the yogin food and drink, after which, as the yogin preached to him, the king and his entire court sat before him and made him an object of reverence.

The king then said, "As a yogin, you must have gone through many lands. Have you ever seen such flowers or such a king as me?" The yogin replied, "The scent of the campaka flowers is excellent, but it is not so with the smells of your body. Your Majesty's kingdom may be superior to other kingdoms, but when you die, you will have to go without it."

The king, recognizing this fact, turned away from his fondness for his own body, and asked for instructions. The yogin first taught him about the cause and effect of karma, then gave him initiation and the instructions for the Developing and the Perfecting Stage. But the king's thoughts turned to the flowers and he did not want to meditate. So the yogin gave him instructions which took his conceptions as path:

> Since appearances themselves are empty,
> consider the guru's instructions as a flower;
> make the skandhas and your own mind the ground.
> Contemplate as having one nature
> the three rivers of pure nectar,
> and the great bliss will arise as a result.

These are the words of the great Vajradhara;
so meditate with conviction.

The king meditated for twelve years, and having realized that the precepts, his experience, and the original state of his own mind were inseparable, he obtained siddhi. From then on, he became known as Campaka. He explained the Dharma to his queen along with innumerable followers, and finally went to the realm of the Ḍākas in this very body.

# Bhikṣana

Bhikṣana, 'the Man with Two Teeth', lived as a man of low caste in Saliputra. As he lacked both wealth and fortune, he went begging from town to town. One day, not having obtained anything and feeling very disheartened, he went to a lonely place. A ḍākinī came to him and asked him what he was doing there. He told her the truth: "If there is some way of acquiring what I desire, I really want it," he said. "Well then, what will be my payment?" asked the ḍākinī. He then bit together his upper and lower teeth, and offered them. Understanding that he had an unwavering mind, she gave him initiation and instructions on the conjoining of wisdom and method.

He meditated in such a way, and in seven years he experienced the truth. Stainless qualities arose in him. He went from town to town narrating his experiences for the benefit of those to be trained, and became famous under the name of Bhikṣana. After many years, he went in this very body to the realm of the Ḍākas.

# Telopa

Telopa made his living in the city of Saliputra as an oil merchant. Since he was able to sell his oil at a good price, he became very rich. As his good fortune continued, he became as wealthy as Kubera, the god of wealth. He enjoyed his prosperity, eating the eighty-four vegetables, the twelve foods, and the five drinks just like a king. Then one day the scholar Bahana came by and preached to him the sorrow of samsara and the means to escape it. The merchant took faith and, asking for the Dharma, he made reverence to the yogin. The yogin Bahana, seeing Telopa preparing the oil, said to him, "Your wealth is due to good fortune, but it will not produce liberation." The merchant answered, "O guru, please then tell me the method which will produce liberation." So the yogin gave him initiation and instructions on how to produce his own radiance in the darkness of night:

> Free the oil of your conceptualizations
> from the kernels of sesame seeds, your own body,
> and then fill up the vessel
> which is your own mind.
> The wick is the inseparability
> of emptiness and appearances;
> if you apply the fire of knowledge,
> you will dispel the darkness of ignorance.
> In the highest joy of liberation,
> you will live in stainless bliss.

The merchant piously meditated, and in six years, when he joined the Developing Stage and the Perfecting Stage, he obtained siddhi. Light streamed from his body and filled the area all around.

Others saw this and reported it to the king. The king asked, "Can this be so?" And he saw that it was. The king also enjoyed stainless bliss, and the others, though they did not have an equal joy, took faith. The merchant then gave instructions, speaking about their world and its emptiness. After many years, together with a large circle of followers, he went to the realm of the Ḍākas.

# Kumaripa

Kumaripa, 'the Potter', lived in the country of Jomanaśrī, where he made his living by making pots. Because he had time for nothing but work, he became quite despondent. A yogin then came and begged alms from him. The potter brought food to him, saying, "O guru, I work strenuously at my task but no great benefit comes from it. I am disheartened because the work is never completely finished. I am disheartened because there seems to be no end to it."

Thereupon the yogin answered, "O benefactor, do you not understand? The living beings of the world have pleasure only with suffering. A few do not have any pleasure at all. From beginningless time, even without working, the pain alone has no end. You have reason to be depressed." The potter took faith and asked from his guru a method of liberation. Thereupon the yogin gave the potter initiation and instructions on the Developing Stage and the Perfecting Stage:

Remove the mud of misery and conceptions
from the clay of ignorance.
By the wheel of the world,
form the pots of the six Tantric families;
then fire them by the fires of knowledge.

By these words, the potter understood the instructions which cleared away his misconceptions. Having meditated for six months, he purified himself of the stains of worldly delusions, and obtained siddhi. While he sat in meditation, the potter's wheel turned by itself and the pots were formed as he desired. When the citizens of the city saw that he had the qualities of the Tantric families, he became known as the guru Kumaripa. Having narrated his experiences, he went in this very body to the realm of the Ḍākas.

# Caparipa

In a certain city in Magadha, there was a herdsman of immeasurable wealth who owned a thousand buffalo and horses, and sheep without number. When his old father died, he gave a large wake—larger than had ever been seen before. He invited all the people of the land, and much food and drink was given out for many days. One day, these people went to bathe in the River Ganges, while the herdsman's wife stayed at home with their three-year-old daughter to watch over things. At this time, the guru Caparipa suddenly appeared and asked for food.

When the woman talked to him honestly and with little artfulness, Caparipa said to her, "If your husband or the others become angry, then come to me. I will be up in the forest making a fire. But if they do not get angry, it will be all right to stay. So you must give me food and drink!"

She listened to the guru, and when he returned to the forest, she was in a very relaxed frame of mind. When the others returned, her mother-in-law, who came also, saw that she had given away most of the food, so that there was little left. She flamed up and fought with her. In anger, the woman, carrying her child on her back, fled to the yogin. When she arrived, the yogin said, "Very good!" He then sprinkled them with mantra water, and both mother and child turned into stone—so that they would not need food or anything else any more.

When her husband returned home he asked, "Where did she go?" The people did not know. Hurrying around, asking about her everywhere, finally he went to the yogin and told him what had happened. He too was sprinkled with mantra water and became what his wife and child had become.

A place was made available for the three of them. The relatives then came one by one, following the others. There were about three hundred of them, who came bleating like buffalo calves; and everyone met with the same treatment.

The child of that woman had certain qualities: from his scrotum came the siddhis of the Ḍākas. From his penis came the power to transform things into gold. From his anus came the elixir of immortality. From his eye, the eight great siddhis: walking on air and the others.

This family became famous everywhere, and the king of Campaka came with buffaloes and other animals. The king, out of faith, built a temple to the three: the child, and the husband and wife. He then built a temple to the other three hundred called 'Many-named'. Those who have bad thoughts cannot enter that temple; if they do, the images will beat them or worse.

This temple has become a center of practice, and it is said that even now there are many yogins who reside there. At that place practice has quick results. You can attain the worldly siddhis there, and while waiting for the appearance of the Victorious One, Maitreya, you can be working for the benefit of living beings.

# Maṇibhadrā

Maṇibhadrā is also called the yoginī Bahuri. In the city of Agartse, there lived a wealthy householder who had a thirteen-year-old daughter who had been given in marriage to a man of her own caste. As she was visiting the home of her parents one day, the guru Kukkuripa came up to her and asked for food. "You are well-formed," she said. "Why do you live like this, begging for food and wearing patched clothes? Surely you should take a wife who is chaste and of your own caste." He replied:

I am frightened by samsara;
and since I am afraid,
I am working to accomplish
the great joy of liberation.
If I do not accomplish liberation
in this auspicious life time,
how will I be able to meet with it
in my next life?
If this precious life,
which is like a jewel,
were to be wrapped in impurity—
such as a spouse—
the desire of my life would be defeated.
All sorts of ills would arise.
Because I know this would happen,
I avoid taking a wife.

When the girl heard this, she took faith in him, and giving him alms, she asked, "Show me a method of obtaining liberation." "My home is in the cemetery," he said. "You must come there if you want it." Even though it was extremely difficult to do, she went to the cemetery that evening before midnight. He saw that she was ready for the teachings, and he initiated her into Cakrasamvara. He gave her instructions on the Developing Stage, the Perfecting Stage, and Total Integration. She then practiced for several days.

When she returned to her parents, they beat her and spoke harsh words to her. She said to them, "There is no one in the three realms of the cosmos who has not been my mother and father. Even with caste and great family lineage, you cannot escape from samsara without falling back. I have taken the guru as my support and am working toward liberation. So hit me . . . I will take that as path."

Her parents believed this to be a trifling matter, and so they said nothing more. But she meditated on the instructions of the guru and in her mind gave up all the results of karma. She practiced for one year, and then her husband came for her and took her back with him. At his house, she did the deeds and duties of the world as they are usually done; she spoke pleasing words and was restrained in body and speech.

Eventually she gave birth to a boy and two girls. Then as things happen, one day while she was taking her son for a blessing, she met with her guru. Twelve years had passed.

She went to draw water and was returning home when she tripped at the foot of the tree and broke her water pot. She just stood there, looking at the broken pot. At noon, when she did not return, her husband went out and saw her there. If anyone said anything to her, she did not seem to hear. She only stared. Then she finally said, "What are you saying? Are you all possessed?" And at sundown she said:

Living beings without beginning,
break the pot of the body.
Why should I return home?
My pot is now broken.
I will not return to my home in samsara;
now I will go to the great bliss.
Behold, O guru, a great wonder:
desiring great bliss, I have recourse to you.

Then she rose up in the air, and for twenty-one days she gave instructions to those in Agartse. Then she went to the realm of the Ḍākas.

# Mekhalā

There was a householder in Devīkoṭa who had two daughters. There was also a great merchant who had two sons—and the two families were to be joined. But everyone gossiped about the two girls—even though they had not done anything wrong. The younger of the two said to her sister, "People are talking about us without cause. We should go somewhere else." But the elder daughter replied, "Even if we went elsewhere, it would not make any difference, since we do not have a good accumulation of karma."

The guru Kāṇhapa then came to that area with a circle of seven hundred yogins and yoginīs. He manifested numberless prodigies such as umbrellas suspended over his head and the ceaseless resounding of the damaru. The two sisters said to themselves, "Since the townspeople have gossiped about us both, we should ask for instructions from the guru and practice them." So they told their stories to him and asked for instructions. The guru granted their request and gave them initiation. He also gave them instructions of Vajravārāhī regarding seeing, meditation, practice, results, and Total Integration.

These two practiced energetically, and in twelve years attained siddhi. They then went back to their guru and presented offerings to him. But he responded by asking, "Who are you? I do not know you." So they gave an account of what had happened previously. "Well then," he said, "you must give me my fee." "O guru, we will give as fee whatever you request," they replied. "Then," said the guru, "give me your heads, both of you." "We will give what the guru requests." Out of each of their mouths came a sharp sword of knowledge. They then each cut off their own head with their own weapon and then presented the heads to the guru, saying, "We are repaying the words of the guru."

We have cut off the illusion
of samsara and crossed over
by the Total Integration
of the Developing and Perfecting Stages.
We have cut off the illusion

of acquiring and renouncing
by the Total Integration
of vision and activity.
We have cut the illusion
of self and other
by the Total Integration
of knowledge and space.
We give you the illusionless
with this gesture.

Having said this, as they began to dance with their heads in their hands, Kāṇhapa exclaimed, "Behold, two great yoginīs! You are happy because you have attained most excellent qualities. But to remain merely in your own tranquility is the inferior way. You should work for the benefit of living beings." Saying this, he restored their heads without leaving any trace of a wound, at which everyone was amazed.

These two sisters, following in the steps of Kāṇhapa, became famous. They attained the siddhi of Mahāmudrā and after working for the benefit of living beings for many years, they went to the realm of the Ḍākas.

## Kanakhalā

She was the younger of the two sisters who, following the guru Kāṇhapa, cut off their own heads as is told in the previous story. The younger sister became known as the yoginī Kanakhalā.

# Kalakala

Kalakala, 'the Chatterbox', was born of a low-caste family in the city of Bhilira. As a result of karma in a previous life, Kalakala was very talkative. The townspeople all found him obnoxious, and therefore ostracized him. He became very downhearted and finally went to live in a cemetery.

While he sat there in his misery, a yogin came along. "Why are you in this cemetery?" he asked. Kalakala told the yogin truthfully about how his life had been, and the yogin said in reply, "If you are depressed, couldn't you use a method of liberation from the misery of the world?" "Who would I ask if I needed it?"asked Kalakala. The yogin indicated he would be the one to ask. After the chatterbox did reverence and made offerings, the yogin initiated him into the Guhyasamāja and gave these instructions for liberation from appearances:

> Meditate as having one nature, without distinction,
> the sound of self and other as sound itself.
> Then, during meditation, your own voice will be the sound
> of thunder in the sky—and flowers will rain down.

Exerting himself, Kalakala meditated and lost the sound of other people's anger in the sound of his own voice; his own voice was lost in a rain of flowers; he lost the idea of flowers in the emptiness of the sky; and the Mahāmudrā of all appearances arose. Having liberated himself from all appearances, he attained siddhi, and in all directions he became known as guru Kalakala. Narrating his experiences, he worked for the benefit of many of those to be trained. Then, together with a circle of three hundred followers, he went to the realm of the Ḍākas.

# Kantali

In the city of Maṇidharā, Kantali, 'the Tailor', lived a life devoid of both wealth and enjoyment. To support himself, he could only sew clothes and beg. One day, while sewing, he stuck himself with the point of a needle. Blood spurted forth, and the hurt was so great that he could not endure it. He therefore returned home.

The ḍākinī Veṭalī took the form of a young girl, who asked him, "What are you doing?" When he told her what had happened, she said to him, "You undergo suffering in this life because of previous lives. Because of this life, you will experience suffering again and again in future lives." To this, Kantali replied, "I would like a method to escape from that suffering if you have one." "Are you able to practice it?" she asked. "I cannot unless I am shown how," he replied. So she initiated him into Hevajra. She instructed him on the immeasurables, the Yoga of the Guru, and the Developing Stage of yoga. Yet while meditating, he became conscious of his sewing. When the ḍākinī returned again, she gave him instructions as to how to take his conceptions as path:

> Meditate sewing together
> emptiness and appearances
> with the needle and thread
> of knowledge and mindfulness.
> When you have sewn these clothes
> with the needle of compassion,
> meditate clothing
> the beings of the world.

Meditating in this way, he realized that all existing things are empty. Developing great compassion for all unenlightened beings, he obtained Total Integration and the siddhi of Mahāmudrā. Becoming famous everywhere as the guru Kantali, he worked for the benefit of living beings, and finally, having narrated his experiences, he went to the realm of the Ḍākas.

# Dhahuli

There lived a man of low caste in Dhakara, who made his living by making rope out of grass. One day, while he was rolling up and tying the ropes, a large blister appeared on his hands. It became so painful that he just stood there wailing. A yogin came along and said, "What ails you?" The rope-maker told him what had just occurred, and the yogin replied, "If you cannot endure this much pain now, what will you do when you are reborn into an unpleasant destiny in a later life?" "O guru," asked Dhahuli, "is there a method to free myself from that?" The yogin then gave him the initiation which transfers spiritual strength, and then told him these instructions for practicing the path of realization:

From the beginning
there is no intrinsic nature
in either the kusha grass
of accustomed appearances
or in the things
which tie appearances together.
So meditate
with increasing energy.

For twelve years he meditated with faith and vigor on what he had been told. Having realized that all binding notions are without foundation, and having realized that the power of other things is dependent, and the essential nature is the space of the Dharma, he obtained siddhi. He became famous everywhere as the yogin Dhahuli, and for seven hundred years, he worked for the benefit of many living beings. Then, together with a following of five hundred, he departed for thc realm of the Ḍākas.

# Udheli

Udheli, 'He Who Flies', was a nobleman of the land of Devīkoṭa, who, as a result of his charity in former lives, was very rich. Once, while he was living in his palace and enjoying his pleasures, clouds of five different colors gathered in the sky. As he lay gazing at them, the clouds appeared to take the shapes of various living things. One looked like a goose flying in the sky, and he reflected, "O, if I could only fly like that!"

While he was reflecting about birds, the guru Karṇaripa came by asking for food. After giving him food and water, the nobleman bowed down to him and said, "Do you have a method for flying in the sky for one who gives alms to yogins?" "Indeed I have," said the yogin. And he gave the nobleman the initiation of the Catuḥpīṭhamahāyoginī-tantra. And these were the instructions:

"In the twenty-four great places, there are twenty-four medicines. Go to each of these places and recite a thousand times the mantra of each ḍākinī. When you have recited them, then take the medicines." "Once I have done that, then what should I do?" asked the nobleman. "First pour the medicines into a copper vessel, then into a vessel of silver, and then pour them into a vessel of gold. Then you will be able to go into the sky," was the yogin's reply.

In twelve years the nobleman completed the admixture of medicines, and having done as instructed, he flew into the sky. He became famous everywhere under the name Udheli, and having narrated his experiences, he went in this very body to the realm of the Ḍākas.

# Kapalapa

Kapalapa, which means 'the Man with a Skull', was a man of low caste in the country of Rājapuri who had five sons. Because of previous karma, his wife died. He carried the corpse to the cemetery, and as he was standing there grieving, he was told that his five sons had also died. He brought their bodies to the cemetery as well, and remained to grieve even more.

The yogin Kṛṣṇacāri came up to him and said, "What are you doing here?" "I have lost my wife and sons, yogin. I am torn by misery. I just stand here, unable to forget these bodies." To which Kṛṣṇacāri replied, "Everyone in the world is in the same condition, and you are not alone. But being miserable is of no benefit from the standpoint of the Dharma. Are you not afraid of birth and death in samsara?" "I indeed fear life and death," said Kapalapa. "And if you have a method of escaping it, please give it to me." So the yogin initiated him into the mandala of Hevajra and gave him instructions on the Developing and Perfecting Stages; then he set him to practicing.

The man made six sets of ornaments from the bones of his sons, and by splitting the head of his wife, he made a cup. This skull cup was the Developing Stage; that it was empty inside the skull showed him the Perfecting Stage. In nine years, he achieved the Total Integration, and having attained siddhi, he then spoke to those to be trained:

I am the yogin of the skull.
The nature of all existing things
I know to be like this skull.
So I behave according to my inner power.

He danced in the sky, and the people all took faith in him. He became famous as the guru Kapalapa; he then narrated his experiences and worked for the benefit of living beings for five hundred years. Then, with a circle of six hundred, he went to the realm of the Ḍākas.

# Kirava

In the city of Grahara, there was a king as wealthy as Kubera, who enjoyed an extensive domain. But that did not satisfy him—he had to pillage the realms of other kings and enjoy them as well. At one time, he led his army into another land; all who were able to flee did so, but the women were not able to get away. When the king heard the women wailing, he asked his minister about it. The minister spoke to him straightforwardly, and the king grew very sad. Compassion arose in him, and he said, "Let the women be reunited with their fathers and husbands."

The minister carried out the king's instructions, and so the men all returned to their homes. The king decreed a great bell for gift-giving, and gave many gifts to those who had no food. The king then reflected that it might be necessary to practice the Dharma, and while he was so thinking a yogin came there asking for food and drink. The king gave the yogin an abundance of both. The yogin then taught him the doctrine of the Four Immeasurables. The king then asked for more teachings of the Buddha, and the yogin initiated him into Cakrasamvara and set him to meditating on the Developing and the Perfecting Stages.

However, his path was hindered by thoughts of his army and his realm, so he received these instructions on how to overcome these thoughts:

> Contemplate that all sentient beings
> of the three realms are like an heroic army.
> A limitless hero comes forth from your own mind—
> which is as expansive as the sky.
> Having removed all distinctions between these two
> heroes,
> you will conquer your enemies;
> then you yourself will become a great king.
> Once you obtain the joy of victory by meditation,
> you will achieve the pinnacle of life.

After twelve years, the king envisioned and experienced this truth, and after he obtained siddhi, the palace was pervaded by light. When he realized that his queen and the court had obtained siddhi as well, he ordered a great ceremony, saying:

> For sentient beings practicing the Four Immeasurables,
> obsessions can be abandoned
> even by acts which look like desire.
> The hero, by what looks like great fury,
> can destroy all enemies.

Becoming famous as the guru Kirava, he narrated his experiences, and for seven hundred years he worked for the benefit of living beings. With a circle of six hundred, he went to the realm of the Ḍākas.

# Sakara

In the land of Kañci, there was a king named Indrabhūti who ruled over 400,000 cities. Though he was a great king, he had no son; so he prayed to both the worldly and the transmundane deities for a son to be born to him. One day, a being took residence in his wife's womb and thoughts of joy arose in her. She had a dream that in six months the child carried the sun and moon on his shoulders, drank the ocean, ate Mount Meru, and put his foot on the three realms of the cosmos. She asked the king about this dream, and he said to her, "I do not know what to make of it. You will have to ask the honored scholars and Brahmans."

Offering gifts, she put her question to them, and they replied, "These are signs that a Bodhisattva will be born, a king of the Dharma-realm, a source of perfections who will bring joy to the people of this world and joy to the next world as well." Everyone was elated upon hearing this.

Nine months later, in the waxing fortnight, a child was born in the center of a lotus, on a great lake of accomplished deeds and merit. There fell a rain of desirable things in the area. Everyone was amazed, and wondered by whose power this was occurring. At noon, they realized that the power was the child's, and they gave him the name 'Lake-born Youth'. Through his power, the inhabitants all obtained and enjoyed all that could be desired.

After this son was born, there came two other sons. When the mother and father died, the people gave the kingdom to the eldest son; but he gave it to the younger sons and became a monk. He then went to Śrīdhana. On the way, the holy Avalokiteśvara appeared to him in the form of a monk, so the prince would not recognize him. "Do you wish to meet with the Sambhogakāya?" he asked the prince. "If I do not have a method, how can I realize this desire?" "If you take me as your guru and pay respect to me, I have a method." And so the prince did reverence and asked for instructions. Avalokiteśvara manifested the hosts of deities of Hevajra by his magic power and then revealed his own form. He then initiated the prince and gave him instructions. Whereupon the Holy One disappeared.

The prince came to Śrīdhana, and while he was practicing, a man desiring to be a yogin came to him and said, "What are you doing?" The monk answered him straightforwardly, at which the man responded, "Then I must serve you. But when you attain siddhi you must give instruction to me." The prince agreed to this, after which he went to an empty cave and practiced for twelve years.

During this time, there occurred a great famine in the land, and many people died. Afraid that he would disturb his guru, the servant lived on the leftovers of the guru's food. One day he went to get food, but there was none to be had, so he went to the king's palace where he managed to get a bowl of rice gruel. As he brought it back to his guru, because he had not eaten, he fell on the ground in front of the cave and spilled some of the rice. "Have you been drinking wine?" the guru asked. "How could I be drinking wine!" exclaimed the servant. "I collapsed because I am weak from hunger." "Why could you not get food?" asked the guru. "I did not say anything for fear of disturbing the guru," the man replied. "There has been a famine for twelve years and many people have died. The others are suffering considerably." "Is it part of the secret practice to say nothing?" asked the master Saroruha. "I have a method of alleviating hunger."

He collected a large amount of rice and made a torma beside a river. He stirred up the eight great nāgas by meditating on their symbols and mantras; he then brought these nāgas overhead by the power of his thoughts. "We are here," said the nāgas. "What do you wish to be done?" "There has been no rain in Jambudvīpa," said the guru. "People are dying and it is your fault. Therefore on the first day, rain down food. On the second day, grain. On the third day, rain down jewels. After you have done that, rain down water."

They did what he had instructed them to do, and the

people were freed from their sufferings. Thoughts about the yogin pervaded every direction: "This was done through the power of Saroruha," the people said. And everyone took faith in him.

Saroruha then initiated his former servant, whose name was Rāma, and gave him instructions whereby he obtained the worldly powers of siddhi. The guru then said, "Since you have been given the instructions for the Developing and the Perfecting Stages of Hevajra, do not just go into the sky, but work for the benefit of living beings. Go to the Śrīparvata and do what you need to do."

The guru went to the realm of the Ḍākas. Rāma brought the daughter of a king to the neighborhood of the Śrīparvata by his power. They both built temples and finally went to the realm of the Ḍākas themselves.

# Sarvabhakṣa

Sarvabhakṣa, whose name means 'the Man Who Eats Everything', was born of low caste, a subject of King Siṇhacandra in the city of Abhara. He had an enormously large stomach, and whatever was put before him, he ate. One day, he could find nothing to eat, so he wandered off to another place where he just sat, thinking about nothing but food. Saraha came along and asked him, "What are you doing here?" Sarvabhakṣa replied, "My stomach burns with a great fire and I cannot find enough food to satisfy me. Today I cannot find anything to eat at all, and so I suffer." "If you cannot endure hunger for such a short time, what will it be like when you are reborn as a preta, a hungry ghost?" The man asked what a preta was like, and the yogin, saying "Look there!" pointed one out. "You will be reborn as a being just like that." Recognizing that indeed this was so, Sarvabhakṣa begged the guru for a method of liberation.

The guru first gave him initiation and then taught him the *Bodhicaryāvatāra* of Śāntideva. He gave instructions as follows:

> Contemplate that your stomach is as empty as the sky.
> Let the fire burn as when you are hungry.
> Let all the visible world be edible and drinkable,
> and let it be consumed as you eat it.

Sarvabhakṣa meditated with such devotion that the sun and moon became afraid and hid themselves in the valley of Mount Meru. Everyone cried out in one voice, "Alas, the light is going out!" Aroused by the ḍākinīs, Mahābrahma came down to Sarvabhakṣa and said, "You have eaten all the food; now meditate without it." So Sarvabhakṣa did. The sun and moon reappeared, and everyone was again happy.

Realizing the integration of appearances and emptiness, Sarvabhakṣa attained siddhi. He narrated his experiences and brought great blessings to all living beings for six hundred years. Then, with a circle of a thousand, he went to the realm of the Ḍākas.

# Nāgabodhi

Once when the holy Nāgārjuna was living in the hermitage of Suvarna, there came from the west of India a Brahman who was a thief. He looked at the guru through the door and saw him eating luxurious food from a golden plate. The thought came into his mind to steal the plate, but the guru recognized the thought and threw the golden plate out of his room onto the ground.

"Why did he do that?" thought the thief. He went into the house and spoke humbly. "I was thinking of stealing the golden plate, but now you have made that unnecessary. Why did you throw it to me?"

"My name is Nāgārjuna," the guru answered. "All my wealth is for the benefit of others. I threw out the plate because when we die there is no use in having wealth. Remain here. Eat and drink all you need so that you do not have to steal."

The man, believing in that kind of behavior, asked for the Dharma. Then Nāgārjuna initiated him into the Guhyasamāja and gave him instructions on freeing himself from attachment to things:

> Contemplate that all the things you desire
> are like large horns on your head.
> Jewels have no inherent nature whatsoever,
> so meditate on the radiant clear light.

Nāgārjuna filled a corner of the house with large jewels and left the thief with them. Nāgabodhi lived in the house and meditated according to the instructions. In twelve years, great horns grew on his head—so that whenever he moved about, they bumped into things. He became very unhappy.

When Nāgārjuna returned, he asked the thief: "Are you happy now?" "I am not happy," replied the man. Nāgārjuna then laughed and gave him further instructions:

> Just as one who grows horns by meditating
> finds they destroy all his joy,
> so longing for a 'basic nature'
> causes all beings to suffer.

Existent things have no actual being,
but they arise like clouds in the sky.
Birth, life, death, benefit, and injury
arise from what? By means of what?
What can benefit you? What can injure you
if the mind itself is pure?
From the beginning, there is nothing to be done,
because everything is empty of substance.

When this was said, the man realized that emptiness is the basic condition of things. Sitting in meditation for six months, having realized the inseparability of samsara and nirvana, he attained siddhi. He became famous under the name Nāgabodhi, and was selected as the successor to the guru. He attained the eight great powers of siddhi for the benefit of living beings: the siddhis of walking underground, of the sword, of binding and letting loose, of the pill and eye medicine, of the winged feet, and of the elixir of immortality. These eight powers will bring whatever is desired.

"Remain on the Śrīparvata," said Nāgārjuna, "teaching and working for the benefit of living beings." Then Nāgārjuna left him there. It is said he will live for two thousand years.

# Dārika

In the land of Saliputra, there was a king named Indrapāla. One day when he was out hunting, at about noontime he came upon a group of people gathering for the market. He saw the people all giving reverence to the yogin

Lūyipa sitting there. The king said to the yogin, "A man such as you with such good appearance and good family should not be eating fish-guts, which are unclean. I will give you whatever you need to eat, and whatever else you want. If you want my kingdom, I will give it to you."

The guru answered, "If you have a method of liberation from old age and death, that I can use. But if you do not, even your kingdom and your daughter would be of no use to me." "Why not?" asked the king. "The kingdom brings little benefit and is a great hindrance. I have renounced everything," Lūyipa said.

Thereupon King Indrapāla himself grew weary of his kingdom and said to his Brahman minister, "I wear a crown in this world, but for what? Let us go to the Dharma. There is sufficient food and clothing for my wife, and I can give the kingdom to my son." The minister saw that such a course would be fitting, and so the king gave the kingdom to his son.

Both the king and the minister went to the cemetery where Lūyipa lived and knocked on his door. "Who is there!" called the master. When the king and his minister answered, the master said, "Well then, come in!" And they entered. The master then initiated them both into the mandala of Cakrasamvara, and the two offered themselves as the initiation fee.

Then the three of them went to another land, Orissa, and there they stayed and begged alms. After that, they went to the land of Bhirapura to a city called Jintapura. In the city, they went to the house which belonged to the woman in charge of the three hundred dancing girls who gave service in the temple.

Lūyipa asked at each of the three hundred doors, "Would not your mistress like to buy a servant?" "Perhaps I may buy him," said the madam. She opened her door and looked out, and when she saw that he was a handsome man, she wanted him and asked, "What is his price?" "Five hundred gold coins," the master answered. When she bought the prince the master said to her, "Do not let anyone sleep with him at night, and do not chain him. He is worth the price you paid for him." Then he and the Brahman left.

The prince worked for twelve years in the house of the prostitute, washing the women's feet and massaging their bodies. However, he did not forget the words of his guru. Along with all his other work, he took on work that was being neglected. All the other servants of the place greatly admired him for that.

One day, a king named Janapa, also known as King Kunji, came to the house with five hundred gold coins which he intended to spend on worldly pleasures. When the master served him, Kunji gave him seven gold coins as payment. Then Kunji spent the entire day in joy and in filling his stomach; as a result of his overeating, he got indigestion. He was pacing back and forth in the middle of the night, when he noticed a pleasant aroma coming from a lighted place within the garden. He went to investigate, and there he saw the servant sitting on a throne, being venerated by fifteen maidens. The king was quite amazed.

He retraced his steps to the house, and told the madam what he had seen. They both went out into the garden and saw the same scene as before. The madam became penitent and prostrated herself before the master, saying, "We poor souls have made an error; we did not know that you had these abilities. I have incurred a great sin by treating you as my servant. We beg you to be patient with us. I will make you an object of reverence for twelve years." When the master assented to this, the madam and King Kunji asked to be his students. He rose in the middle of the air and came down above the town, saying:

A worldly king has a parasol
and sits on an elephant throne.
My kingdom is more distinguished
and my position more exalted.
I have the parasol of liberation
and ride the Mahāyāna.
Dārika enjoys himself
on the throne of the three worlds.

Because he was the servant of a prostitute, he was known as Dārika. Later, with a circle of seven hundred, he went to the realm of the Ḍākas.

# Putali

One day, a guru yogin came and begged alms from a man of low caste who made his home in Bengal. The man brought the yogin food and drink and, taking faith in him, took him as guru. He was initiated into Hevajra and given instructions. The yogin also gave him a thanka of Hevajra, about which the yogin said, "Practice and use the thanka as you beg alms from city to city." Putali practiced accordingly for twelve years and attained siddhi, though he did not have a complete realization.

One day, Putali went to the king's palace. The king saw him as he was putting each god in its place on the thanka, and the king reviled him, saying, "This is not a painting. Only icon-painters make proper paintings." The yogin replied, "These are the genuine gods. My gods are highest because they have taken the place of your gods in the thanka."

The king, thinking that maybe this was true, summoned his icon-painter. The yogin said to him, "Even if you paint your god in the place of my god, how can it be right?" "What will happen?" asked the king. "My god will become the god of gods," the yogin replied. "How can we demonstrate that?" asked the king. "Paint the king's god above and place the Buddhist deity below. Soon the Buddhist god will be on top," the yogin said.

"If that occurs," said the king, "I will accept your system and become a Buddhist."

The yogin reflected on these words. Later, when they looked at the painting, the king's god had left its place and the other one was there instead. The king was astonished. He took the yogin as guru and entered the Dharma. The yogin became famous as the guru Putali, and for five hundred years he worked for the benefit of living beings. Having narrated his experiences, finally, with six hundred followers, he went to the realm of the Ḍākas.

# Panaha

Panaha, whose name means 'the Bootmaker', was a man of low caste in Sandhonāgara who supported himself by making boots. One day, the bootmaker saw a yogin who had great magical powers begging alms. He took faith in that yogin and followed him into a quiet cemetery. "Why did you come here?" asked the guru. "I have come to ask for the Dharma," the bootmaker replied. And so the yogin preached the misery of samsara and the benefits of liberation. The bootmaker became very despondent about samsara, and asked, "O guru, please give me a method of liberation from samsara." After the yogin gave the initiation which transfers blessings, he gave these instructions to take desirable objectives as the path:

> Put on the ornamented boots;
> hasten along in your walking and a sound will arise.
> Concentrate on this sound alone; then meditate
> that the sound and emptiness are inseparable.

Panaha understood the meaning and meditated on it. After nine years he purified the stains which obstruct the path of sight, and attained siddhi. Becoming famous as the guru Panaha, he narrated his experiences. Having worked for the benefit of living beings for eight hundred years, he went to the realm of the Ḍākas with a circle of eight hundred.

# Kokalipa

Once there was a king in the city of Campara who could not endure the heat. So he stayed in the shade of a grove of asmra trees, near a stream of clear water where there grew sweet-smelling brightly colored flowers and fruits of all varieties. Here the princes and nobility did him reverence. And, of course, the king had many young maidens to serve him—some fanned him, some sang, some danced for him, while others scattered flowers.

While he was enjoying his kingdom—which did not lack for any delights—a true monk came to the garden. There were three hundred doors to the pleasure grove, and he did not know which one to enter. The king himself heard him, called "come inside," and had the monk admitted.

The king gave the monk food and provisions and then asked him, "Can your Dharma be as happy as my Dharma?" "From the point of view of a child, you are very happy," said the monk. "But from the point of view of the wise, all this is poison." "How can you say poison?" asked the king. The monk then explained to the king about the three poisons. "The kingdom is a composite of these poisons," said the monk. "It is destined for an unpleasant end. It is by nature painful; it is like a man who eats and drinks delicious food that had been laced with poison." The king, a person of spiritual inclinations, took this monk as guru and requested instructions. He was initiated into Cakrasamvara and was shown the path.

The king then abdicated in favor of his son. But though he was able to renounce his previous mode of life, the sound of the cuckoo birds in the asmra trees distracted him, so he asked to be instructed in a way that would free him completely from distractions. The monk said to him:

Just as in the empty sky,
the thunderclouds gather;
and when the rainfall occurs
the sap extends through to the fruit,
likewise in the emptiness of the ear,
the 'thunder' of the cuckoo sounds,

and from the clouds of concepts and perceptions
comes the poisonous rain of misery
which makes the leaves of obsession grow.
The wise man cuts off his childish nature.
From the empty nature of the mind itself,
the thunder of the inseparability of sound
and emptiness,
the clouds of unstained great bliss collect,
and from the rainfall of the radiant true nature,
the fruit of the five knowledges grows.
Behold such a wonder for one who understands.

He meditated on these words and attained siddhi in six months. He became famous as the guru Kokalipa, and working for the benefit of living beings, he went to the realm of the Ḍākas in this very body.

# Anaṅga

Anaṅga was born a person of low caste in the land of Gahura. Because he had meditated on patience in a previous life, he was very handsome, and because everyone was always gazing at him, he became very proud. A disciplined monk who practiced the appropriate behavior came to where he lived, asking for food. "Come in," Anaṅga said. "I will serve you every day." And he asked the monk to return.

Anaṅga washed the monk's feet, placed cushions for him to rest on, and satisfied him with food and drink. "Your reverence," he said, "it is very difficult to beg alms and food. Why do you do it?" "Since I am afraid of samsara, I wish a method of liberation from it," the monk replied. "Your Reverence, what is the difference between the support we two have?" "There is a great difference," the monk replied. "The Dharma does not arise from the pride which is your support. Measureless good things arise from the faith which is my support." "Your Reverence, what is the quality of faith?" Anaṅga asked. And the monk replied, "Those whose support is the practice of the Dharma are not hindered by either human or non-human forces. They attain the body of a Buddha and cross over from world to world."

Anaṅga then asked the monk to give him a method to obtain such qualities, and the monk replied, "Are you able to give up worldly activities such as dressing and cooking?" "Any man can do that," Anaṅga responded. "Well then, having first done that, can you meditate?" "I can," said Anaṅga, and so he was initiated into Cakrasamvara and given these instructions on how to clarify the six sense fields:

All various appearances
have the nature of the mind.
Nothing whatsoever
exists apart from it.
Arrange the objects of the six senses
in their own place;
penetrate to their indestructible nature
without lusting for them.

He meditated, and having attained siddhi in six months, he became known as the guru Anaṅga. He worked for the benefit of living beings and finally went in that very body to the realm of the Ḍākas.

# Lakṣmīnkarā

Lakṣmīnkarā was the sister of King Indrabhūti who ruled over the 250,000 cities of Sambola in Uḍḍiyāna. From her youth, she had enjoyed the many advantages of her noble class. She learned doctrines from the great siddha

Kambala, and she knew many of the Tantra collections. Her brother, King Indrabhūti, had given her in marriage to the son of Jalendra, King of Laṅkā. When the messenger arrived to take her to Laṅkā, she carried her stainless wealth with her, her great knowledge about the Dharma.

When she arrived at the city of Laṅkāpura, Lakṣmīnkarā became very sad, for all of the many people she saw were non-Buddhists. Because it was said that the stars were unfavorable, she was not permitted to enter the king's palace. So she stayed in town. The entourage of the prince, just returning from a hunt and carrying much meat with them, came into her presence and greeted her.

"What is all this?" asked the princess. "Where did these animals come from? Who killed all of them?" The hunters answered, "We have just come back from the hunt. Your husband, the prince, went into the wilds to hunt and kill."

The princess felt a great revulsion at the talk of the hunt and of eating just to stuff their bellies. She thought to herself, "My brother is a king who protects the Dharma. Can I permit myself to be married to someone who is like a pagan?" Thereupon she fainted. After she recovered from her faint, she gave her wealth to the citizens of the city and her ornaments to her retinue. She then returned to the place where she was staying. Giving orders that she would not receive anyone for ten full days, she remained inside the house. She cut her hair and stripped herself naked; then she smeared ashes and coal on her body. Although she acted demented, she unwaveringly set about her heart's aim.

The king and his court were oppressed by sorrow. They sent for a doctor who prepared medicines for her, but she struck out at all who came near her, tossing brass ornaments in the air. Although they sent a message to her brother about this turn of events, she remained very unhappy.

The princess considered plans for escape, for she had

turned her heart from samsara. She acted like a demented ascetic. Escaping from Laṅkāpura and staying in a cemetery, she consummated her heart's aim. In seven years she attained siddhi. A sweeper of the king did reverence to her, and she gave him instructions. He attained some of the necessary qualities and was working to experience the others when King Jalendra and his entourage came by one day on a hunt.

The king lost his way and wandered about; unable to find his way out of that wild place, he looked for a place to rest. He came to the cave where Lakṣmīnkarā slept. Thinking to himself, "What is the crazy woman doing?" he looked in. There was a bright light inside, and in all directions he saw numberless divine maidens who were doing reverence and making offerings. Though he went back to his palace, a pure faith arose in the king, and he returned to that place and did reverence.

"Why do you do reverence to a woman like me?" Lakṣmīnkarā asked. The king then asked for instructions, but she said:

All beings who dwell in samsara partake of pain.
There is no happy or blissful state of being.
Birth, old age, and death; even the gods,
chief among beings, are not free but are stricken by them.
The three evil destinies are painful in themselves.
Though you eat here and there, you will always be hungry.
You are tormented by fire and frost endlessly.
O king, seek the bliss of liberation.

Then she said, "You cannot become my pupil. Your sweeper is my student, and will be your teacher. He has just attained siddhi and will be your auspicious friend." "Since there are so many sweepers," said the king, "how will I know him?" "The right sweeper will be giving food to the people. Go to him at night."

When the king saw the proper sweeper he checked him carefully. He then put him on a throne, did him honor, asked for instructions, and was given the initiation which transfers spiritual power. Finally the sweeper and the princess manifested many miracles in Laṅkāpura, teaching the Developing and Perfecting Stages of Vajravārāhī. Finally, in this very body, they went to the realm of the Ḍākas.

# Samudra

In a land called Sarvatira, there lived a man of low caste who gained his sustenance by collecting things from the sea. One day he found nothing, and growing depressed about his life, he sat down in a cemetery. The yogin Acinta came along and asked him, "What are you doing here?" The man told him what had happened previously, and expressed his unhappiness.

"All sentient beings in the world have measureless misery," the yogin said. "You will find the previous misery unendurable, but more pain will come, and you may not find even a word of pleasure." "O yogin," the man said, "I ask for any method of being liberated from misery." The yogin then initiated him, and gave him instructions on the Four Inner Joys and the Four Outer Immeasureables:

> Friendliness, compassion, joy, and equanimity,
> are the Four Immeasureables.
> Happiness will flow from the center
> and from worldly things in equal measure.
> The four cakras are the four joys.
> Happiness and emptiness are quite inseparable.
> If you meditate correctly,
> not only will you have undefiled bliss,
> but there will not be a word of misery.

After he understood what was said, the man meditated and in three years attained siddhi. He became famous in all directions as the guru Samudra. Having narrated his experiences, he worked for the benefit of living beings and with a circle of eight hundred, went to the realm of the Ḍākas.

# Vyali

In a place called Apatrara, there lived a wealthy Brahman named Vyali who made many experiments in order to make the elixir of life. He bought a lot of mercury and many drugs; he then pulverized the drugs and mixed them together. But he could not find the key to the elixir. When nothing resulted from all this, and as no signs of progress had appeared, in a fit of rage he threw his book into the river Ganges and gave up his efforts.

After working for twelve years on the elixir, and having used up all of his wealth, he went as a beggar to the city where the vihāra of King Rāma was situated. In that same city, a prostitute went to the banks of thc Gangcs to bathc, found the book the old Brahman had thrown away, and showing it to him, asked, "What is this?" He saw that it was his old alchemy book, and told her of his previous attempts to produce the elixir. "If I had a little bit more gold, I would be able to do it," he said. She then gave him money, but under the same delusions as before, he followed the same procedures. He was powerless. He bought a lot of mercury and practiced again for a year, but since he did not know about the red Skyurura, the signs of transformation did not occur.

One day, while the prostitute was bathing, a flower which was self-formed attached itself to her finger. As she was plucking it off, a particle of the flower fell into the mixture of substances, and immediately the signs of transformation appeared. The Brahman asked the woman what had gone into the mixture, because he was himself careful not to allow foreign substances into it. "What caused this?" he asked. "The signs of success are here. The eight marks of good fortune have arisen." They indeed had great fortune.

The prostitute put a drop of the elixir into the Brahman's food and served it to him. On previous days when they had added drops to food and drink, he had not detected any difference. But this day he did. The prostitute had accomplished what he had not.

The Brahman, the prostitute, and a horse all ate the elixir, and all three attained the successful power of living without death. But the Brahman had a very selfish nature, and he wanted to go where he would not have to give the elixir to anyone. He went to the realms of the gods, and even the gods did not know he had it. He then went to the country of a king named Kilambe and lived there.

There was a rock a mile high and ten shouting distances in extent surrounded by a swamp. On the top of it, there was a tree. The Brahman lived in the secluded shade of this tree, where he would not have to reveal the recipe for the elixir to anyone.

Now the holy Nāgārjuna, after attaining the successful power of going through the air, came to that place, wearing a pair of magic shoes. He did reverence and asked for instructions. "How did you get here?" asked Vyali. Nāgārjuna showed him the power of the magic shoes, and explained how he had got them. Vyali gave him the recipe for the elixir and then said, "Give me those boots for a fee." Nāgārjuna gave him one shoe, and with the other went back to Jambudvipa. Nāgārjuna completed his practice on the Śrīparvata and he worked for the benefit of living beings.

Nāgārjuna then said, "Attachment to gold is an evil unless you are able to attain the proper qualities. If you are not able to produce these qualities, you should seek the spiritual counsel of a guru; you will then become a great man."

# Colophon

Here, then, are the stories of the world-famous eighty-four siddhas, Lūyipa and the rest. These are the genuine histories set forth according to *The Hundred Thousand Songs* of Abhayaśri who, ornamented with true qualities, was born in Magadha of holy lineage.

May the merit of these stories bring those who are tormented by the poisons to a guru. May they experience the essential nature of the medicine which relieves these poisons.

The great guru Abhayadattaśrī from Campara in India narrated the lives of the eighty-four siddhas and the monk sMon-grub Shes-rab has correctly translated it into Tibetan.

# Appendices

# Iconography

The student of Tibetan Buddhism is most likely to meet the siddhas in Tibetan art, primarily in thankas, Tibetan paintings. One can find the siddhas either as the main subject of a thanka, or as subordinate to another figure. If the siddhas are in a subordinate position, perhaps in a line above or below the main subject, or in the corners of a thanka, they are usually there to represent the transmission of their tradition, which has come down both through their teachings and their lineages.

Thankas devoted to the siddhas are usually done in a series, each of the paintings portraying a certain number of the eighty-four siddhas. Each siddha is shown with the implements of his or her trade, or with some symbol connecting him or her with the higher levels of being.

Siddhas can be portrayed as monks or laymen, but are most frequently shown as yogins, since it is success in yoga that is the distinguishing feature of the siddha. Yogins *per se* have particular iconographic features: they are usually portrayed with long hair, often but not always tied in a top-knot, and they are frequently bearded. They are usually dressed in short trousers, although sometimes they are shown wearing a white cloth or even just a loin cloth. Occasionally they are adorned with Tantric ornaments: tiaras and elaborate strings of beads made of bone. They are usually portrayed seated on cushions of leaves or animal skins, although occasionally they are shown seated on corpses or human skins. The yogin is almost always shown with a cord, used to maintain his meditative posture, which is placed over his shoulder and around his body. Some pictures actually show the cord in use. Yogins who are siddhas are frequently shown carrying a skull-cup which holds either a red or blue substance. As in Western iconography, the skull represents mortality and death; it also symbolizes emptiness.

Not all of the siddhas are shown as yogins. Siddhas such as Nāgārjuna, Āryadeva, or Ratnākaraśānti, who are scholastic masters as well, are portrayed as monks. Several of the siddhas, particularly those who are kings, are usually shown as laymen.

On thankas devoted to siddhas, the principal figures are almost always accompanied by smaller figures, either assisting them or offering veneration to them. This is strongly suggestive of the circle of followers attributed to many of the siddhas in the stories, and represents the siddhas working for the benefit of others in the world.

In the following section, I have compiled basic iconographical data from a few of the siddha thankas available, and have described the principal iconographic features of each siddha. The main sources for this section are a set of thirteen thankas in the Ethnological Museum of Stockholm, referred to here as the Stockholm thankas; a series of thankas from the Hamburg Museum, referred to here as the Hamburg thankas; and paintings of the siddhas on two strings of cloth flaps in the American Museum of Natural History of New York, referred to here as the AMNH panels.

The Stockholm thankas have been reproduced and described in Toni Schmid's *The Eighty-five Siddhas*; however, the artist was working with a somewhat different list of siddhas than in our stories, so not all of our siddhas are represented. The Hamburg thankas, found in Grünwedel's 1916 German translation of the lives of the siddhas, come from a larger set showing the masters of the Nyingmapa sect of Tibetan Buddhism. Not all of the siddhas are to be found in this series, since one thanka is missing.

An excellent set of siddha thankas is also to be found in the fifth volume of *Crystal Mirror* (Dharma Publishing, 1977). Not surprisingly, being in the Nyingma tradition, they are similar to the Hamburg thankas.

In this section, to aid in identifying the siddhas, some of the common variants of the siddha's names—both in Sanskrit and in Tibetan—are also given. Generally the name by which the siddha is best known or by which he or she is known in the text is used for discussion purposes (for example, Nāropa rather than Naḍapāda). The names of the siddhas vary greatly in different sources. One finds Tibetan translations of the siddhas' names, Prakrit forms, and Sanskrit forms or reconstructions. In the Sanskrit reconstructions, for example, the ending *-pāda* is very common—frequently added to proper names or titles as a token of respect.

Almost every possible variation of a name seems to occur, and in many cases syllables are reversed. Sometimes an 's' is found for 'p' in a name (for example, Saṅkaja for Paṅkaja), and 'b' is often substituted for 'v' (Birvapa for Virūpa). Very common is 'ts' for 'c' (Tsaurangi for Caurāṅgi) and 'dz' for 'j'. Names of the siddhas may also vary widely in the different traditions. The form the siddhas take upon themselves may differ as well.

1. LŪYIPA The text gives the Tibetan form of his name, which is Nya'i-rgyu-ma za-ba or Nya'i-rgyu lto-gsol-ba, both meaning 'Eater of Fish Intestines'. The name Lūyipa itself is probably derived from the Old Bengali rendering of the Sanskrit Lohitapāda, *lohita* meaning a type of fish. Some of the variations on his name include Luipa, Lohipa, Lūhipāda, and Lūhipa.

Iconographically, Lūyipa is usually shown eating fish entrails, generally shown as rope-like coils. On the Stockholm thanka, Lūyipa is shown seated on the belly of a large frog-like reptile, holding a fish in his right hand and pulling out its intestines with his left. To Lūyipa's right there is a man eating entrails that are coming out of a fish's mouth.

On the AMNH panels, Lūyipa is shown in yogin's garb. He has a pointed beard, wears a long white scarf, and is seated on a lotus throne with a *kalaśa* or initiation vase to his left. He holds a skull-cup filled with blood in his left hand. A long red coil is shown coming out of the cup and entwining around his right arm; he holds the end of the coil in his right hand.

2. LĪLAPA Līlapa is a shortened form of the Sanskrit Līlāpāda, which in Tibetan is rendered as sGeg-pa.

On the Hamburg thankas, Līlapa is shown wearing a long robe. He is seated under a tree with one leg drawn up and the other leg hanging down as if he were sitting on a throne. His left hand is concealed, his right hand is down, palm out, in a gesture of giving. Beside him is shown a figure with long hair playing a flute and dancing with the left leg in the air.

3. VIRŪPA Virūpa, 'the Man of Diverse Forms', probably received this name because of his many and varied activities.

Alternative forms of his name are Birvapa, Birūpa, Bhirbapa, and Bhirvapa.

On the Stockholm thankas Virūpa is shown with a moustache, wearing a turban with a flower wreath around it. He is seated on a green mat. He holds a skull-cup in his right hand, and his left hand is pointed to the sun. There is a smaller figure nearby, holding a skull-cup in both hands. From a *kalaśa*, a liquid runs into a third skull-cup, and what appears to be a river is shown pouring down from the sky.

On the AMNH panels, Virūpa is depicted as a yogin. Along with the yogin's cord he wears a cord of flowers, and has a similar flower garland in his hair. He is seated on an animal skin, and is shown staring up to his right with an angry expression. His right hand is raised toward the sun, and is connected to it by golden rays; in his left hand he holds a skull-cup filled with a blue substance. There is a male figure standing to his left who holds an umbrella over him.

Virūpa is particularly important to the Sakyapa lineages. On a thanka depicting several Sakyapa monks, he is shown with a pink complexion, a moustache and a small beard, his hair curled elegantly on his forehead and chin. He is wearing large earrings and a decorated cloak around his shoulders, and is seated on an animal skin. He holds a skull-cup in his left hand.

There is also a fourteenth century bronze statue of Virūpa showing a trousered man seated cross-legged on a lotus seat that has a deerskin placed over it. He has a small goatee, and his hair is piled up on the top of his head. His earlobes are long, and there are small ear-plugs in each ear. There is a string of flowers hanging from his right shoulder, and a similar crown of flowers on his head. He is portrayed with wide eyes 'to strike terror'. His hands are in the *mudrā* of 'turning the Wheel of the Law'.

4. ḌOMBIPA Ḍombipa's name is reconstructed in Sanskrit as Ḍombipāda, but he is more frequently called Ḍombi Heruka. A *ḍombi* is a low-caste musician.

Ḍombipa is usually portrayed holding a snake and riding on the back of a tiger. He is usually adorned with Tantric ornaments: earrings, headband with skulls and ropes of beads, bones, or pearls strung about his body. There is usually a halo around his head. He is often shown with his consort.

5. ŚAVARIPA In its full Sanskrit form, Śavaripa is Śabaripāda, 'the Man of the Śabara Tribe'. Variations of his name are Śābari, Sabari, and Mahāśabara. Our story mentions that he is also called the 'Mountain Lord', Ri-khrod dbang-phyug, the 'Man Who Wears Peacock Feathers', rMa-bya gos-can, and the 'Mountain Hermit', Ri-khrod mgon-po.

Śavaripa is generally depicted holding a bow and arrow. He is sometimes shown with a deer or deer's carcass; he is also sometimes shown dancing. He is often shown with his hair in a bun on the top of his head, and with a moustache and beard. Although in some thankas he wears trousers, he is usually depicted wearing a loincloth, sometimes of peacock feathers. He is often shown with one or two women, and sometimes with a male companion.

6. SARAHA Saraha, 'the Arrow Shooter', is from the Sanskrit *śara*, arrow; the Tibetan is mDa'-snun. He is also called Sāraha, Sarahapāda, and Śrīsaraha. Another name frequently attributed to him is Rāhula or Rāhulabhadra, rendered in Tibetan as sGra-gcen-'dzin.

Saraha's iconography is unmistakable. He is almost always shown holding an arrow, often sighting down it in the manner of an arrow maker. He is usually shown as a yogin, wearing tantric ornaments, and seated on an animal skin, and he is often accompanied by a woman. The sun and moon often appear in his depiction.

7. KANKARIPA Kankaripa is probably, in its Sanskrit form, Kankālipāda, 'the Skeleton-man', from *kankāla*, 'skeleton'. However, there is also the word *kankara* meaning 'vile'; hence he could be considered 'the Disgusting One'.

Iconographical data is scarce since he is an obscure siddha. He may be portrayed as a yogin gazing at a skull.

8. MĪNAPA Mīnapa in its fuller Sanskrit form is Mīnapāda, from the Sanskrit *mīna* meaning fish. In Tibetan he is called Nya-bo-pa. Mīnapa is usually depicted standing within a fish, although in the Stockholm thanka a Mīnapa is shown seated on an antelope skin, his left hand holding a skull-cup.

9. GORAKSA Goraksa means 'the Cow-protector' or 'the Cowherd'. In Tibetan this is rendered as Ba-glang-bsrung or Ba-glang-rdzi. Goraksa is often shown dancing and holding a drum and bell; in other thankas he may be shown with his herd of cows.

10. CAURĀṄGI Despite the folk-etymology which interprets his name as Caur-angi, 'Member of the Robbers', in Tibetan Chom-rkun-gyu yan-lag, this name is more likely to be a prakritization of the Sanskrit *Caturāṅgi*, 'the Four-limbed'. Variations of his name include Tsaurangi, Tsorangipa, Tsaurangapa, Tsaurakhampa, and Coraghi.

Caurāṅgi is often shown as a yogin seated on an animal skin with legs crossed and with knees raised off the ground. In this volume he is shown with a dragon pouring liquid into a skull cup.

11. VĪNAPA Vīnapa is a shortened form of Vīnapāda, 'the Luteplayer'. The name is derived from *vīna*, a type of stringed musical instrument still quite popular in India. Variations of Vīnapa's name are Binapa, Bhinapa, and in Tibetan, Pi-vang-pa or Pi-vang-brdung. Vīnapa's instrument provides his distinctive iconographical mark.

12. ŚĀNTIPA Śāntipa is better known as Ratnākaraśānti —the famous Mahāyāna master; although he is also known as Akarchinta. Iconographically, Śāntipa is shown as a monk, usually with peaked scholar's hat, and with various other objects associated with his scholarship.

13. TANTIPA Tantipa in fuller Sanskrit form is Tantipāda, which in Tibetan is Thags-mkhan, 'the Weaver'. Tantipa's iconographical mark is the loom.

14. CAMARIPA Camaripa, 'the Leather-worker', is also known as Tsamaripa, Tsamarapa, Camara, and in Tibetan, lHam-mkhan. Camaripa's iconography reflects his occupation, and he is usually shown working with leather, or with leather-work beside him.

15. KHAḌGAPA Khaḍgapa means 'the Swordsman', and is from the Sanskrit *khaḍga* meaning 'sword'. Variations of his name are Pargapa and Saḍgapa. He is called Ral-gri-pa in Tibetan. Khaḍgapa is usually depicted with a sword and a snake.

16. NĀGĀRJUNA Nāgārjuna in Tibetan is known as Klu-grub, although some Tibetan transliterations of his name have it as Nāgārdzuna. Nāgārjuna is virtually unmistakable in iconography. He is almost always shown with monk's robes and with a halo with seven snakes within it, which most likely derives from the nāga, 'serpent', in his name.

17. KĀṆHAPA Kāṇhapa is more commonly called Kṛṣṇācāri, meaning 'He of Dark Practice' (dark meaning 'hidden' rather than 'evil'). A variation of his name is Kṛṣṇācarya, 'the Dark Master'. He is also called Kanapa or Kahnapa, and the Tibetan versions of his name include Nag-po spyod-pa, Nag-po-pa, and brTul-zhugs spyod-pa chen-po.

Kāṇhapa has no unique iconographical features, although he may be shown dancing with various objects in his hands. In one thanka he is shown with a bowl and coil of rope, in another with drum and skull-cup. He may also be shown with a parasol over his head, and is sometimes shown with a halo. He may be shown meditating, with a human skin as a cloak, and holding a skull-cup; he may also be shown dancing on the prostrate form of a human being.

18. KARṆARIPA Karṇaripa is better known as Āryadeva, 'Phags-pa-lha in Tibetan. He is also called Kaneri, Āryadheva, and Mig-gcig-pa, 'the One-eyed'. Āryadeva, like his guru Nāgārjuna, is usually shown as a monk, dressed in monk's robes, and wearing the peaked scholar's hat.

19. THAGANAPA Thaganapa is a corrupted form of Sthagana from *sthaga* meaning 'sly'. Variations of his name are Thagapa, Thegana, and Thakhana. His name in Tibetan is rDzun-smra-ba and rTag-tu-rdzun-smra-ba, meaning 'the Liar' or 'He Who Always Lies'. Thaganapa's iconographical form is varied. He may be shown leaning against a tree, and sometimes with his left hand to his ear.

20. NĀROPA In full Sanskrit Nāropa is Nāḍapāda, probably from *naḍa*, meaning 'reed'. He is also called Naro, Narotapa, Narota, and in Tibetan, rTsa-bshad-pa.

Nāropa has no distinguishing iconographical features. On the Stockholm thankas, Nāropa is bearded—he is wearing a monastic hat, and has a rosary around his neck. He is seated western style. His left hand is on his left knee, and his right hand is raised. On the Hamburg thanka, Nāropa is shown dressed as a yogin, sitting on a hill and holding a flayed human skin stretched out behind him. In another thanka, Nāropa is shown seated on a cloth, holding a conch shell and bell. In this volume he is shown holding a skull in his hand.

21. SHALIPA Shalipa, in reconstructed Sanskrit, is known as Śṛgalapāda from the Sanskrit *śṛgala* which means 'jackal'. In Tibetan his name is sPyan-ki-pa, 'the Wolf-man'. Variations of his name are Siyalipa, Silāli, Śyalipa, and Śalipa.

Shalipa's iconography usually centers on his relation with jackals and wolves, which are usually shown nearby him. He is also often shown with a corpse nearby. In this volume he is shown seated on a corpse with other corpses nearby.

22. TILOPA Tilopa is also known as Tillo, Tillipa, Tailopa, or Telopa. In Tibetan he is known as sNum-pa, Mar-nag 'tsong-mkhan, or Til-brdung-mkhan. Tilopa has no distinguishing iconographical features. In one thanka he is shown with a vajra and skull-cup; in this volume he is shown holding a fish.

23. CATRAPA Catrapa, in reconstructed Sanskrit, is known as Cattrapāda. Variations of his name are Tsatrapa, Catapa, and Chatrapāda. Iconographically Catrapa is usually shown carrying a book.

24. BHADRAPA Bhadrapa, in full Sanskrit, is Bhadrapāda, from *bhadra* meaning 'auspicious'. He is also known as Bhadra, Bhatapa, Badapa, and in Tibetan as bZang-po.

Bhadrapa's iconography varies. On the Stockholm thanka, he is shown seated on a tiger skin, wearing no ornaments, but accompanied by two musicians, one of them playing the flute, the other a lute. On the Hamburg thanka, Bhadrapa is shown as a yogin seated on a black pelt with his hands at his chest. There is a vessel with a pouring spout in front of him. On another thanka he is shown in the gesture of blessing. In this volume he is shown holding a skull cup, which an attendant is filling.

25. DHUKHANDI Dhukhandi is probably from the Sanskrit *Dvikhandin*, meaning 'One Who Has Two Sections'; he is also called Dvakanti, Khandipa, Dokhandi, Dhosanti, and in Tibetan, gNyis-gcig-tu-byed-pa. One common version of his name is rDo-khan-do, a Tibetanization of the Sanskrit. Iconographically Dhukhandi is shown with the objects of his trade: cloth, scissors, etc.

26. AJOKIPA Ajokipa in full Sanskrit is Āyogipāda, 'He Who Does Not Make Effort'; variations of his name are Adzogi, Azogipa, and Ajoki. In Tibetan he is called Le-lo-can, 'the Lazy One'. Ajokipa has no distinguishing iconographical features, although he may be shown reclining. In this volume he is shown as a stout man with food in front of him.

27. KALAPA The probable Sanskrit reconstruction for Kalapa is Kaḍapāda from *kaḍa* meaning 'mute'; the Tibetan rendition is sMyon-pa, 'Madman'. Kalapa does not seem to have any distinguishing iconographical features. He may be shown as yogin, monk, or layman.

28. DHOMBIPA Dhombipa comes from the Sanskrit *dhobi*, meaning 'washerman'. He is also called Dhobipa, Dhombhi,

and in Tibetan, Khrus-mkhan, 'the Washerman'. Dhombipa is sometimes spelled 'Ḍombipa'—but these two siddhas cannot be confused iconographically. Dhombipa is usually shown washing clothes.

29. KAṄKANA Kaṅkana comes from the Sanskrit *kaṅkaṅa* which means 'bracelet'. Variations of his name are Kakani and Kikipa; in Tibetan he is called gDu-bu-can, 'the Bracelet-wearer'. Iconographically Kaṅkana is shown as a layman staring at a bracelet on his arm.

30. KAMBALA Kambala derives from the Sanskrit *kambala* meaning 'wool garment' or 'blanket'. Variations of his name are Khaṃbala and, in Tibetan, Ba-wa-pa or more often Lva-ba-pa or Lva-va-pa. Kambala has no distinguishing iconographical features. The Stockholm thanka shows him wearing trousers and boots, seated in a grass hut on a tiger skin. He is staring at a rock which is hanging in mid-air, and a book, wrapped in a cloth, is hanging from the ceiling. In this volume Kambala is simply shown as a scholar, with peaked pandit's hat.

31. ṬEṄGIPA Ṭeṅgipa is also called Dinkapa, Tiṅkapa, Tenki, and in Tibetan, 'Bras-rdung-ba, meaning 'the Rice-pounder'. Ṭeṅgipa is usually depicted with a mortar and pestle.

32. BHANDHEPA Bhandhepa is probably from the Sanskrit *bhandara*, meaning 'storehouse'; his name also appears as Bade, Batalipa, and Bhadepa. In Tibetan he is known as Nor-la 'dzin-pa. Bhandhepa has no distinguishing iconographical features. In this volume he is shown with a canvas.

33. TANDHEPA Tandhepa is also called Tandhi, Tentana, and in Tibetan, Cho-lo-pa, 'the Dice-player'. Tandhepa is usually depicted with a gaming board.

34. KUKKURIPA Kukkuripa is from the Sanskrit *kukkura* which means 'dog'. Iconographically Kukkuripa is shown with his dog.

35. KUCIPA Kucipa, in full Sanskrit form, is probably Kubjikapāda, from *kubjika*, meaning 'bent' or 'hump-backed'. Variations of his name are Kujiba, Kutsipa, and Kubjipa. In Tibetan he is known as lTag-lba-can. Kucipa does not seem to have any distinguishing iconographical characteristics. In this volume he is shown seated in a rather hunched position.

36. DHARMAPA Dharmapa, in full Sanskrit form, is Dharmapāda, 'the Man of the Dharma'. Variations of his name are Dhamapa, Damapa, and in Tibetan, Thos-pa'i shes-rab bya-ba, 'He Who Has the Wisdom Gained by Hearing'. Dharmapa does not seem to have any distinguishing iconographical features, although he is usually shown as a scholar.

37. MAHIPA Mahipa is a short form of Mahipāda, which means 'the Strong Man', and is from *mahiṣa*, which means 'strong' or 'mighty'. Variations of his name are Makipa, Mahilapa, and Mardila. In Tibetan he is known as Ngar-rgyal-can, 'the Man of Pride'.

Mahipa does not seem to have any distinguishing iconographical features. In this volume he is shown seated in a cemetery amongst corpses; a dragon is coming down from the sky.

38. ACINTA Acinta, 'the 'Inconceivable', is also known as Atsinta. In Tibetan he is known as bSam-mi-khyab-pa, 'the One not Covered by Thought' or Dran-med-pa, 'the One without Thoughts'. Acinta is usually shown with a bundle of wood, although in one thanka he is shown holding a blue gem in his right hand and a skull-cup filled with blood in his left.

39. BABHAHI Babhahi is also called Baha and Bapabhati; in Tibetan he is known as Chu-las 'o-mo-len, 'He Who Draws Milk from Water'. Iconographically he is usually shown with his consort.

40. NALINA Nalina is from the Sanskrit *nalina*, which is a type of lotus. He is also called Nalana, Nili, Nali, and in Tibetan is known as Pad-ma'i rtsa-ba, 'Root of the Lotus'. Iconographically Nalina is usually depicted looking at a lotus.

41. BHUSUKU Bhusuku is better known as the Ācārya Śāntideva; he is also called Bhusukupa. In Tibetan he is called Zhi-lha or Sa'i-snying-po. Bhusuku is shown in different ways iconographically. In some thankas he is depicted as a monk holding a sword; in others he is shown flying through the air holding books, etc. In this volume he is depicted as a scholar floating above his seat.

42. INDRABHŪTI Indrabhūti, whose name means 'He Whose Majesty Is Like Indra', is also sometimes called Indrabodhi, Indrabhodhi, or even Andrachoti. In Tibetan he is called dBang-po'i-blo. Indrabhūti is usually depicted as a king.

43. MEKOPA Mekopa, in its longer Sanskrit form, is Meghapāda, from *megha*, meaning 'cloud'. Megopa is a variation on his name. Iconographically Mekopa is usually shown with a vessel.

44. KOṬALI Koṭali is also known as Kodalipa, which is reconstructed as Kuṭhārin or Kutharapāda, from *kuṭhāra*, meaning 'axe'. Variations of his name are Kuṭali and Kutharī. He is also known as Togcepa. In Tibetan he is known as Tog-rtse-zhabs, Tog-rtse-pa, 'Dzor-'dzin, and sTa-re-'dzin, 'the Axe-man'. Iconographically, Koṭali is usually shown carrying a hoe which often has a blade shaped like a fish.

45. KAṂPARIPA Kaṃparipa probably comes from the Sanskrit Karmarapāda, from *karmara* meaning 'artisan' or 'blacksmith'. Variations of his name include Kamari and Kamripa. In Tibetan he is known as mGar-pa. Iconographically Kamaripa is usually shown with sheets of metal and other tools of his trade.

46. JĀLANDHARI Jālandhari probably comes from the Sanskrit *jāla*, meaning 'net'. Variations of his name are Dzalandara and Jārilandha. In Tibetan he is known as Dra-ba 'dzin-pa, 'the Net-bearer'.

Jālandhari's iconography varies, although he is usually shown standing with one leg hooked up on his arm and his hands raised over his head. In this volume he is shown standing in a similar position, although his arms are not over his head.

47. RĀHULA Rāhula is a name connected with *rāhu*, 'the dragon's head', which, according to Classical Indian belief, causes eclipses. In Tibetan he is known as sGra-gcan-'dzin.

Rāhula does not seem to have any distinctive iconographical features, although he is shown in one thanka with his hands raised over his head, holding a bundle with a circular design, probably the moon. In this volume he is shown with an image of the Buddha in the background.

48. DHARMAPA Dharmapa in Tibetan is known as Chos-pa or Thos-pa-can or Thos-pa shcs-rab-can. Iconographically Dharmapa is depicted as a monk; he is also often shown with a ḍākinī looking on from the clouds.

49. DHOKARIPA Dhokaripa is also called Tukkari, Dokari, Tokri, and rDo-ka-ri, a Tibetanization of his name. Dhokaripa is interpreted to mean 'the Man Who Carries a Pot'. Iconographically Dhokaripa is usually depicted carrying a vessel. In this volume he is shown carrying a bundle.

50. MEDHINA Medhina is from the Sanskrit which means 'earth'. He is also called Medhini and, in Tibetan, Thang-lo-pa, which means 'Man of the Plains'. Medhina is usually depicted plowing a field with oxen.

51. PAṄKAJA Paṅkaja means 'the Lotus-born'; his name is sometimes spelled Saṅkaja, and variations of his name are Pakaja, Paṅkadza, Saṅkhadza, and Paṅkaza; in Tibetan he is known as 'Dam-skyes. Iconographically Paṅkaja is usually shown with water and flowers.

52. GHAṆḌHAPA Ghaṇḍhapa is a shorter version of the Sanskrit Ghaṇṭapāda, 'the Man of the Bell'. He is also frequently known as Vajraghaṇṭa. Variations of his name are Ghandopa, Gandapa, and Ganthapa. In Tibetan he is known as Dril-bu-pa or rDo-rje dril-bu-pa, 'the Man with the Bell and Dorje'.

Ghaṇḍhapa is usually shown with his consort. He is often depicted standing in a cloud, holding a bell in his right hand.

53. YOGIPA Yogipa is a shorter form of the Sanskrit Yogipāda; a variation of his name is Dzogipa. Yogipa does not seem to have any distinguishing iconographical features. In this volume he is shown as a yogin wearing a human skin.

54. CALUKI Caluki is probably from the Sanskrit *caluka*, meaning 'a small pot'. Variations of his name are Tsaluki, Culiki, and Celupa. Caluki does not seem to have any distinguishing iconography, although in one thanka he is shown holding a skull-cup and a damaru. In this volume he is shown meditating.

55. GORURA Gorura is also known as Vajura, which is from the Sanskrit *vāgura*, meaning 'net'. He is also known as Godhura. In Tibetan he is called Bya-ba, 'the Bird-man'. Gorura's iconography usually shows him with birds or with a net.

56. LUCIKA Lucika is probably from the Sanskrit *luñcaka*, meaning 'One Who Pulls Out'; he is also called Luñcaka and Lutsikapa. Lucika does not seem to have any distinguishing iconography. In this volume he is shown as a yogin, dancing.

57. NIGUṆA Niguṇa is a corrupted form of the Sanskrit *nirguṇa*, which means 'devoid of virtue' or 'devoid of attachments'. Variations of his name are Naguna and Nerguna. In Tibetan he is known as Yon-tan-med-pa. Niguṇa does not seem to have any distinctive iconographical marks.

58. JAYĀNANDA Jayānanda means 'He Who Delights in Victory'. Variations of his name are Jayānanta, Dzayā-nanta, and Dzānanta. The Tibetan form of his name is rGyal-ba mtha'-med, meaning 'Endless Victory'. Jayānanda does not seem to have any distinctive iconographic features. In this volume he is shown looking at birds.

59. PACARI Pacari is probably from the Sanskrit *pacala* which means 'cook'. He is also called Patsari, and in Tibetan, 'Khur-ba 'tsong-ba, 'the Pastry-seller'. Pacari does not seem to have any distinguishing iconographical features. In this volume he is shown cooking pastries.

60. CAMPAKA Campaka is Sanskrit for a type of flower. Variations of his name include Tsampala and Cambaka. Iconographically Campaka is usually shown with a flower; or he may be shown dancing, holding both a flower and a skull-cup.

61. BHIKṢANA Bhikṣana may come from the Sanskrit *viṣana*, which means 'horn' or 'tusk'. Variations of his name include Bhikṣana, Bhakhana, and Bhekhepa. In Tibetan he is known as So-gnyis-pa, 'He with Two Teeth'. Bhikṣana does not seem to have any distinguishing iconographical features, although he may be shown as if pulling out his teeth.

62. TELOPA Telopa is a shorter form of the Sanskrit Tailopāda, from *taila*, meaning 'sesame-seed oil'. He is also called Dhili, Delipa, Tailopa, Telī, and in Tibetan, Mar-nag 'tshong-mkhan, 'the Seller of Black Butter'. Telopa is usually shown with oil-making apparatus.

63. KUMARIPA Kumaripa is probably derived from the Sanskrit *kumbhakāra*, which means 'the Potter'. He is also

called Kumara, and in Tibetan is known as rDza-mkhan. Kumaripa is usually depicted shaping clay on a potter's wheel.

64. CAPARIPA Caparipa perhaps comes from the Sanskrit *carpaṭa*, meaning 'ear'. Variations of his name are Tsaparipa, Tsapalipa, and Tsarwaripa. Caparipa does not seem to have any distinguishing iconographical features. In this volume he is shown as a scholar.

65. MAṆIBHADRĀ Maṇibhadrā, which means 'Auspicious As a Jewel', is also called the yoginī Bahura. Iconographically Maṇibhadrā is usually shown flying through the air.

66. MEKHALĀ Mekhalā may come either from the Sanskrit *Mahākhalā* which means 'Elder Mischievous Girl' or *mekhala* which means 'belt' or 'sacred cord'. Mekhalī is a common variant on her name. Iconographically, Mekhalā is usually shown with a sword coming from her mouth.

67. KANAKHALĀ Kanakhalā means 'Smaller Mischievous Girl'. Iconographically, Kanakhalā is usually shown with her head in one hand and a sword in the other.

68. KALAKALA Kalakala is also known as Kalākapa and Kalakepa. In Tibetan he is known as Ku-co-can. Iconographically Kalakala is usually shown with a forefinger raised. In this volume he is simply shown as a yogin.

69. KANTALI Kantali may come from the Sanskrit *kanthadi*, meaning 'rag-wearer'; the name may also be related to *caṇḍala*, meaning 'an outcaste group'. He is also known as Kantalipa, Kanthari, and in Tibetan, Tshem-bu-pa, which means 'the Tailor'. Iconographically, Kāntali is usually depicted sewing.

70. DHAHULI Dhahuli is also called Dharuri and Dekara. In Tibetan he is known as rTsva-thag-can, 'the Man of the Grass-rope'. Iconographically, Dhahuli is usually shown holding a length of rope.

71. UDHELI Udheli probably comes from the Sanskrit *uddiya*, which means 'flying' or 'soaring'. Variations of his name are Udhilipa, Udhili, and Uddaripa; in Tibetan he is known as Phur-pa. Iconographically, Udheli is usually shown with a whisk in his hand. In this volume he is shown flying over the ocean.

72. KAPALAPA Kapalapa is from the Sanskrit *kapāla*, which means 'skull'. He is also known as Kapalipa. In Tibetan he is known as Thod-pa-can. Kapalapa is usually shown carrying a skeleton or a skull-cup.

73. KIRAVA Kirava is also known as Kirapa, Kilapa, and Kiraba. In Tibetan he is known as rNam-rtog spang-ba, 'He Who Abandons Conceptions'. Iconographically, Kirava is usually shown holding a sword and a shield.

74. SAKARA Sakara probably comes from the Sanskrit *puskara*, which means 'blue lotus'. He is also called Pukara, Padmavajra, and Saroruha. In Tibetan he is known as mTsho-skyes, 'the Lake-born'. Iconographically, Sakara is usually shown with his consort, holding a vajra in his hand; however, he occasionally is shown as a monk holding a vajra and skull-cup.

75. SARVABHAKṢA Sarvabhakṣa means 'He Who Eats Everything'. In Tibetan he is known as Thams-cad-za-ba. Sarvabhakṣa is usually shown with a bowl or eating from a bowl.

76. Nāgabodhi Nāgabodhi is known in Tibetan as Klu'i-byang-chub. Nāgabodhi is often shown as a yogin meditating in a cave. In the Stockholm thanka he is shown holding a skull-cup, and there are two elephants depicted with him. He is also often shown with cows. In this volume he is shown as a yogin leaning on a stick.

77. Dārika Dārika is also known as Darika. In Tibetan he is known as sMad-'tshong-can, 'Man of the Prostitutes' or sMad-'tshong-ma'i-g'yod, 'Servant of the Prostitutes'. Iconographically, Dārika is shown in various ways. Although he is often shown flying through the air, he may be shown as a king or a yogin seated on an animal skin and holding a skull-cup.

78. Putali Putali is also known as Sutali, Tali, Satapa, and Purali. In Tibetan he is known as rGyan-slang-ba, 'He Who Raises the Ornaments'. Putali is usually shown holding a vajra, with a thanka depicted beside him.

79. Panaha Panaha may come from the Sanskrit *Upanahi*, 'He Who Ties Together'. He is also known as Panha, Pahana, and Sanaka. In Tibetan he is known as mChil-lham-can, 'the Bootmaker'. Iconographically, Panaha is usually shown running or dancing and wearing ornamental boots. In this volume he is shown with a needle and thread.

80. Kokali Kokali comes from the Sanskrit *kokila*, which means 'cuckoo'. Variations of his name are Kokilipa, and Kokala. In Tibetan he is known as Ko-la-la'i skad-du-chags. Iconographically, Kokali does not seem to have any distinguishing features. In this volume he is shown holding a vajra and bell and looking into the sky.

81. ANAṄGA Anaṅga, which literally means 'without limbs', is a name for Kama, the Indian cupid. He is frequently called Anango, and is also known as Anangi, Arangi, and Anigo. Although Anaṅga does not seem to have any distinguishing iconographical features, he is often shown meditating or listening to a monk.

82. LAKṢMĪNKARĀ Lakṣmīnkarā means 'She Who Makes Fortune'. Her name is often Tibetanized as Legs-smin-kara, 'the Well-ripened'. Lakṣmīnkarā's iconography does not seem to have any distinguishing features, although she is often shown with small blossoms surrounding her.

83. SAMUDRA Samudra means 'the Beachcomber'; in Tibetan he is known as rGya-mtsho-nas nor-bu-len-mkhan, 'He Who Draws Wealth from the Sea'. Samudra is often depicted in a houseboat.

84. VYALI Vyali is also known as Byali, Byari, Balipa, and Vyadi. Iconographically, Vyali is usually shown with a woman and a horse.

# Comparative Chart of the Siddhas

Many of the stories follow a standardized form giving the name, the caste or occupation, the place, the guru, and often the particular Tantric tradition in which the protagonist was initiated. These details are gathered together in the following chart. The name of the siddha is given first, then his city or area, his occupation or whether he is Brahman, kṣatriya, etc., his guru if known from the story, the Tantric system if mentioned, and how long it took to gain siddhi. This chart is similar to, but expands upon, the one found in Sankṛtyāyana's *Recherches Bouddhique*, pp. 220–225.

## Comparative Chart of the Siddhas

| *No.* | *Name* | *Place* | *Occupation* | *Guru* | *Tantra* | *Time* |
|---|---|---|---|---|---|---|
| 1. | Lūyipa | Saliputra | prince | ḍākinī | Cakrasamvara | 12 yrs |
| 2. | Līlapa | S. India | king | yogin | Hevajra | 12 yrs |
| 3. | Virūpa | Somapurī | monk | Vajravārāhī | Hevajra | 12 yrs |
| 4. | Ḍombipa | Magadha | king | Virūpa | Hevajra | 12 yrs |
| 5. | Śavaripa | Mt. Vikrama | hunter | Avalokiteśvara | nm | 12 yrs |
| 6. | Saraha | Roli | Brahman | ḍākinī | nm | 12 yrs |
| 7. | Kankaripa | Maghahura | sudra | yogin | nm | 6 yrs |
| 8. | Mīnapa | Kāmarūpa | fisherman | Śiva | nm | 12 yrs |
| 9. | Goraksa | E. India | herdsman | Acinta | nm | nm |
| 10. | Caurāṅgi | E. India | prince | Acinta | nm | nm |
| 11. | Vīnapa | Ghahuri | prince | Buddhapa | Hevajra | 9 yrs |
| 12. | Śāntipa | Vikramaśīla | monk | Togcepa | nm | 12 yrs |
| 13. | Tantipa | Sandhonāgara | weaver | Jālandhari | Hevajra | 12 yrs |
| 14. | Camaripa | Viṣṇunagara | cobbler | yogin | nm | 12 yrs |
| 15. | Khaḍgapa | Magadha | thief | Carpati | nm | 21 days |
| 16. | Nāgārjuna | Kahora | monk | Tārā | Guhyasamāja | 12 yrs |
| 17. | Kāṇhapa | Somapurī | monk | Jālandhari | Hevajra | 12 yrs |
| 18. | Karṇaripa | Nālandā | monk | Nāgārjuna | Guhyasamāja | nm |
| 19. | Thaganapa | E. India | sudra | monk | nm | 7 yrs |

*(continued)*

Comparative Chart of the Siddhas (*Continued*)

| *No.* | *Name* | *Place* | *Occupation* | *Guru* | *Tantra* | *Time* |
|---|---|---|---|---|---|---|
| 20. | Nāropa | E. India | wine-seller | Tilopa | Hevajra | 6 mos |
| 21. | Shalipa | Vighāsura | sudra | yogin | nm | 9 yrs |
| 22. | Tilopa | Bhigunagara | monk | nm | nm | 10 yrs |
| 23. | Catrapa | Sandhonāgara | beggar | yogin | Hevajra | 6 yrs |
| 24. | Bhadrapa | Maṇidhara | Brahman | yogin | nm | 6 yrs |
| 25. | Khandipa | Ghandapura | sudra | yogin | Cakrasamvara | 12 yrs |
| 26. | Ajokipa | Saliputra | nm | yogin | Hevajra | 9 yrs |
| 27. | Kalapa | Rājapura | nm | yogin | Cakrasamvara | nm |
| 28. | Dhombipa | Saliputra | washerman | yogin | Cakrasamvara | nm |
| 29. | Kaṅkana | Viṣṇunagara | king | yogin | nm | 6 mos |
| 30. | Kambala | Kankarāma | prince | ḍākinī | Cakrasamvara | 12 yrs |
| 31. | Ṭeṅgipa | Saliputra | minister | Lūyipa | Cakrasamvara | 12 yrs |
| 32. | Bhandhepa | Śrāvastī | painter | Kṛṣṇacāri | Guyasamāja | nm |
| 33. | Tandhepa | Kausāmbī | sudra | yogin | nm | nm |
| 34. | Kukkuripa | Kapilaśakru | Brahman | ḍākinī | nm | nm |
| 35. | Kucipa | Kari | sudra | Nāgārjuna | Guhyasamāja | nm |
| 36. | Dharmapa | Vikramāsura | Brahman | yogin | nm | nm |
| 37. | Mahipa | Magadha | sudra | yogin | nm | nm |
| 38. | Acinta | Dhanarūpa | wood-seller | Kambala | Cakrasamvara | nm |
| 39. | Babhahi | Dhanjura | kṣatriya | yogin | nm | 12 yrs |
| 40. | Nalina | Saliputra | nm | yogin | Guhyasamāja | 9 yrs |

| | | | | | | |
|---|---|---|---|---|---|---|
| 42. | Indrabhūti | Uḍḍiyāna | king | Kambala | Cakrasamvara | 12 yrs |
| 43. | Mekopa | Bengal | food-seller | yogin | nm | 6 mos |
| 44. | Koṭali | Rāmeśvara | farmer | Śāntipa | nm | 12 yrs |
| 45. | Kaṃparipa | Saliputra | smith | yogin | nm | 6 yrs |
| 46. | Jālandhari | Thod-tha | Brahman | ḍākinī | Hevajra | 7 yrs |
| 47. | Rāhula | Kāmarūpa | sudra | yogin | nm | 16 yrs |
| 48. | Dharmapa | Bodhinagara | monk | ḍākinī | nm | 5 yrs |
| 49. | Dhokaripa | Saliputra | sudra | yogin | Hevajra | 3 yrs |
| 50. | Medhina | Saliputra | sudra | yogin | nm | 12 yrs |
| 51. | Paṅkaja | nm | Brahman | Nāgārjuna | nm | 7 days |
| 52. | Ghaṇḍhapa | Nālandā | monk | nm | Cakrasamvara | nm |
| 53. | Yogipa | Odantapuri | caṇḍala | Śavaripa | Hevajra | 12 yrs |
| 54. | Caluki | Maṅgalapura | sudra | Maitripa | Cakrasamvara | 9 yrs |
| 55. | Gorura | nm | bird-catcher | yogin | nm | 9 yrs |
| 56. | Lucika | Bengal | Brahman | yogin | Cakrasamvara | 12 yrs |
| 57. | Niguṇa | Pūrvadeśa | sudra | yogin | nm | nm |
| 58. | Jayānanda | Bengal | minister | nm | nm | nm |
| 59. | Pacari | Campāra | baker | Avalokiteśvara | nm | nm |
| 60. | Campaka | Campaka | prince | yogin | nm | 12 yrs |
| 61. | Bhikṣana | Saliputra | sudra | ḍākinī | nm | 7 yrs |
| 62. | Telopa | Saliputra | oil merchant | Bahana | nm | 6 yrs |
| 63. | Kumaripa | Jomanaśrī | potter | yogin | nm | 6 mos |
| 64. | Caparipa | Magadha | yogin | nm | nm | nm |

(*continued*)

Comparative Chart of the Siddhas (*Continued*)

| *No.* | *Name* | *Place* | *Occupation* | *Guru* | *Tantra* | *Time* |
|---|---|---|---|---|---|---|
| 65. | Maṇibhadrā | Agartse | housewife | Kukkuripa | Cakrasamvara | nm |
| 66. | Mekhalā | Devīkoṭa | woman | Kāṇḥapa | Hevajra | 12 yrs |
| 67. | Kanakhalā | Devīkoṭa | woman | Kāṇḥapa | Hevajra | 12 yrs |
| 68. | Kalakala | Bhilira | sudra | yogin | Guyasamāja | nm |
| 69. | Kantali | Maṇidharā | tailor | ḍākinī Veṭalī | Hevajra | nm |
| 70. | Dhahuli | Dhakara | sudra | yogin | nm | 12 yrs |
| 71. | Udheli | Devīkoṭa | kṣatriya | Karṇaripa | nm | 12 yrs |
| 72. | Kapalapa | Rājapuri | sudra | Kṛṣṇacāri | Hevajra | 9 yrs |
| 73. | Kirava | Grahara | king | yogin | Cakrasamvara | 12 yrs |
| 74. | Sakara | Kañci | prince | Avalokiteśvara | Hevajra | nm |
| 75. | Sarvabhakṣa | Abhara | sudra | Saraha | nm | nm |
| 76. | Nāgabodhi | Suvarna | Brahman | Nāgārjuna | Guhyasamāja | 12 yrs |
| 77. | Dārika | Saliputra | king | Lūyipa | Cakrasamvara | nm |
| 78. | Putali | Bengal | sudra | yogin | Hevajra | 12 yrs |
| 79. | Panaha | Sandhonāgara | cobbler | yogin | nm | 9 yrs |
| 80. | Kokalipa | Campāra | king | monk | Cakrasamvara | 6 mos |
| 81. | Anaṅga | Gahura | sudra | monk | Cakrasamvara | 6 mos |
| 82. | Lakṣmīnkarā | Uḍḍiyāna | princess | Kambala | nm | 7 yrs |
| 83. | Samudra | Sarvatira | sudra | Acinta | nm | 3 yrs |
| 84. | Vyali | Apatrara | Brahman | nm | nm | nm |

# Bibliography

## Sanskrit Works

The works of the siddhas as contained in this bibliography are all in the Tantric section of the bsTan-'gyur. Many of the siddhas, for example Nāgārjuna, have texts included elsewhere in the bsTan-'gyur.

1. Lūyipa has six works in the bsTan-'gyur:
2144 Śrī-bhagavad-abhisamaya-nāma
2171 Śrī-vajrasattva-sādhana-nāma
3147 Buddhodaya
3170 Tattva-svabhāva-dohakoṣa-gītikā-ḍṛṣti-nāma
4665 Buddhodaya-nāma
3195 Lūyipāda-gītikā

2. Līlapa has one work in the bsTan-'gyur:
3171 Vikalpa-parihāra-gītikā-nāma
There are two works attributed to Līlavajra who may or may not be connected with our Līlapa:
2679 Vajrasattva-sādhana-nibandha
2867 Śrī-yamāntaka-mūla-mantrārtha-vajra-prabhedha-nāma

3. Virūpa has a number of works in the bsTan-'gyur:
2263 Chinna-muṇḍa-sādhana-nāma
2873 Raktayamāri-sādhana
2874 Raktayamāntaka-sādhana

2875 Prabhāsodaya-krama
2876 Suniṣprapañca-tattvopadeśa-nāma
2878 Yamāri-yantrāvali
2900 Amṛtādhiṣṭāna-nāma
3197 Virūpa-gītikā
3130 Dohakoṣa-nāma
3133 Amṛta-siddhi-mūla-nāma
3172 Karma-caṇḍālikā-dohakoṣa-gītikā-nāma
4691 Guhyābhiṣeka-prakriyā-nāma
5026 Amara-siddhi-vṛtti-sanātana-siddhi-nāma
3129 Śrī-virūpa-pāda-caturaśīti

4. Ḍombipa has a number of works in the bsTan-'gyur:
2133 Guhya vajra-tantrarāja-vṛtti
2181 Ekavīra-sādhana-nāma
2358 Daśatattva
2359 Yoga-yoginīnām asādhāraṇārthopadeśa-nāma
2360 Gaṇacakra-vidhi-nāma
2361 Śrī-hevajra-sādhana
2363 Bhikṣa-vṛtti-nāma
2422 Trikramopadeśa-nāma
2435 Nairātmā-yoginī-sādhana
2448 Ārya-tārā-kurukullā-stotra
3067 Śrī-sahaja-siddhi-nāma
3196 Ḍombī-gītikā
3365 Nāmasaṃgīti-vṛtti
4622 Ekavīra-sādhana-nāma
4705 Catus-tattva
4983 Śrī-gaṇapati-cakra-sūrya
4816 Mṛta-vidhi-nāma

5. Śavaripa has a number of works in the bsTan-'gyur:
2271 Vajrayoginy-abhiṣeka-saṃkṣepa-nāma
2631 Adhiṣṭhāna-mahākāla-sādhana-nāma
3204 Śūnyatā-dṛṣṭi-nāma
4925 Akṣobhyānuṣaṅgikanātha-vighna-nibarhaṇa
4926 Nātha-maṅgala-guṇasāgara-nāma

4927 Rakta nāthāyuḥ-parirakṣā-mukhāgama
4936 Sādhiṣṭhāna-śrīmahākāla-sādhana-nāma
4941 Mahākāla-stotra

Under the name of Mahāśabaripāda or Mahāśabara there are the following works:

2174 Śrī-sahajopadeśa-svādhiṣṭhāna-nāma
2175 Śrī-sahaja-śambara-svādhiṣṭāna-nāma
2270 Śiṣyānugraha-vidhi-nāma
2272 Vajrayoginī-gaṇacakra-vidhi-nāma

Under the name of Śabarīśvara, who may or may not be our siddha, are the following works:

2091 Yogaṣaḍaṅga-nāma
3135 Mahāmudrā-vajra-gīti-nāma
3276 Citta-guhya-gambhīrārtha-gīti-nāma
4934 Svadhiṣṭāna-mahākāla-sādhana-nāma

Under the name Śrī Mahāsabara Saraha there is the following work:

3119 Dohakoṣa-nāma-mahāmudropadeśa

6. Saraha has many works in the bsTan-'gyur:

2524 Śrī-buddha-kapāla-tantrasya pañjikā jñānavatī-nāma
2527 Śrī-buddha-kapāla-sādhana-nāma
2528 Sarvabhūta-bali-vidhi
2529 Śrī-buddha-kapāla-nāma-maṇḍala-vidhi-krama-pradyotana
3068 Dohakoṣa-gīti
3110 Dohakoṣa-nāma-caryā-gīti
3111 Dohakoṣopadeśa-gīti-nāma
3113 Kakhasya doha nāma
3114 Kakhasya doha-ṭippaṇī
3115 Kāya koṣāmṛtavajra-gītā
3117 Cittakoṣā-ajavajra-gītā
3118 Kāya-vāk-cittāmanasikāra-nāma
3121 Dvādaśopadeśa-gāthā
3122 Svādhiṣṭhāna-krama
3123 Tattvopadeśa-śikharadoha-gīti-nāma
3173 Bhāvanā-dṛṣṭi-caryā-phala-dohagītikā-nāma

3179 Vasantatilaka-dohakoṣa-gītikā-nāma
3268 Mahāmudropadeśa-vajra-guhya-gīti
3985 Trailokya-vaśaṃkara-lokeśvara-sādhana
3986 Trailokya-vaśaṃkara-lokeśvara-sādhana-nāma
4192 Trailokya-vaśaṃkarāvalokiteśvara-sādhana
4248 Trailokya-vaśaṃkara-lokeśvara-sādhana
4935 Adhiṣṭhāna-mahākāla-sādhana-nāma
4940 Mahākāla-stotra

7. Kankaripa has one work in the bsTan-'gyur:
3217 Ṣoḍaśa-bindu-bhāvanā-nāma

8. Mīnapa has one work in the bsTan-'gyur:
3218 Bāhyāntara-bodhicitta-bandhopadeśa-nāma

9. Goraksa has one work in the bsTan-'gyur:
3219 Vāyu-tattva-bhāvanopadeśa-nāma

10. Caurāṅgi has one work in the bsTan-'gyur:
3220 Vāyu-tattva-bhāvanā-nāma

11. Vīnapa has two works in the bsTan-'gyur:
2396 Guhyābhiṣeka-prakaraṇa-nāma
3221 Vajraḍākinī-niṣpanna-krama

12. Śāntipa (Ratnākaraśānti) has many works listed in the bsTan-'gyur:
2141 Khasama-nāma-ṭīkā
2374 Bhramahāra-nāma-sādhana
2375 Sahaja-yoga-krama-nāma
2376 Sahaja-sadyoga-vṛtti-garbha-prakāśikā-nāma
2456 Vajratārā-sādhana
2495 Guṇavatī-śrīmahāmāyā-ṭīkā
2515 Mahāmāyā-sādhana
2690 Piṇḍīkṛta-sādhanopāyikā-vṛtti-ratnāvalī-nāma
2714 Kusumāñjali-guhyasamāja-nibandha-nāma
2782 Śrī-kṛṣṇayamāri-mahātantrarāja-pañjikā-ratnapradīpa-nāma
2798 Kṛṣṇayamāri-sādhana-protphullakumuda-nāma

2848 Vajrabhairava-gaṇacakra-nāma
3301 Abhiṣeka-nirukti
3450 Śrī-sarvarahasya-nibandha-rahasya-pradīpa-nāma
3205 Sukha-duḥkha-dvaya-parityāga-dṛṣṭi-nāma
3939 Pratisarā-rakṣā-cakra-lekhopāya
3947 Pañca-rakṣā-vidhi
4312 Vajra-tārā-sādhana
4535 Triyāna-vyavasthāna-nāma
5087 Maṇḍala-vidhi-nāma
5088 Maṇḍala-vidhi

13. Tantipa has one text in the bsTan-'gyur:
3222 Caturyoga-bhāvanā-nāma

14. Camaripa has one work in the bsTan-'gyur:
3223 Prajñopāya-viniścaya-samudaya-nāma

15. Khaḍgapa does not have any works attributed to him in the bsTan-'gyur.

16. Nāgārjuna has seventy works listed in the Tantric section of the bsTan-'gyur:
2010 Dharmadhātu-stotra
2011 Nirupama-stava
2012 Lokātīta-stava
2013 Cittavajra-stava
2014 Paramārtha-stava
2015 Kāyatraya-stotra-nāma
2016 Kāyatraya-stotra-nāma-nirvaraṇa
2017 Sattvā-rādhana-stava
2018 Prajñā-pāramitā-stotra
2019 Acintya-stava
2020 Stutyatīta-stava
2021 Niruttara-stava
2022 Ārya-bhaṭṭārakamañjuśrī-paramārtha-stuti-nāma
2023 Ārya-mañjuśrī-bhaṭṭāraka-karuṇā-stotra
2024 Aṣṭa-mahāsthāna-caitya-stotra
2025 Aṣṭa-mahāsthāna-caitya-stotra

2026 Dvādaśakāra-nāma-naya-stotra
2027 Vandanā-stotra-nāma
2028 Narakoddhāra-nāma (Naragoddira in original)
2336 Saṃdhi-bhāṣā-ṭīkā
2555 Tārā-sādhana
2556 Mahākāruṇikāryatārā-sādhana-sāmānyābhisamaya-nāma
2644 Śrī-mahākāla-stotra-padāṣṭaka-nāma
2645 Śrī-mahākālasya-stotra-aṣṭamantra-nāma
2646 Vajra-mahākālāṣṭaka-stotra
2648 Śrī-guhyasamāja-tantrasya-tantraṭīkā-nāma
2649 Aṣṭādaśa-paṭala-vistara-vyākhyā
2661 Piṇḍīkṛta-sādhana
2662 Śrī-guhyasamāja-mahāyogatantrotpattikrama-sādhana-sūtra-melāpaka-nāma
2663 Śrī-guhyasamāja-maṇḍala-vidhi-nāma
2664 Seka-catuḥ-prakaraṇa
2665 Bodhicitta-vivaraṇa-nāma
2666 Bodhicitta-vivaraṇa
2667 Pañca-krama
3033 Caṇḍa-vajra-krodhadeva-pañca-nāma-maṇḍala-vidhi
3034 Vajrapāṇi-mārgāṅgāṣṭaka
3048 Tattva-pradīpa-nāma-vajrapāṇi-sarvasādhana-pūrṇālaṃkāra
3224 Svabhāvāsiddhy-upadeśa-nāma
3307 Vajrayāna-sthūlāpatti
3500 Ārya-nīlāmbaradhara-vajrapāṇi-kalpa-nāma-dhāraṇī-ṭīkā
3525 Mañjuśrī-vajra-prajñā-vardhana-nāma
3555 Ārya-sahasrabhujāvalokiteśvara-sādhana
3556 Ārya-lokeśvara-ṣaḍakṣara-sādhana
3671 Lokeśvara-sādhana
3688 Nīlāmbaropasiddhi-nāma
3689 Prāyaścittāmṛta
3690 Vajra-pavitra-karma-saṃbhāra
3691 Saptāṅga-sādhana

3712 Vajrapāṇi-maṇḍala-vidhi
3891 Kalyāṇa-kāmadhenu
4189 Kalpokta-kurukullā-devī-sādhana
4310 Vajra-tārā-sādhana
4340 Ekajaṭā-sādhana
4384 Muktakena-tārākalpodbhava-kurukullā-sādhana
4467 Nāgeśvararāja-sādhana
4487 Khadiravaṇī-tārā-sādhana
4551 Avamāna-pradīpa-nāma
4710 Trailokya-vijayārya-tārā-sādhana
4792 Ṣaḍaṅga-yoga-nāma
4828 Piśācī-yakṣiṇī-ḍākinī-kalpottha-kuṇḍalī-sādhana-nāma
4829 Yakṣiṇī-kuṇḍalī-sādhana-piṇḍārtha-vṛtti
4847 Caṇḍa-mahāroṣaṇa-vajrapāṇi-nāma-sādhana
4878 Tārā-stotra
4881 Khadiravaṇī-tārā-stotra
4898 Śrī-nātha-mahākāla-sādhana-krama
4900 Śrī-mahākāla-sādhana-nāma
4942 Caturbhuja-mahākāla-sādhana
4954 Vajra-mahākālābhicāra-homa-nāma
4971 Hasti-ratna-dhana-deyopadeśa-nāma
5100 Praṇidhāna-ratna-rāja-nāma

17. Kāṇhapa (Kṛṣṇacāri) has many works in the bsTan-'gyur:
2164 Bhagavac-chrī-cakraśambara-maṇḍala-vidhi
2165 Śrī-cakraśambara-homa-vidhi
2166 Vasantatilaka-nāma
2167 Guhyatattva-prakāśa-nāma
2168 Āli-catuṣṭaya
2169 Ālicatuṣṭaya-vibhaṅga-nāma
2170 Saptākṣara-sādhana
2177 Saṃvara-vyākhyā
2251 Ālokacatura-ṭīkā-nāma
2313 Yoga-ratnamālā-nāma-hevajra-pañjikā
2317 Hevajra-nāma-mahātantrarāja-dvikalpamāyā-pañjikā-smṛti-nibandha

2325 Ārya-ḍākinī-vajrapañjara-nāma-mahātantrarāja-kalpa-mukhabandha
2381 Śrī-hevajraikavīra-sādhana
2382 Hevajra-sādhana-tattvoddyotakara-nāma
2383 Śrī-hevajra-paddhati-maṇḍala-vidhi
2384 Homa-vidhi
2385 Hevajra-homa-vidhi
2386 Pratiṣṭhā-vidhi-nāma
2387 Gaṇacakra-pūjā-krama
2388 Stūpa-vidhi-nāma
2389 Mṛtyu-vidhi-nāma
2430 Sarvabhūta-bali-vidhi-nāma
2507 Śrī-buddha-ḍākinī-sādhana
2508 Mahāmāyā-maṇḍala-vidhi-krama-bodhana-nāma
2509 Sāmānya-dharma-caryā
2512 Sapta-parva-vidhi
2604 Raktaikajaṭy-adhiṣṭhāna-vidhi
2683 Śrī-guhyasamāja-maṇḍalopāyikā
2684 Śrī-vajrasattva-pūjā-vidhi
2685 Bali-vidhi
2686 Pratiṣṭhā-vidhi-nāma
2811 Kṛṣṇayamāri-buddha-sādhana-nāma
2819 Kṛṣṇayamāri-śmahoma-vidhi-nāma
2820 Gaṇacakra-vidhi-nāma
2810 Bhaṭṭāraka-mañjuśrī-yamāri-pūjā-vidhikrama-nāma
3032 Guhyapati-vajrapāṇi-nīlāmbaradhara-sādhana
3035 Guhyapati-vajra-sādhana
3127 Pañca-sarga-nāma
3139 Vajra-gīti
3215 Asaṃbandha-dṛṣṭi-nāma
3318 Gaṇacakra-vidhi
4398 Kurukullā-sādhana
4543 Mahāyāna-melayāna-pradīpa
4664 Mṛtyupati-pramathanī-nāma-sādhanopāyikā
4667 Śrī-vasantatilaka-nāma
4818 Sarvapreta-vajra-pāśa

4822 Śrī-yamakālāyuṣpati-maṇḍala-vidhi
4961 Śrī-mahākāla-siddhi-rakṣā-pratyaṅgiraḥ-sādhana-nāma
4973 Vināyakarāja-sādhana-nāma
4974 Karmīramaṇi-cakraśambara-sādhana-nāma
4975 Śrī-vajraḍākinī-sādhana-nāma
4976 Vināyakarāja-sādhana-nāma
4977 Ārya-gaṇapati-stuti
4978 Mahāvināyaka-rūpopadeśa-cintāratna-nāma
4979 Ārya-gaṇapati-bali-vidhi
4980 Vināyaka-homa-vidhi
4987 Ārya-gaṇapati-cintāratna-sādhana
4989 Ārya-gaṇapati-stuti
5060 Mahāḍhunḍhana-mūla-nāma
5062 Rathacakra-pañcadaśa-yantra
5067 Caṇḍālī-yantra
5134 Vajrayoginī-sādhana
5180 Bhagavad-vajrasattva-sādhana-svādhiṣṭhānopadeśa-krama-nāma
5181 Jihma-saralīkaraṇopadeśa

18. Karṇaripa (Āryadeva) has a number of works in the bsTan-'gyur:
2481 Śrī-catuḥpīṭha-yoga-tantra-sādhanopāyikā
2483 Jñāneśvarī-sādhana
2484 Śrī-catuḥpīṭha-tantrarāja-nāma-maṇḍalopāyikā-vidhi-sāra-samuccaya-nāma
2485 Śrī-catuḥpīṭha-gūḍhārtha-nirdeśa-ekadruma-pañjikā
2486 Vajraghaṇṭa-pūjā-sādhana-krama
2659 Pradīpoddyotana-nāma-ṭīkā
2668 Caryā-melāpaka-pradīpa
2669 Cittāvaraṇa-viśodhana-nāma-prakaraṇa
2670 Svādhiṣṭāna-krama-prabheda
2671 Abhibodhi-kramopadeśa
2672 Marahoma-vidhi
2673 Śrī-guhyasamāja-niṣpanna-kramāntaka
3126 Nirvikalpa-prakaraṇa

3189 Karṇari-gītikā
3285 Atiguhyācintya-nāma-pañca-viṣa-gupta-mārga
3526 Bhagavan-mañjughoṣa-vicāraṇa
4695 Pratipattisāra-śataka
4707 Nairātmā-pañcadaśadevī-stotra
5005 Krodha-bhaya-nāśanī-sādhana-nāma
5006 Bhaya-śṛlinī-sādhana
5007 Pralayābhiṣeka-vidhi
5008 Krodha-bhaya-nāśanī-samaya-guhya-sādhana
5009 Krodha-bhaya-nāśanī-homa-vidhi-nāma
5011 Mahādevatraya-sādhana

19. Thagana has three works in the bsTan-'gyur:
2708 Śrī-guhyasamāja-tantra-vivaraṇa
2731 Śrī-samantabhadra-sādhana-vṛtti
3174 Dohakoṣa-tattva-gītikā-nāma

20. Nāropa has a number of works in the bsTan-'gyur:
2068 Paramārtha-saṃgraha-nāma-sekoddeśa-ṭīkā
2194 Ekavīra-heruka-sādhana-nāma
2290 Vajrayoginī-sādhana
2316 Vajrapāda-sāra-saṃgraha-pañjikā
2415 Śrī-hevajra-sādhana
2474 Ratna-prabhā-nāma
2618 Dharmābhiṣeka-mārga-saṃhati
2647 Śrī-devīmahākālī-sādhanopāyikā
3136 Vajra-gīti
3137 Vajra-gīti
3225 Śatākṣara-bhaṭṭārakasya sattvatraya-bhāvanā
4623 Śrī-guhya-ratna-cintāmaṇi-nāma
4628 Śrī-cakraśambara-vikurvaṇa Caturviṃśati-deśa-pramāṇa-śāsana
4632 Karṇa-tantra-vajragāthā-nāma
4668 Śrī-vajrayoginī-guhya-sādhana-nāma
4673 Vajrayoginī-sādhana
4789 Śrī-guhyasamājopadeśa-pañcakrama-nāma
4790 Pañcakrama-saṃgraha-prabhāva

4929 Śrīmatī-devīmahākālī-guhya-sādhana-nāma

21. Shalipa has two works in the bsTan-'gyur:
3226 Ratnamālā-nāma
4969 Bhairava-mahākāla-sādhana

22. Tilopa has the following works in the bsTan-'gyur:
2193 Śrī-sahajaśambara-svādhiṣṭhāna-nāma
2371 Tattvacaturopadeśa-prasannadīpa-nāma
3128 Dohakoṣa
3132 Mahāmudropadeśa
3227 Karuṇā-bhāvanādhiṣṭhāna-nāma
4630 Ṣaḍdharmopadeśa-nāma
4635 Acintya-mahāmudrā-nāma
5014 Guru-sādhana
5015 Bāhya-siddhi-pratītyasamutpāda

23. Catrapa has one work in the bsTan-'gyur:
3208 Śūnyatā-karuṇā-dṛṣṭi-nāma

24. Bhadrapa has no works attributed to him in the bsTan-'gyur.

25. Dhukhandhi has two works in the bsTan-'gyur:
3228 Mahāyāna-sthiti-niścaya-nāma
4846 Catur-akṣarapadeśa

26. Ajokipa has one work in the bsTan-'gyur:
3229 Citta-saṃpradāya-vyavastāna-nāma

27. Kalapa may have one work in the bsTan-'gyur under the name Kalākapāda:
2218 Śri-vajraḍāka-nāma-mahātantrarājoddhṛta-sādhanopāyikā-bodhicittāvaloka-mālā-nāma

28. Dhombipa has two works in the bsTan-'gyur:
3231 Nāḍī-bindu-dvāre yogacaryā-nāma
3232 Akṣaradvikopadeśa-nāma

29. Kaṅkanapa is credited with one work in the bsTan-'gyur:
3175 Caryā-dohakoṣa-gītikā-nāma

30. Kambala has a number of works in the bsTan-'gyur:
2160 Bhagavacchrī-cakraśamvarasya-sādhana ratnacūḍāmaṇi-nāma
2377 Bhagavad-hevajra-sādhana-tattva-caturkrama-nāma
2161 Śrī-cakraśambara-maṇḍalopāyikā-ratna-pradīpodyota-nāma
3206 Asaṃbandha-dṛṣṭi-nāma
3207 Asaṃbandha-sarga-dṛṣṭi-nāma
3466 Ārya-prajñāpāramitopadeśa-nāma
4580 Maṇḍala-vidhi
5123 Ārya-prajñāpāramitopadeśa-nāma

31. Ṭeṅgipa has no works in the bsTan-'gyur, but it is said that he revised Lūyipa's Buddhodaya. Taranatha p. 178 note 14.

32. Bandhepa has one work in the bsTan-'gyur:
3176 Sahajānanda-dohakoṣa-gītikā-dṛṣṭi-nāma

33. Tandhepa has no works attributed to him in the bsTan-'gyur.

34. Kukkuripa has the following works in the bsTan-'gyur:
2499 Mahāmāyā-tantrānusāriṇī-heruka-sādhanopāyikā
2500 Vajrasattva-sādhana
2501 Moha-taraṇa-kalpa-nāma
2502 Mahāmāyā-sādhana-maṇḍala-vidhi
2503 Mahāmāyā-maṇḍala-devā-stotra
3233 Tattva-sukha-bhāvanānusāri-yoga-bhāvanopadeśa
3234 Sarvaparicchedana-upadeśa-nāma
4782 Śrī-mahāmāyā-bali-vidhi

35. Kucipa has no works in the bsTan-'gyur.

36. Dharmapa has one work in the bsTan-'gyur:
3177 Sugata-dṛṣṭi-gītikā-nāma

37. Mahipa has one work in the bsTan-'gyur:
3178 Vāyu-tattva-doha-gītikā-nāma

38. Acinta is credited with one work in the bsTan-'gyur:
3235. Tīrthika-caṇḍālikā-nāma

39. Babhahi is credited with one work in the bsTan-'gyur:
2119 Śrī-cakrasaṃvara-pañjikā-nāma

40. Nalina is credited with one work in the bsTan-'gyur:
3236 Dhātuvāda-nāma

41. Bhusuku (Śāntideva) is most famous as a writer on the Mahāyāna, but he has some Tantric works attributed to him as well:
2688 Śrī-guhyasamāja-mahāyogatantra-bali vidhi-nāma
3169 Sahaja-gīti
4662 Cakraśambara-ṭīkā
4663 Cakraśambara-sādhana-nāma

42. Indrabhūti has a number of works in the bsTan-'gyur:
2157 Śrī-cakrasaṃvara-stotra
2172 Śrī-cakraśambarānubandha-saṃgraha
2257 Śukla-vajrayoginī-sādhana
2253 Siddhi-vajrayoginī-sādhana
2254 Śrī-vajrayoginī-mantratattva-svādhiṣṭhāna-nirdeśa-nāma
2324 Ḍākinī-vajrapañjara-mahātantrarājasya pañjikā-prathama-paṭala-mukha-mukhabandha-nāma
2327 Śrī-saṃpuṭa-tilaka-nāma-yoginī-tantrarājasya ṭīkā smṛti-saṃdarśanāloka-nāma
2468 Śrī-ānanda-puṣpamālā
2469 Śrī-tattvāmṛtopadeśa
2533 Śrī-sarvabuddha-samayoga-nāma-tantra-pañjikā
2544 Sarvabuddha-samayoga-gaṇa-vidhi-nāma
2552 Vajrasattvopāyikā
3063 Jñāna-siddhi-nāma-sādhanopāyikā
3210 Tattvāṣṭaka-dṛṣṭi-nāma
3300 Ratna-cakrābhiṣekhopadeśa-krama
4035 Kurukullā-sādhana
4394 Aṣṭabhuja-kurukullā-sādhana

4563 Śrī-ajñā-vinivarta-gaṇapati-sādhana-nāma
4626 Vajrayāna-mūlāṅgāpatti-deśanā
4771 Śrī-guhyagarbha-krama-dvayoddeśa
4830 Aparājitā-meruvarā-bhadraṃkara-ratna-sādhana
4997 Aparājitā-ratna-bhadra-sādhana-nāma
5028 Citta-ratna-viśodhana

43. Mekopa has one work in the bsTan-'gyur:
3237 Citta-caitanya-śamanopāya-nāma

44. Koṭalipa has one work in the bsTan-'gyur:
3258 Sahajānanta-svabhāva-nāma

45. Kaṃparipa has one work in the bsTan-'gyur:
3239 Soma-sūrya-bandhanopāya-nāma

46. Jālandhari has several works in the bsTan-'gyur:
2173 Śrī-cakrasaṃvara-garbha-tattva-siddhi
2278 Vajrayoginī-sādhana-nāma
2366 Hevajra-sādhanasya ṭippaṇī-śuddhi-vajrapradīpa-nāma
3240 Hūṃkāra-citta-bindu-bhāvanā-krama-nāma
4627 Bhagavac-chambatra-stotra
4838 Śrī-mahākāruṇikābhiṣeka-prakaraṇopadeśa-nāma

47. Rāhula has several works in the bsTan-'gyur:
3241 Acintya-paribhāvanā-nāma
4636 Dharma-caryāparādha-svayaṃmukti-nāma
4930 Vajra-khecarī-sādhana
4939 Nātha-samaya-stotra

48. Dharmapa has one work in the bsTan-'gyur:
3242 Hūṃkāra-citta-bindu-bhāvanā-krama-nāma

49. Dhokaripa has one work in the bsTan-'gyur under the name Ṭukkarī:
3243 Prakṛti-siddhi-nāma

50. Medini has one work in the bsTan-'gyur:
3244 Sahajāmnāya-nāma

51. Paṅkaja has two works in the bsTan-'gyur:
3230 Sthāna-mārga-phala-mahāmudrā-bhāvanā-nāma
Under the name Baṅgaja there is:
3245 Anuttara-sarva śuddhi-krama-nāma

52. Ghaṇḍhapa has a number of works in the bsTan-'gyur:
2148 Śrī-cakrasaṃvara-seka-prakriyopadeśa-nāma
2149 Śrī-cakrasaṃvara-sādhana
2150 Śrī-cakrasaṃvara-pañcakrama
2151 Upadeśa-kāyamaṇḍalābhisamaya
2152 Śrī-cakrasaṃvara-pañcakrama-vṛtti
2153 Sahaja-śambara-sādhana
2154 Śrī-bhagavac-cakraśambara-sādhana-ratnacintāmaṇi-nāma
2155 Śrī-dvibhuja-sahaja-śambara-sādhana
2156 Gaṇacakra-vidhi
2158 Maṇḍala-deva-stotra-ratna-māyādāna-nāma
2279 Vajravārāhī-sādhana
2355 Śry-ekavīra-nāma-sādhana
2958 Ārya-mañjuśrī-gambhīra-vyākhyā
3246 Ālikāli-mantra-jñāna-nāma
4624 Śrī-cakraśambara-pañcakrama
4654 Śrī-cakrasaṃvaropadeśa
4956 Abhiṣeka-vidhi-ratnamālā-saṃnibha-nāma

53. Yogipa has one work in the bsTan-'gyur:
2345 Aṣṭa-śmaśāna-nāma

54. Caluki has two works in the bsTan-'gyur:
2090 Ṣaḍaṅga-yogopadeśa
2709 Ratnavṛkṣa-nāma-rahasya-samāja-vṛtti

55. Gorura has no work in the bsTan-'gyur.

56. Lucika has one work in the bsTan-'gyur:
3251 Caṇḍālikā-bindu-prasphāraṇa-nāma

57. Niguṇa has one work in the bsTan-'gyur:
3252 Śarīra-nāḍikā-bindu-samatāmnāya-nāma

58. Jayānanda has no works in the Tantric section of the bsTan-'gyur; there are, however, two works in the Sūtra section by a Jayānanda.

59. Pacari has no work in the bsTan-'gyur.

60. Campaka has one work in the bsTan-'gyur:
3254 Ātma-parijñāna-dṛṣṭy-upadeśa-nāma

61. Bhikṣana has one work in the bsTan-'gyur:
3255 Aṣṭabhaya-mūḍha-karaṇopāya-nāma

62. Tailopa has one work in the bsTan-'gyur:
3256 Viṣāntarabāhya-nivṛtti-bhāvanā-krama-nāma

63. Kumaripa has one work in the bsTan-'gyur:
2656 Pradīpadīpa-ṭīppaṇī-hṛdayādarśa-nāma

64. Caparipa has three works in the bsTan-'gyur:
3253 Caturbhūta-bhavābhivāsana-krama-nāma
3546 Āryāvalokiteśvarasya carpaṭiracita-stotra
5098 Sarva-siddhi-kara-nāma

65. Maṇibhadrā has two works in the bsTan-'gyur:
2132 Śrī-vajraḍāka-tantrasya tattvasusthira-nāma-pañjikā
2135 Vajraḍāki-vivṛtti-nibandha-nāma

66. Mekhalā has one work in the bsTan-'gyur written with her sister:
3257 Nandyāvarta-traya-mukhāgama-nāma

67. Kanakhalā has one work in the bsTan-'gyur, written with her sister:
3257 Nandyāvarta-traya-mukhāgama-nāma

68. Kalakala has no works in the bsTan-'gyur.

69. Kantali has one work in the bsTan-'gyur:
3258 Sahajānanta-svabhāva-nāma

70. Dhahuli has one work in the bsTan-'gyur:
3212 Śoka-vinoda-dṛṣṭi-nāma

71. Udheli has no work in the bsTan-'gyur.

72. Kapalapa has no work in the bsTan-'gyur.

73. Kirava has one work in the bsTan-'gyur.
3203 Doha-caryā-gītikā-dṛṣṭi-nāma

74. Sakara has a number of works in the bsTan-'gyur:
2311 Hevajra-tantra-pañjikā-padminī-nāma
2337 Gīti-tattva-nāma
2349 Śrī-hevajra-pradīpa-śūlopamāvavādaka-nāma
2350 Hevajra-maṇḍala-vidhi
2352 Homa-vidhi
2354 Śrī-hevajra-bhaṭṭāraka-stotra-nāma
2419 Hevajra-maṇḍala-karma-krama-vidhi

75. Sarvabhakṣa has one work in the bsTan-'gyur:
3214 Karuṇā-caryā-kapāla-dṛṣṭi-nāma

76. Nāgabodhi has a number of works in the bsTan-'gyur:
2675 Śrī-guhyasamāja-maṇḍalopāyikā-viṃśati vidhi-nāma
2676 Karmānta-vibhaṅga-nāma
2677 Karamāntarbhāvopadeśa-nāma-prakaraṇa
2697 Pañcakrama-ṭīkā-maṇimālā-nāma
2702 Pañcakramārtha-bhāskaraṇa-nāma
2827 Kṛṣṇayamāri-cakropadeśa
2871 Yamāri-siddha-cakra-sādhana
3044 Ārya-nīlāmbaradhara-vajrapāṇi-nāma-tantra-ṭīkā
3052 Balyālaṃkāra
3054 Ārya-nīlāmbaradhara-vajrapāṇi-sādhanapāyikā
3055 Ārya-nīlāmbaradhara-vajrapāṇi-sādhanopāyikā-ṭīkā
3259 Atiyoga-bhāvanā-nāma
4606 Sarvatathāgata-stava-nāma

77. Dārika has a number of works in the bsTan-'gyur:
2072 Śrī-kālacakra-tantrarājasya sekaprakriyā-vṛtti-vajra-padodghaṭi-nāma
2145 Śrī-cakrasaṃvara-sādhana-tattvasaṃgraha-nāma
2146 Śrī-cakrasaṃvara-maṇḍala-vidhi-tattvāvatāra-nāma

2147 Śrī-cakrasaṃvara-stotra-sarvārtha-siddhi-viśuddha-cūḍāmaṇi-nāma
2273 Yogānusāriṇī-nāma-vajrayoginī-ṭīkā
2275 Vajrayoginī-pūjā-vidhi
2276 Kaṃkāla-tāraṇa-sādhana
3065 Śrī-Uḍḍiyāna-vinirgata-guhya-mahāguhya-tattvopadeśa
3105 Saptama-siddhānta-nāma
3216 Tathatā-dṛṣṭi-nāma
3465 Prajñāpāramitā-hṛdaya-sādhana-nāma

78. Putali has one work in the bsTan-'gyur:
3260 Bodhicitta-vāyu-caraṇa-bhāvanopāya

79. Panaha has one work in the bsTan-'gyur:
3261 Caryā-dṛṣṭy-anutpanna-tattva-bhāvanā-nāma

80. Kokalipa has one work in the bsTan-'gyur:
3262 Āyuḥ-siddhi-parirakṣā-nāma

81. Anaṅga has one work in the bsTan-'gyur:
3263 Viṣa-nirvahaṇa-bhāvanā-krama-nāma

82. Lakṣmīnkarā has a number of works in the bsTan-'gyur:
2060 Sadguru-dharmarāja-stotra-nāma
2255 Vajrayoginī-sādhana
3064 Advaya-siddhi-sādhana-nāma
3311 Vajrayāna-caturdaśa-mūlāpatti-vṛtti
3549 Lokeśvara-stotra
3557 Bhaṭṭārakāryaikādaśamukhāvalokiteśvara-sādhana
3560 Āryāvalokiteśvarasya stotra
3561 Āryāvalokiteśvara-stotra
3211 Citta-kalpa-parihāra-dṛṣṭi-nāma

83. Samudra has one work in the bsTan-'gyur:
3265 Sūkṣma-yoga-nāma

84. Vyali has the following works in the bsTan-'gyur:
3266 Bāhyāntarāmṛta-kalpa-nāma

4700 Ekapradīpopadeśa
4702 Upadeśa
4783 Ekasmṛti
4784 Mahāmāyopadeśa

## Tibetan Works

*grub mchog spyi la brten pa'i bla ma'i rnal 'byor rgya gar lugs dngos grub thig le 'khyil ba*

*grub thob brgyad bcu rtsa bzhi'i rdzogs rim rin chen phreng ba rtsa 'grel*

*grub thob chen po brgyad bcu rtsa bzhi'i 'bri yig shin tu dag cing gsal ba legs bshad gser thur*

*grub thob gsol 'debs*

*thugs gsang ba'i doha*

*rnal 'byor bgrub pa thob pa bzhi bcus rdo rje'i mgur nyams kyi man ngag thig le gsel gyi phreng ba*

*phags yul gyi grub chen brgyad bcu rtsa bzhi la mchod cing gsol ba gdeb pa'i cho ga dngos grub kun 'byung*

*bla ma rdo rje 'chang grub thob brgyad bcu rtsa bzhi'i byin rlabs lhan cig tu bya ba'i tshul dngos grub chu rgyun*

## Modern Works

Basham, A. L. *The Wonder That Was India.* Evergreen Encyclopaedia, vol. 1. 11th printing. New York: Grove Press Inc., 1959.

Beyer, Stephan. *The Buddhist Experience: Sources and Interpretations.* Encino, California: Dickenson Co., 1973.

Bharati, Agehananda. *The Tantric Tradition.* New York: Doubleday & Co., Anchor Books, 1970.

Bhattacharya, Benetosh. *An Introduction to Buddhist Esoterism.* London: Oxford University Press, 1932.

Clark, Walter Eugene. *Two Lamaistic Pantheons.* New York: Paragon Book Reprints, 1965. Originally Harvard University Press, 1937.

Conze, Edward. *Buddhist Meditation.* New York: Harper Torchbook, 1969.

———, ed. *Buddhist Texts Through the Ages.* New York: Harper Torchbook, 1964.

———. *Buddhist Thought in India.* Ann Arbor: University of Michigan Press, 1962.

David-Neel, Alexandra. *Initiations and Initiates in Tibet.* 2nd ed. Translated by Fred Rothwell. New York, Rider & Co., 1958.

———. *Magic and Mystery in Tibet.* Baltimore: Penguin Books, 1973.

Dasgupta, S. B. *Obscure Religious Cults as Background of Bengali Literature.* Calcutta: Calcutta University Press, 1950.

Delahaye, Hippolyte. *The Legends of the Saints.* Translated by Donald Attwater. New York: Fordham University Press, 1962.

Eliade, Mircea. *Shamanism: Archaic Techniques of Ecstasy.* Translated by Willard Trask. Bollingen Series vol. 76. Princeton: Princeton University Press, 1964.

———. *Yoga, Immortality & Freedom.* Translated by Willard Trask. Bollingen Series vol. 56. New York: Pantheon Books, 1958.

Evans-Wentz, W. Y. *The Tibetan Book of the Great Liberation.* Oxford, London, and New York: Oxford University Press, 1968.

———. *Tibetan Yoga and Secret Doctrines*. Oxford, London, and New York: Oxford University Press, 1967.

———. *Tibet's Great Yogi, Milarepa*. Oxford, London, and New York: Oxford University Press, 1969.

Gordon, Antoinette. *The Iconography of Tibetan Lamaism*. 2nd. ed. Rutland, Vermont: Chas Tuttle Co., 1959.

Govinda, Anagarika. *The Foundations of Tibetan Mysticism*. New York: E. P. Dutton, 1959.

———. "Siddhas and Zen Buddhism." *Wind Bell* 9 (1970): 42-46.

Grünwedel, Albert. *Die Geschichten der vier und achtzig Zauberers aus dem Tibetishchen ubersetz*. Leipzig: Baessler Archiv V., 1916. A German translation of *The Eighty-four Siddhas*.

Guenther, Herbert V. *The Life and Teachings of Naropa*. Oxford, London, and New York: Oxford University Press, 1963.

———. *The Royal Song of Saraha*. Seattle and New York: University of Washington Press, 1969.

———. *Tibetan Buddhism without Mystification*. Leiden: E. J. Brill, 1966.

Hoffman, Helmuth. *The Religions of Tibet*. Translated by Edward Fitzgerald. New York: Macmillan Co., 1961.

Jan Yün-hua. "Nāgārjuna, One or More? A New Interpretation of Buddhist Hagiography." *History of Religions* 10 (1970): 139-154.

Joshi, Lalmani. *Studies in the Buddhistic Culture of India During the 7th & 8th Centuries*. Delhi: Motilal Banarsidass, 1967.

Pal, Pratapaditya, and Tseng Hsien-chi. *Lamaist Art, the Aesthetics of Harmony*. Boston: Museum of Fine Art.

Ray, Acharya, P. C. *History of Chemistry in Ancient and Medieval India*. Calcutta: Indian Chemical Society, 1956.

Robinson, Richard. *The Buddhist Religion.* Encino, Calif: Dickinson Co., 1970.

Sankrtyayana, Rahula. "Recherches Bouddhique: L'Origin du Vajrayana et les 84 Siddhas." *Journal Asiatique*, Paris, 1934, pp. 209-230.

Schmid, Toni. *The Eighty-five Siddhas.* Sino-Swedish Expedition Publication, *Stateus Ethnografiska*, no. 42, 1958.

Sopa, Geshe, and Jones, Elvin. *A Light to the Svātantrika Mādhyamika.* Unpublished manuscript.

Taranatha. *A History of Buddhism in India.* Translated from the Tibetan by Lama Chimpa and Aloka Chattopadhyaya. Edited by Debipradad Chattopadhyaya. Simla: Indian Institute of Advanced Study, 1970.

Tucci, Giuseppi. "Animadversiones Indicae." *Journal of the Asiatic Society of Bengal* 26 (1930): 125-260.

———. *Tibetan Painted Scrolls.* Rome: La Libreria Dello Stato, 1949.

Waddell, Laurence Austin. *The Buddhism of Tibet or Lamaism.* 2nd ed. London: W. Hefer & Sons, Ltd., 1934.

Walleser, M. *The Life of Nāgārjuna from Tibetan and Chinese Sources.* Reprinted from *Asia Minor*, introductory volume. London: Probstain & Co.

Wayman, Alex. *The Buddhist Tantras.* New York: Samuel Weiser, 1973.

Zimmer, Heinrich. *The Philosophies of India.* Edited by Joseph Campbell. Bollingen 26. Princeton: Princeton University Press, 1969.

# Tibetan Text

The text used for this translation was taken from the Peking edition of the bsTan-'gyur. The Peking edition is not, however, the most readable, so the decision was made to publish the following edition instead of the Peking. This text is reprinted from *Grub thob brgyad bcu rtsa bzhi'i chos skor*, New Delhi: Chophel Legdan, 1973. Although a detailed comparison has not been made between this text and the Peking edition, the two editions seem identical except for the title and prologue.

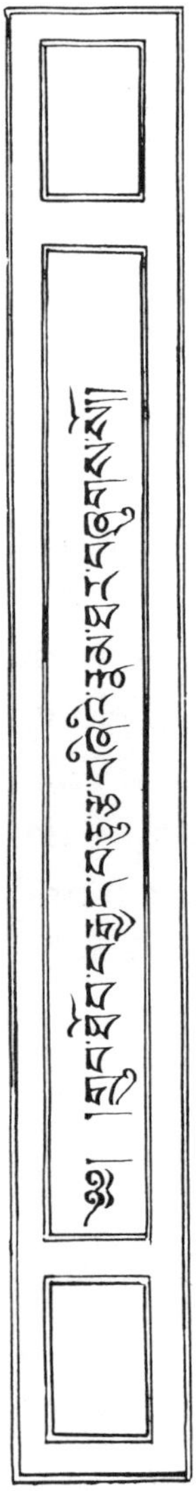

1

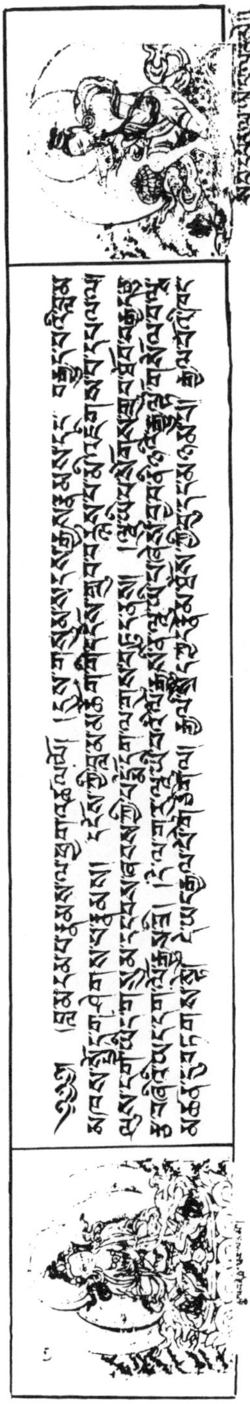

2

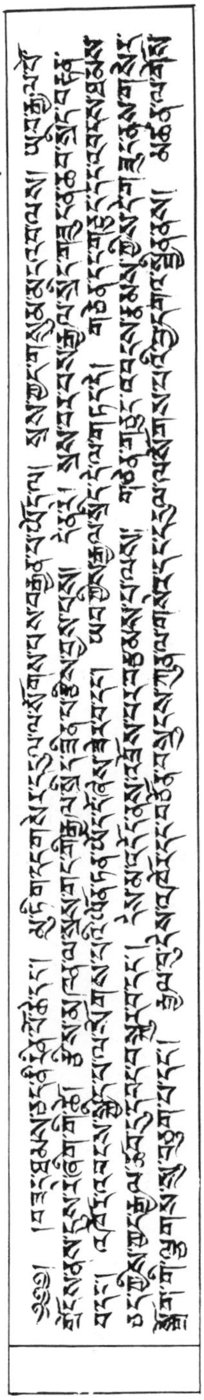

3

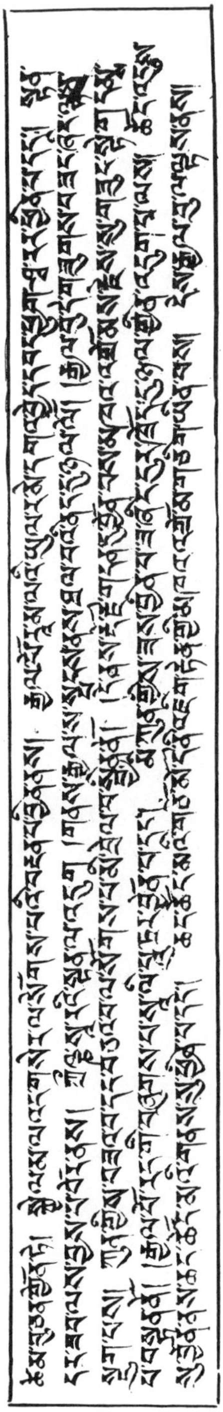

4

5 དེ་ནས་བྲུད་མེ་དང་རི་མ་རྫ་མ་འཕྱིན་དང་ཟས་ཕུལ་བ་བླུགས་ནས་ཞེན་པ་དང་། རྒྱལ་བུས་རེས་བསྐུར་བས་མ་ཁའ་འགྲོ་མ་དེ་འཁྲིས་ནས། ཕྱིར་ཀྱིས་ཟས་བཟང་དང་ནི་ཕྱི་རྣམ་
པར་རྟོག་པ་མ་ཕྱུང་ནས། ཆོས་ག་ལ་འཚོང་ཞེས་སྨྲས་པ་ས། །རྒྱལ་བུ་རེས་རྣམ་རྟོག་དང་མཚན་མ་ཐེ་ཚོམ་རྒྱུ་བ་ཀྱི་གེ་གས་སུ་འདུག་སྨྲ་མ་ནས། རྣམ་རྟོག་དང་མཚན་
མ་སྤྱངས་ཏེ། ཞ་བས་གཙྭན་ས་ཞ་བསྲང་བའི་རྒྱུམ་ས་ལ་སྐྱུར་བ་རྣམ་ས་བླངས་ནས། དེ་ཟ་ཞིང་ལོ་བཅུ་གཉིས་ཀྱི་བར་དུ་བསྒྲུབས་ཏེ། ཞའི་རྒྱུམ་ཟ་བ་ཞ་ཚོང་མ་འི
ཐུང་མེད་ཀུན་གྱིས་མཐོང་ནས། ཐམས་ཅད་ཀྱིས་ལཱུ་ཡི་པ་ཞེས་སྨྲས་པ་དང་། ཧཱུྃ་ཕྱག་ལ་ས་མ་ཆམ་ས་ཐམས་ཅད་དུ་ལཱུ་ཡི་པ་ཞེས་གྲགས་ཏེ་དེ་འི་མིང་དང་དོན་
གྲུབ་ཐོབ་བོ། །འདི་ཡི་འཛིན་དྷཱ་རི་ཀ་པ་དང་། ཌེཾ་ཀི་པའི་སྐབས་སུ་ཡང་འབྱུང་ངོ་། །གྲུབ་ཆེན་ལཱུ་ཡི་པའི་རྣམ་པར་ཐར་པ་རྫོགས་སོ།། ||

6 ༄༅། །གུ་རུ་ལཱི་ལ་པའི་ལོ་རྒྱུས་ནི། རྒྱ་གར་ལྷོ
ཡུལ་གཞན་ཞིག་ནས་རྣལ་འབྱོར་པ་ཞིག་དེའི་ཐད་དུ་བྱོན་པ་དང་།
རེ་མོངས་གསུངས་པས། བདག་མི་སྡུག་སྐྱེ་ཡུ་རང་ཉིན་མོངས།
མ་འགྲུབ་འདི་གསལ་བས་ཉིད་རང་སྡུག་བསྔལ་ལོ། །བདག་ནི
ཆས་པ་དང་འཆི་བའི་སྡུག་བསྔལ་མ་དད་བྱུང་ལྡན་གྱི་ཁང

གུ་རུ་ལཱི་ལ་པ་ལ་ན་མོ།

གྲོགས་ཀྱི་རྒྱལ་པོ་གཅིག་སེང་གེའི་ཁྲི་ལ་བཞུགས་པའི་ཚོ།
རྒྱལ་པོ་ནི། ཕྱིར་རྒྱལ་ཁམས་ཐམས་ཅད་དུ་འཁྱམས་པ་ཉིན
རེ་ཅིས་ཏེ་ན། ཉིད་རྒྱལ་སྲིད་ཤེར་གྱིས་དོགས། འབངས་རྣམ
མི་འི་ནད་དང་ན་ཚ་དང་རྒས་ཀྱང་མི་སྐྱེ་ག །སྡུག་བསྔལ་ཀྱང་མི་འཆི།
དག་ཡོད་གསུངས་པས། རྒྱལ་པོ་དད་ནས། དངོས་ཀྱི་ཉིད

7 ༄༅། །བཞིན་དུ་རྒྱལ་ཁམས་འཁྲིམ་པ་ན་མི་ཉུས། ཙོན་ཀྱང་རང་གི་རྒྱལ་ས་ར་ལྷུན་ལ་འདུག་ནས་བསྒོམ་པར་ནུས་ན། དངོས་ལ་ཉིད་ཀྱི་གདམ
ངག་ཅིག་ཞུ་བྱས་ནས་ཕྱག་བྱས་པས། གནང་སྟེ། ཀྱཻ་རྡོ་རྗེའི་དབང་བསྐུར། གདམས་ངག་སྨིན་ནས་རྫས་པ་ཅིག་པའི་ཏིང་ངེ་འཛིན་བསྒོམ་དུ་བཅུག་གོ །དེ་ནས་རྒྱལ
པོ་རང་ཉིད་ཀྱིས་སེང་གེའི་ཁྲི་ལ་ཟ་འོག་ལ་སོགས་པའི་སྟན་དང་ཆང་ས་ཅན་དང་། རྣམ་ལ་སོགས་པའི་སྟེང་དུ། བཙུན་མོ་དང་བློན་པོའི་ཚོགས་དང་། རོལ་མོའ
ཀྱི་ཕྱག་སྣ་ཚོགས་པས་བསྐོར་ནས་བསྒོམ་ས་པས་མཚན་ཡང་ལོངས་སྤྱོད་པ་འམ། སྣག་པ་ལ་སོགས་པས་ལཱི་ལ་པ་ཞེས་གྲགས་སོ། །གདམས་ངག་དོན
ནི་ཕྱག་གཡས་པའི་སོར་གདུབ་ལ་མ་ཡེངས་པར་བསྒོམ་པའོ། །དེ་མི་འགྱུར་བར་འདུག་བྱས་པས། དེའི་སྣང་དུ་ཤེས་པ་རྡོ་རྗེའི་ལྷ་ཚོགས་བསྒོམ་ནི

8 གདམས་ངག་བྱིན་པ་དང་། དེ་ལ་ངར་མི་འགྱུར་བར་འདུག་ཟེར་ནས། བསྐྱེད་རྫོགས་ཟུང་འཇུག་ཏུ་བསྒོམས་པས་རྟོགས་པ་རང་ཤུགས་སུ་ཤར་ནས་ཕྱག་རྒྱ་ཆེན་པོའི
དངོས་གྲུབ་ཐོབ་བོ། མངོན་པར་ཤེས་པ་ལ་སོགས་པའི་ཡོན་ཏན་དུ་མ་དང་ལྡན་ནོ། །དེ་ནས་བླ་མའི་གདམས་ངག་གི་ངང་གི་བརྟེན་པ། སློབ་མ་འི་ལས་ལ་འགྲོ
བའི་གསུམ་འཛོམ་ས་ན་འདོད་ཡོན་མ་སྤངས་ཀྱང་གྲོལ་ལོ། །དེས་ཀྱང་ར་རྒྱ་དེན་དཔལ་ཀ་ཙ་མི་དང་བ་མཛད་ལ། མི་ང་དུ་ཡང་ལཱི་པ་ཞེས་གྲགས་མཚམས
ཐམས་ཅད་དུ་གྲགས་ཤིང་མཐར་མཁའ་སྤྱོད་དུ་གཤེགས་སོ། ། །གུ་རུ་ལཱི་ལ་པའི་ལོ་རྒྱུས་རྫོགས་སོ།།

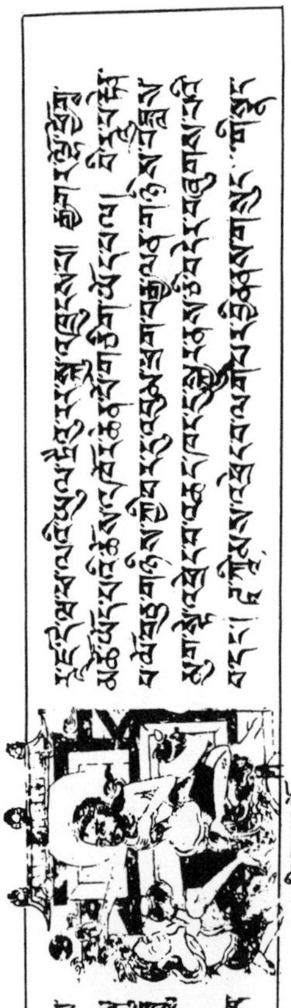

9

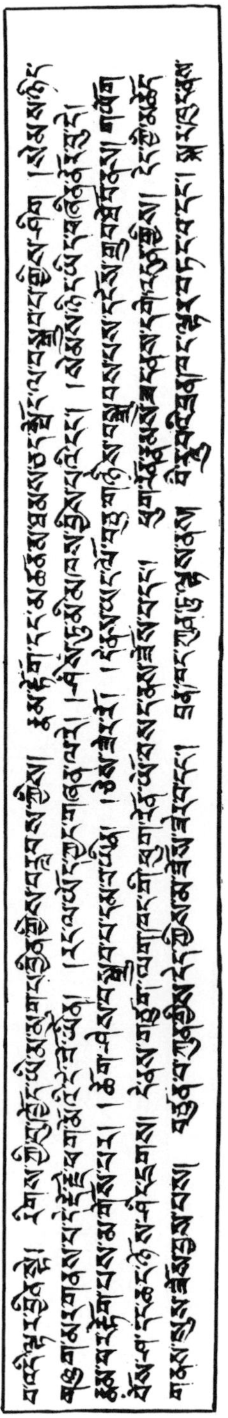

10

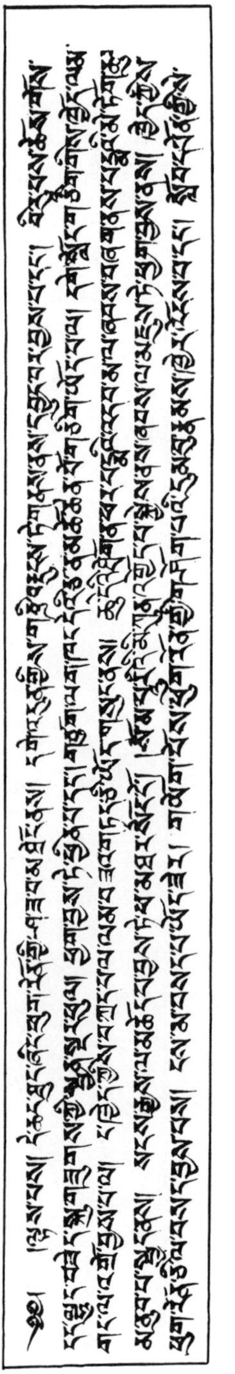

11

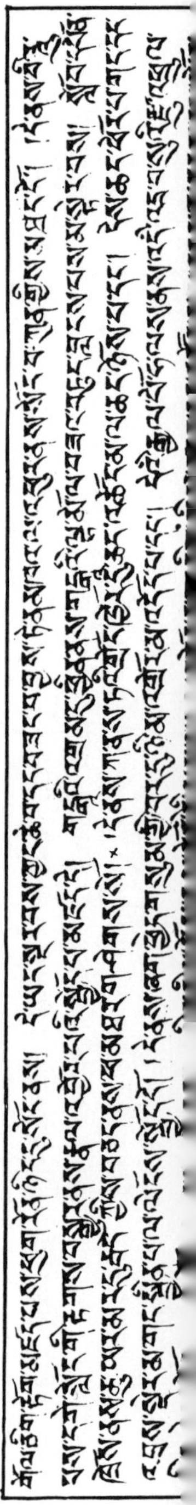

12

13 དེ་ནས་ཨོ་རྒྱན་ཞེས་བྱ་བའི་མུ་སྟེགས་ཀྱི་ཡུལ་དུ་ཕྱིན་པ་དང་། དེའི་ཡུལ་ན་དབང་ཕྱུག་ཆེན་པོའི་སྐུ་བྲུ་བརྒྱད་ཅུ་རྩ་གཅིག་པ་ཅིག་འདུག་པ་ལ་ཕྱག་གིས་ཟེར་བ་ལ། ངོ་བོ
ཡིན་པ་ཕྱི་པོ་ལ་ཕྱག་འཚལ་བའི་ལུགས་མེད་ཟེར་བས། དེ་ན་ཁྱེད་བསོད་དཔ་ཡིན་ཞེས་དེའི་རྒྱལ་པོ་ལ་སོགས་ཀུན་ཟེར་བ་དང་། སློབ་དཔོན་ན་རེ། ངས་འདི་ལ་ཕྱག
བྱས་ན་སྒྲིག་པ་འདོད་པས་ཕྱག་མི་བྱེད་པ་ཡིན་ཞེས་སྨྲས་པ་དང་། རྒྱལ་པོས་དེའི་སྒྲིག་པ་ང་ལ་ཤོག་གཅིག་ཟེར་ནས། སློབ་དཔོན་གྱིས་ཕྱག་ཐལ་མོ་སྦྱར་བ་ལས་མ་ཕྱུ་དེ་བའི
སྐུ་བྲེད་ཆ་ལ་དུ་གས་པ་དང་། བར་སྣང་ནས་སྐུ་གཅིག་ཕྲུར་ནས། དབང་རྣམ་བཅས་པ་བཞིན་དུ་ཞ་ནན་ཟེར། ཕྱོན་མཁར་བོར་བྲོས་པས། མཐའ་འཁོར་བས་ལྷག་ས

14 པ་ཡང་སྒྲ་ར་འབྱུར་རོ། །དེ་ནས་མ་དྷུ་རི་བའི་རྟེན་གྱི་མཆོད་པའི་ཡོ་བྱད་རྣམས་ལ་སློབ་དཔོན་འཕྱུ་ལ་ནས། དེ་ནང་བ་སངས་རྒྱས་པ་གཞན་གྱི་འཚོ་བ་བྲུས་ནས་དུ་དུར་ཡོད
ཟེར་རོ། །དེ་ནས་སློབ་དཔོན་གྱི་རྒྱ་གར་ཤར་ཕྱོགས་ན་ཊི་ཀོ་ཊི་ར་བྱིན་པས་ཡུལ་དེའི་མི་ཐམས་ཅད་ཕྲ་མེན་མ་རངས་ངོ་ནས། ཕྲ་མེན་གཅིག་ཀ་ལམ་ཁ་ར་སྤྱད་ནས་བྲ་སེན་གྱི
སྟ་གས་ཀྱི་སྟ་བས་ཀྱིན་སྟོང་བ་ཚོས་ལུགས་ཡིན་པ་ལ། སློབ་དཔོན་གྱིས་སྟོན་ལ་བྱིན་རླབས་གཙུག་ལག་ཁང་ཞིག་དུ་ཞ་ལ་བར་བྲ་སེ་ནས་འདུག་པ་དང་། ཐམ
ཟེའི་སྦྲུ་གུ་ཞིག་ཕྱི་ནས་འོང་བ་ལ་སྤྱགས་པ་ད་བཟུས་པ་ད་ངས་པས། གྲོང་དེར་ཟས་ནི་རྣ་ད་ལ་ཞལ་ལ་ནི་མི་རྣ་ངང་པ་དང་། དེ་རྣམས་པ་སང་ལ་རྒྱལ་པ་གཅིག་དང་ཕྲ་ང་ནས།
དེས་ཐམ་ཟེའི་སྦྲུ་གུ་ལ་སྣས་པ། ཡུལ་འདི་ན་ཐམས་ཅད་ཕྲ་མེན་མ་རངས་ངང་ནལ་མི་མི་ང་ཅིང་། དེར་ཀུན་གྱི་བར་ཆ་དབྱེང་བ་ཡིན་པས། གཙུག་ལག་ཁང་ཞ

15 ༄༅། །གཞི་སྐོར་ལ་འདུག་ཟེར་ནས་དེར་ཕྱིན་པ་དང་། སློབ་དཔོན་ཡི་དུ་པས་ཐམ་ཟེ་དེ་ལ་སྦྱུགས་རང་ཕྱིན་བཏབ་པས་བྲུས་དེ་ཐོར་བ་དང་། ཕྲ་མེན་མ
ཀུན་འཚོགས་ནས་མཆོད་པའི་ཡོ་བྲད་ཅི་ཡོད་ཟེར་བ་ལ། ཤ་སྣ་རི་ཚོགས་གཞན་ཀྱིན་ཡོད་དེ་ཤ་ཆེན་མ་རྟེད་ཟེར་བ་ལ། དེ་རིན་ང་ནས་གཅིག་ན་རེ། ངས་ཤ་ཆེན
གཉིས་ཁྱུག་ཕྱིན་ཡོད་ཟེར། ཁྱེར་ལ་ཤོག་ཟེར་བས་ལེན་པར་རྩམ་ས་པས། ཐམ་ཟེའི་སྦྲུ་གུ་ཡི་བྱིན་རླབས་མཛོད་པ་དེས་ལ་ཐོར་མ་ཐུབ། ལེན་པར
ཡང་ཡང་བཏང་བས་ཡི་རྒྱ་ཤིང་འགལ་གཅིག་གི་སྤྱི་ཕྲ་ཡོད་པ་ཤིང་དང་བཅས་པ་ཁྱེར་ནས་འོངས་པ་ལ། ཕྲ་མེན་མ་ཀུན་གྱིས་ཕྱག་ཚང་བྱེད་དུ་བྱུང་བས་ང་།
ཡི་རྒྱ་ལ་ཐོ་བ་འི་ཆང་ཀུན་འཐུངས། ཕྲ་མེན་ཀུན་གྱིས་ཡི་རྒྱ་བ་བས་དཔའ་བྲ་སྒྲ་ཐམས་ཅད་ཀྱི་གར་རྒྱ་ངས་ཀྱི་སྐྱ་སྒྲགས་པ་དང་། སློབ་དཔོན་གྱིས་བྲི

16 བོའི་སྐད་དམ་བརྒྱུ་གཉིས་ཆད་པས། ཕྲ་མེན་ཐམས་ཅད་བརྒྱལ་བར་བྱས། ཕྱིས་ཕྲ་མེན་ཐམས་ཅད་དམ་ལ་བཏགས་ནས་ཕྱི་ནང་ཆ་སྐྱབས་འགྲོ་བྱེད་པ
དང་། དལ་དང་བ་འི་སེམས་ཅན་ལ་གནོད་ཆོམ་བྱེད་པར་འདུག་ཅིག །སྐྱབས་འགྲོ་དང་སེམས་བསྐྱེད་མི་བྱེད་པའི་ལུས་ལ་མི་གནོད་པ་ཞིག་བྲག་ཕྱིར་བ
རེ་ཐམ་འབྱུང་ཅིག །རྒྱལ་དམ་ལས་འདས་ན་འཁོར་ལོ་འདོད་ས་རྗེ་ཆོད་ཅིང་། བྱང་གི་གནོད་སྦྱིན་འདེས་བྲག་འཐུངས་ཞིག་གསུངས་པས། དགྲ་ཡར
གནོད་སྦྱིན་དང་འཁོར་ལོའི་གཟུགས་ནམ་མཁའ་ལ་ཡོད་དོ། །བསྒྲུངས་མའི་འཁོར་དུ་བྱས་ནས་དམ་ལ་བཏགས་དེ་སློབ་དཔོན་གཞན་དུ་གཤེགས་སོ།།
སླར་ཡང་གྱི་རལ་ཡོ་གནས་དེ་ཀོ་ཊི་ར་བྱིན་པ་དང་། ལམ་མཁར་མ་དུན་ཕྱ་དང་། ལྷ་མོ་ཨུ་མ་གཉིས་ཀྱིས་སྤྲུལ་པའི་གྲོང་ཁྱེར་འཇུམ་མཆོ་བྱེད་དང

17

18

19

20

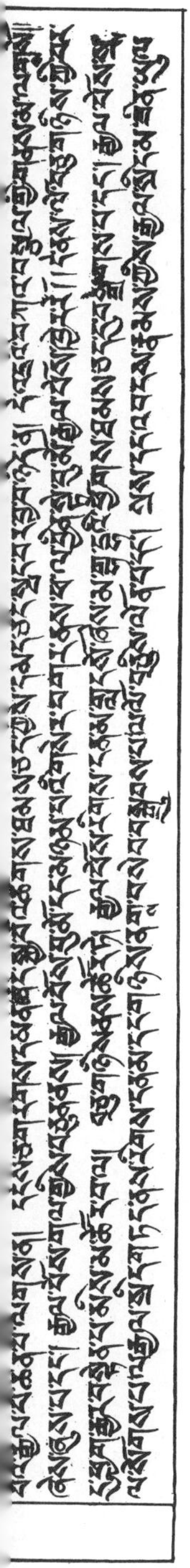

21

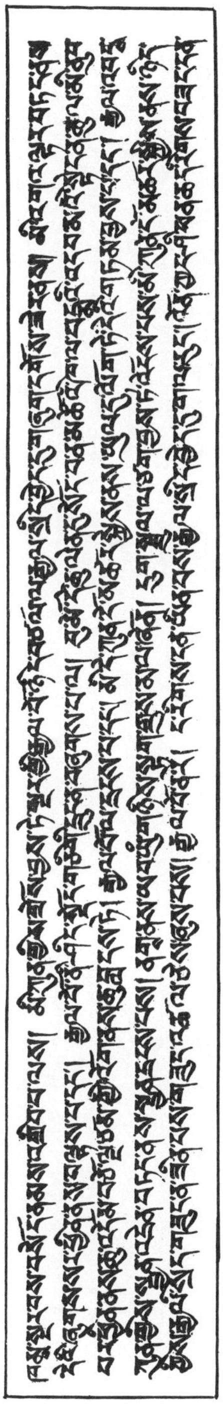

22

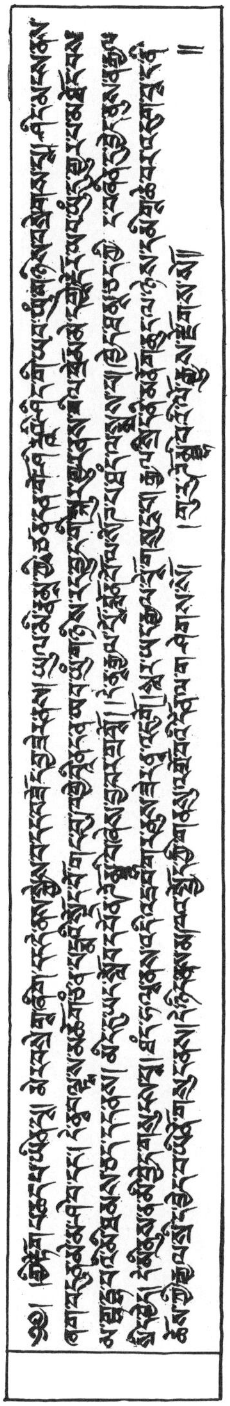

23

24

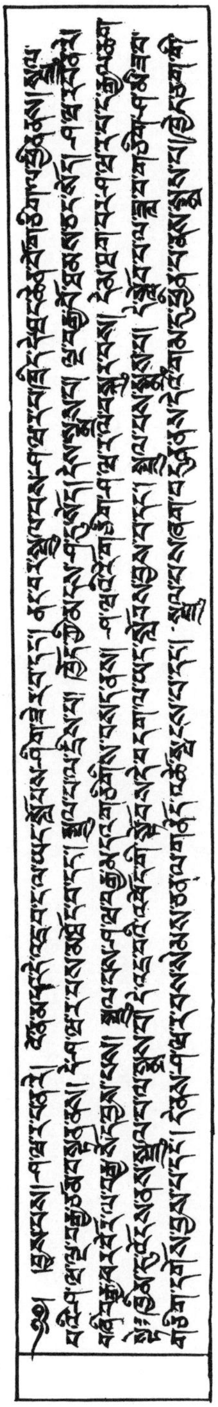

25

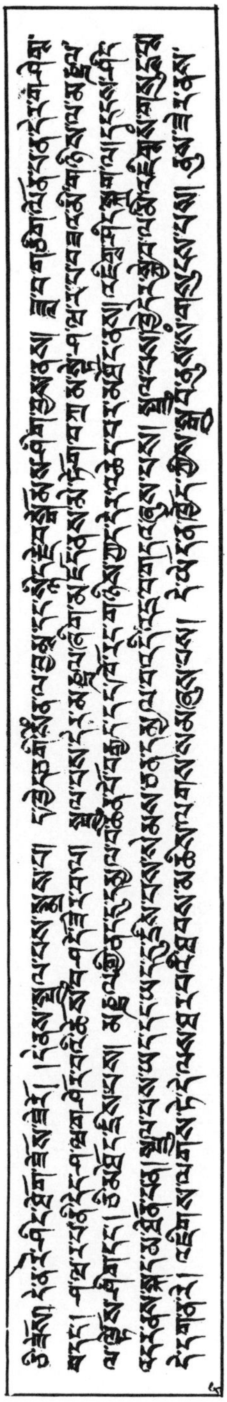

26

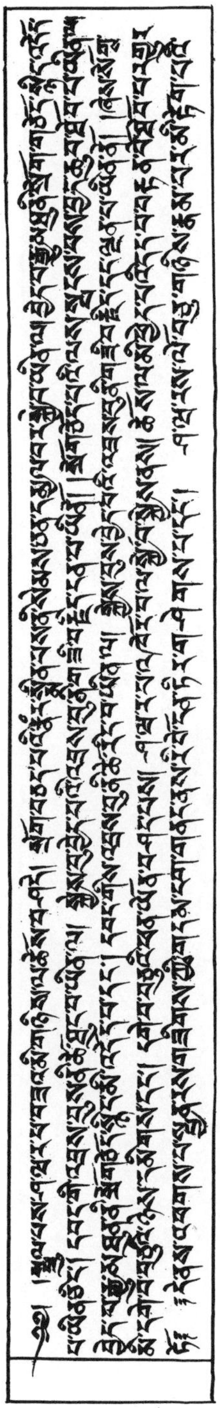

27

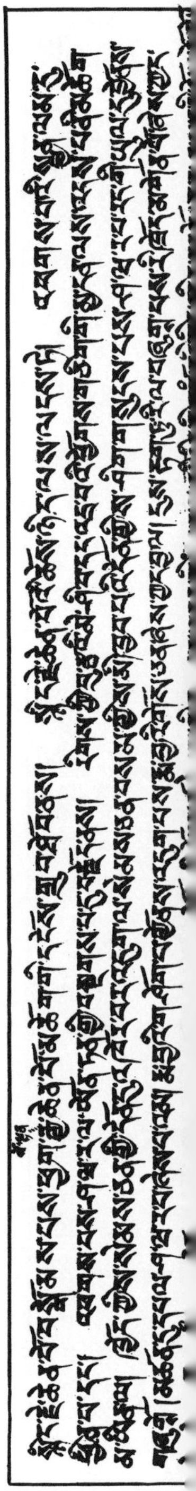

28

29

30

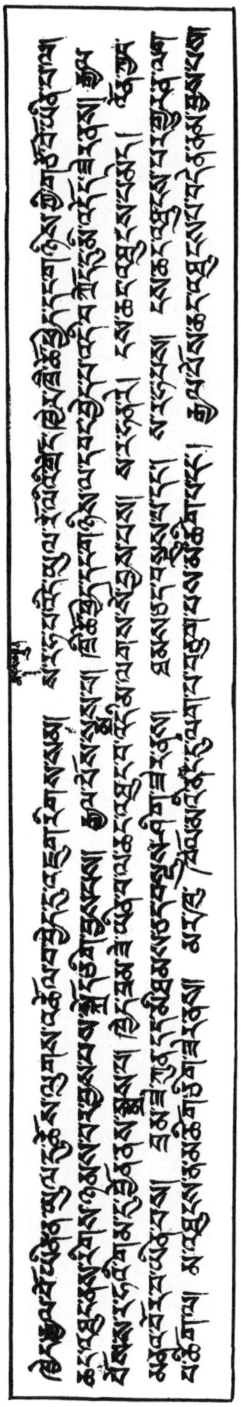

31

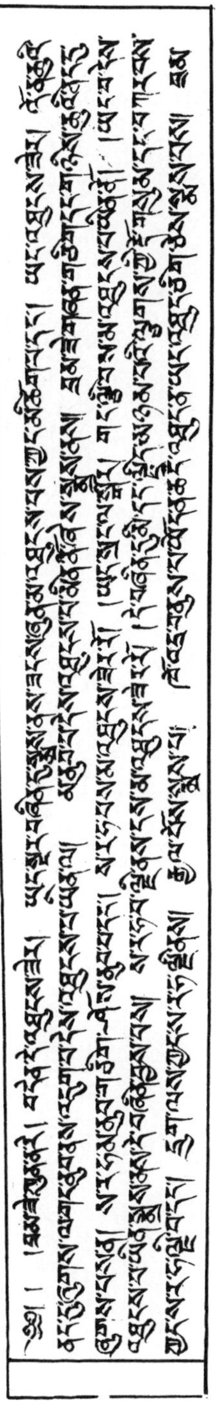

32

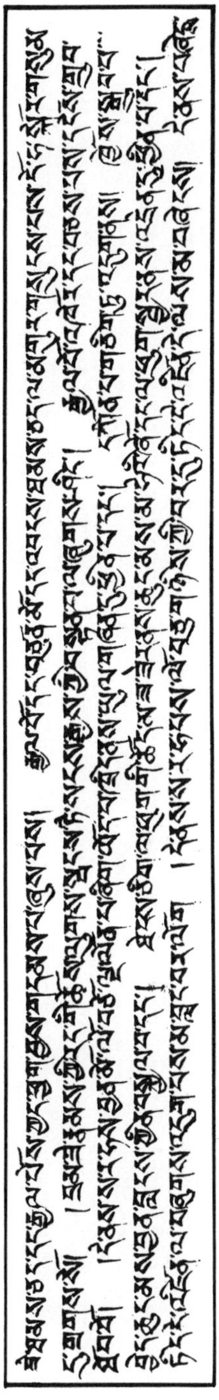

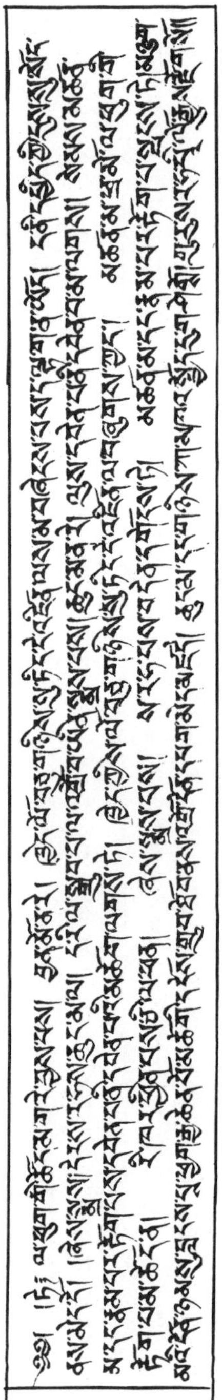

33

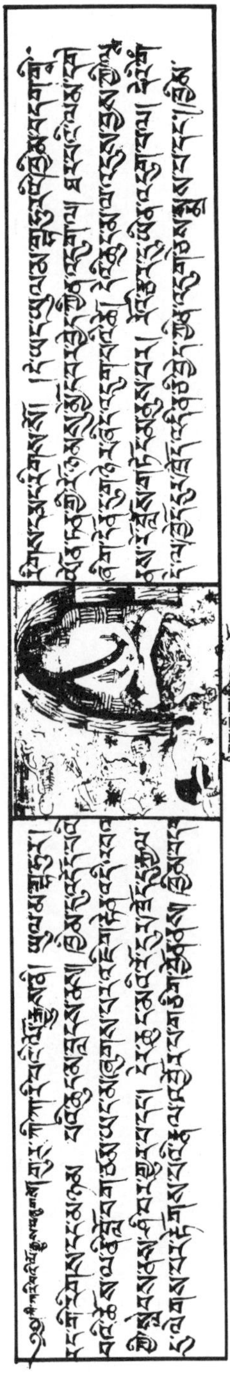

34

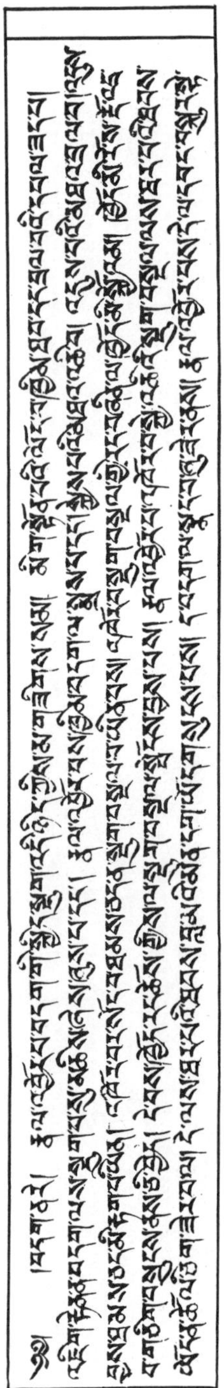

35

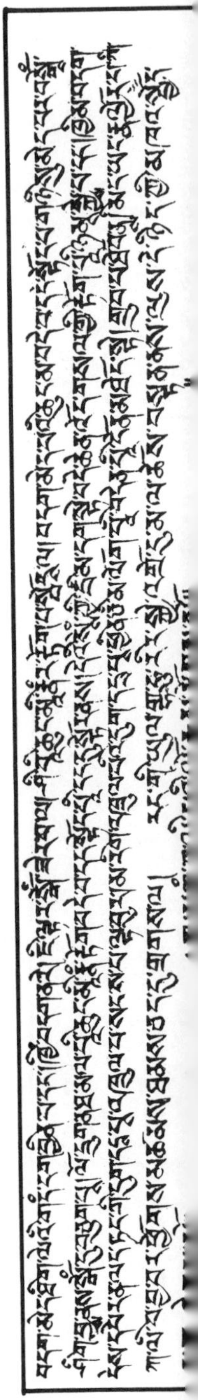

36

37 [illegible]
འཆོང་བ་ཡིན་པ་ལ། ཉ་པ་གཅིག་གིས་ནས་བ་ལ་ཕྱི་ཤུད་དུ་  ལ་ལྷུགས་ཀྱུ་བཏབ་ནས། དེའི་རྣ་མོར་ཤ་དང་བཅས་ཏེ་ཆུར་
རྐྱུར་བ་དང་། ཉ་ཆེན་པོ་ཅིག་ཟིན་ནས་ཐེན་པས། ཉ་པ་ཡང་ གྲུང་ངེ་རྒྱ་མཚོ་ར་ཉ་པ་ཐུབ་ནས། དེ་ར་ཉ་པ་དེ་ཉ་ཆེན་པོ་ཅིག་གི་མིད་
པ་ལ་ལས་ཀྱི་དབང་གི་དེ་རམ་ཤིག་ཡོད་པ། དེའི་རྟུམ་སུ་དབང་ ཕྱུག་ཆེན་པོ་ལ་ལྷ་མོ་སྐུ་མས་ཆོས་ཞུས་པས། དབང་ཕྱུག་ཆེན་

གཟུགས་ཅན་པ་ལ་ནམོ།

38 ཕོ་ན་རེ། དའི་ཆོས་པ་དེ་གང་ན་དང་དུང་ལ་བ་ཤད་པ་མ་ཡིན་ཏེ། ཤི་ཉ་ཆུ་གས་ངང་བ་ཡིན་པས་རྒྱ་མཚོའི་ཉིང་དུ་བང་པ་བཅིག་ས་ཤིག །དེ་རུ་ག་ཤ་དེ་ཟེར་ནས། དེ་བཞིན་
དུ་བྱས་པ་དང་། དེའི་ཉིང་དུ་ལྷ་མོ་ཨུ་མ་ལ་ཆོས་བཤད་པས། དེའི་རྟུས་ཁང་པའི་འོག་ཆུ་ཉ་དེ་འདོད་པ་དང་། ཆོས་ཀྱི་འགྲོ་ལ་ལྷ་མོ་གཉིད་ལོག་དང་མཇུང་ནས་
ནས༔ དབང་ཕྱུག་ཆེན་པོས་ལྷ་མོ་ཨུ་མ་ལ་གོ་འམ་བྱས་པས། ཉ་བས་ཐོ་ལེགས་བྱས་ཀྱི་ན་ཆོས་ཉན་པ་དང་། ཆོས་དེ་ཐོན་པ་དང་ལྷ་མོ་གཉིད་སད་དེ་ཆོས་
ཤོད་བྱས་པས་དབང་ཕྱུག་ཆེན་པོ་ན་རེ། ངས་ཆོས་བཤད་ཟིན་ཟེར། ལྷ་མོ་ན་རེ། ངས་ཀྱི་ཆོས་འདི་བར་དུ་ཐོས། དེ་ནས་གཉིད་ཀྱིས་ཁྱེར་ནས་མ་ཐོས་
ཐུབ་པ་ལ། འོན་ཐོས་ལགས་ཟེར་བ་དེ་སུ་ཡིན་ཟེར་ནས། ལྷ་མོས་དེ་སྐད་ཟེར་བ་བདག་གིས་མ་སྨྲས་ཟེར། དབང་ཕྱུག་ཆེན་པོས་མངོན་ཤེས་ཀྱིས་གཟིགས་པས།

39 ༄༅། །ཁང་པའི་འོག་གི་ཉའི་ལྟོ་བ་ན་མི་གཅིག་འདུག་པ་དེ་ས། ཆོས་ཉན་པ་ར་མ་ཐོང་ནས། དེ་ར་བསམ་པ་ལ་འདི་དའི་སློབ་མ་ར་སེང་བས་དམ་ཚིག་གཅིག་པ་
ཡིན་སྙམ་དུ་དགོངས་ནས། དེ་ར་ཉ་པ་ལ་དབང་བསྐུར་ནས་ཉ་པ་དེ་ལོ་བཅུ་གཉིས་ཉའི་ལྟོ་བ་ར་སྒྲུབ་པ་བྱས་པ་དང་། དེ་ནས་ཡུལ་ཤྲི་ཧ་པ་རི་ཞེས་བྱ་
བའི་ཉ་པ་གཅིག་གིས་ཉ་ཆེན་པོ་གཟུང་ནས་སྦྱོང་པ་དང་། ཉ་པས་བསམ་པ། ཉ་ཆེན་པོ་འདི་དེའི་ལྟོ་ལུགས་ཀྱིས། འདི་ལོ་ཤོག་པར་གསེར་དངུལ་ལ
སོགས་པའི་རྫས་འབ་གཞལ་འབྱུང་ཡང་ངེས་དང་སྙམ་སྟེ། ཉའི་ལྟོ་བ་ཤ་གས་པས་མི་ཅིག་འདུག་ནས། ཁྱོད་སུ་ཡིན་བྱས་པ་ལ། དེ་ན་རེ། བདག་ཀྱང་ཉ་བ
ཡིན་པའི་རྒྱལ་པོ་འདི་ཞེས་བྱ་བའི་དུས་ཉ་བ་དེས་ཁྱེར་སྐྱེ་མེད་པ་ཡིན་ཟེར་ནས། མི་ཀུན་གྱིས་རྩིས་པས་ལོ་བཅུ་གཉིས་ལོན་འདུག་པས། མི་ཐམས་ཅད

40 ངོ་མཚར་སྐྱེས་ཏེ། མི་དེ་རྣམས་ཀྱི་ལ་འཁོར་བ་མི་དེ་པ་ཞེས་བྱ་བར་གྲགས་སོ། །དེ་ནས་མི་ཐམས་ཅད་ཀྱིས་མཆོད་པ་དང་། མི་ན་བས་ས་ལ་གར་བྱས་པ་དང་ནང་
པས་ལ་མ་ནུབ་པ་དང་། རྗེའི་སྙིང་དུ་གར་བྱས་པས་ཀྱང་འདམ་ལྟར་བྱེད་ནུས་ཀུན་ངོ་མཚར་སྐྱེས་སོ། །དེ་ནས་མི་ན་པའི་ཞབས་ནས། སྔར་པ་སུགས་ལས་
ཀྱི་འབྲེལ་བ་དང་། དུས་འདིར་ཚོགས་ལ་མོས་པ་ཡིས། །ཡོན་ཏན་ཕུན་ཚོགས་འདི་ལྟར་བྱུང་། །སེམས་དང་སེམས་ནི་རིན་པོ་ཆེ། །ཅེས་གསུངས་ནས་ལོ་ལྔ་
བརྒྱར་སེམས་ཅན་གྱི་དོན་མཛད་དོ། །མཚན་ཡང་མི་ན་པ་ཛ་ཛའི་ཞབས། །ཉ་ཆེ་ན་པ་ངོ་གསུམ་དུ་གྲགས་ཤིང་། །དང་པོར་འཇིག་རྟེན་གྱི་དངོས
གྲུབ་པ་ཐོབ་ནས་རིམ་གྱིས་ས་ལམ་བགྲོད་དེ་ལུས་དེ་ཉིད་ཀྱིས་མཁའ་འ་སྤྱོད་དུ་གཤེགས་སོ། །གུ་རུ་མི་ན་པའི་ལོ་རྒྱུས་རྫོགས་སོ།། །

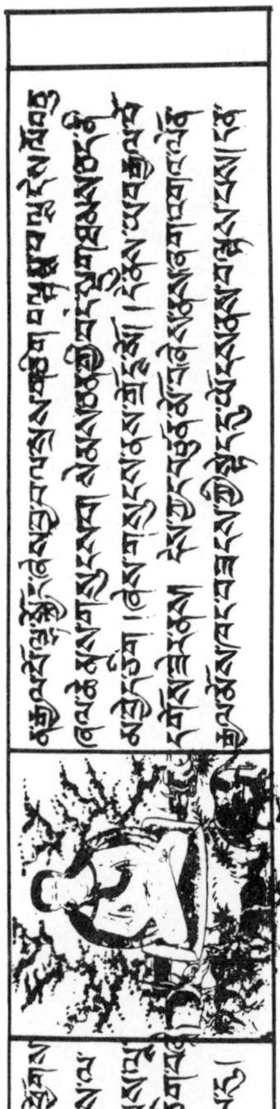

41

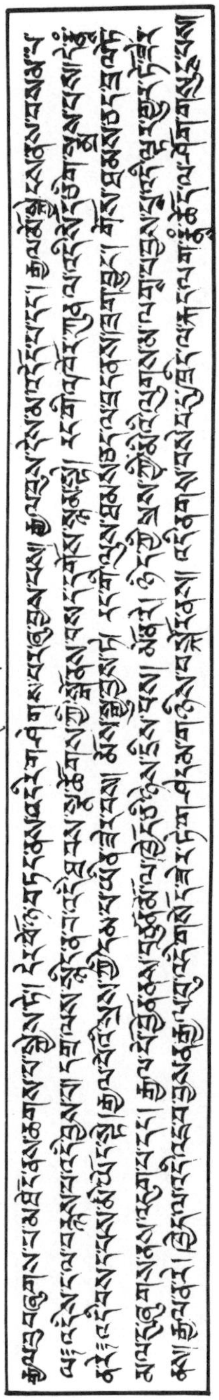

42

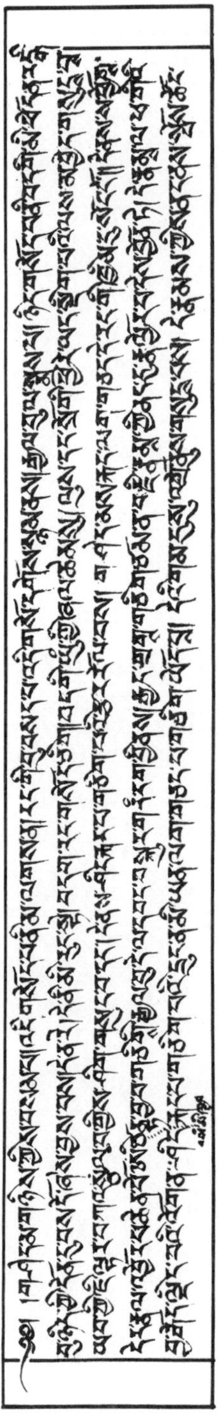

43

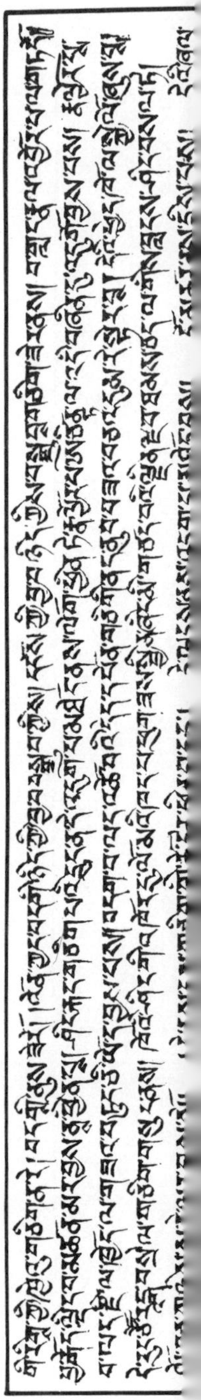

44

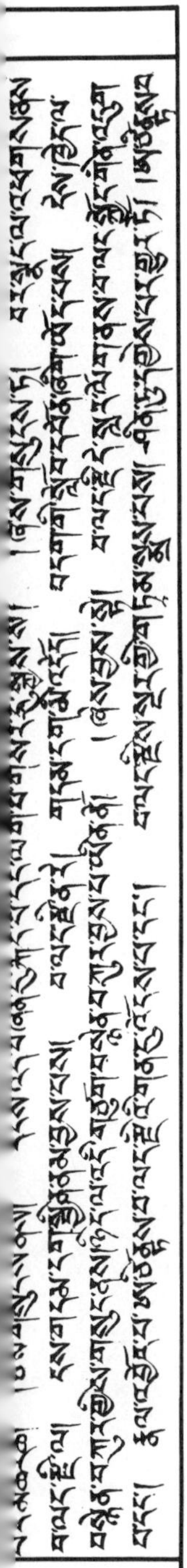
45

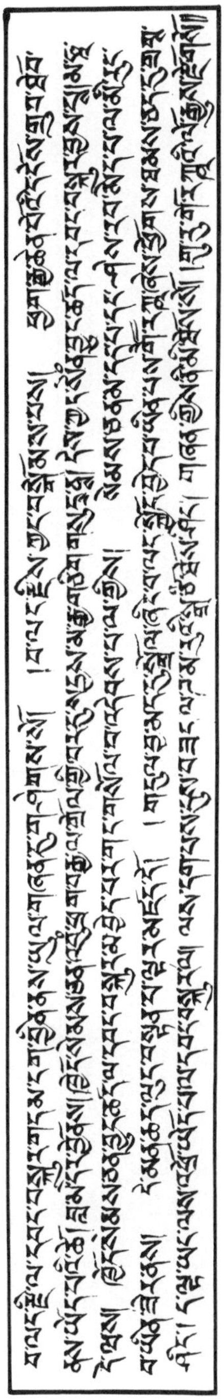
46

47

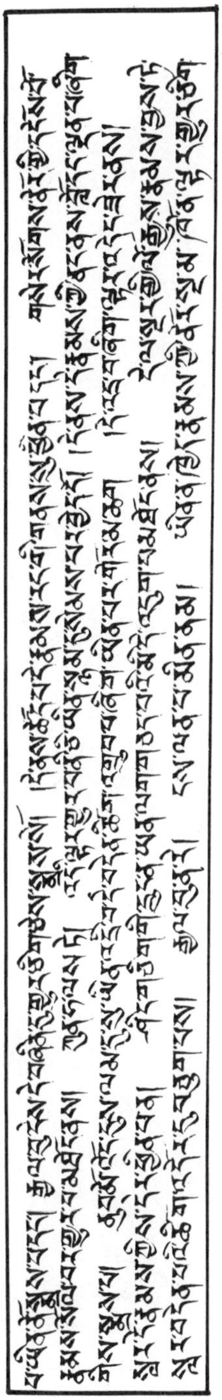
48

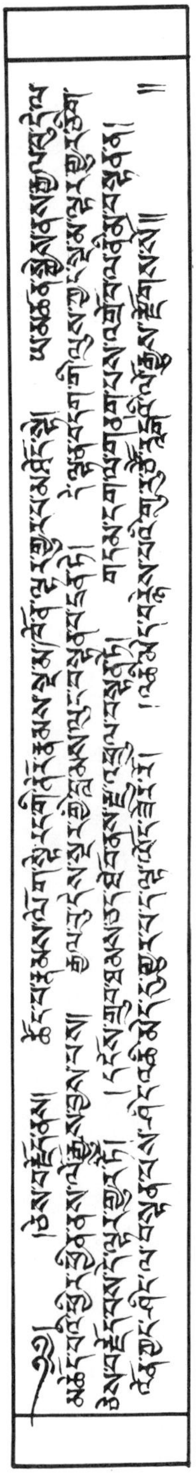

49

50

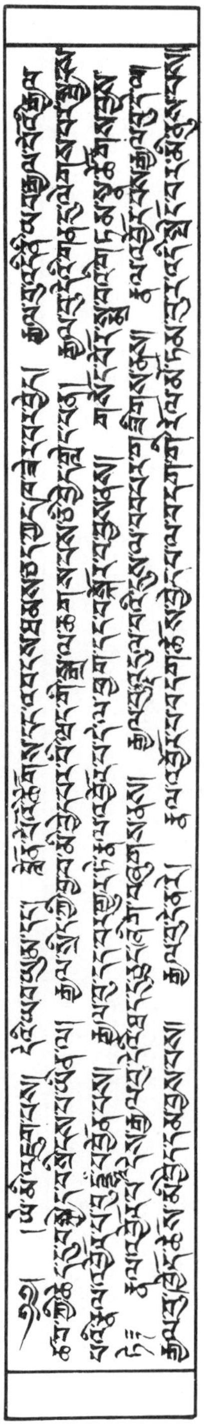

51

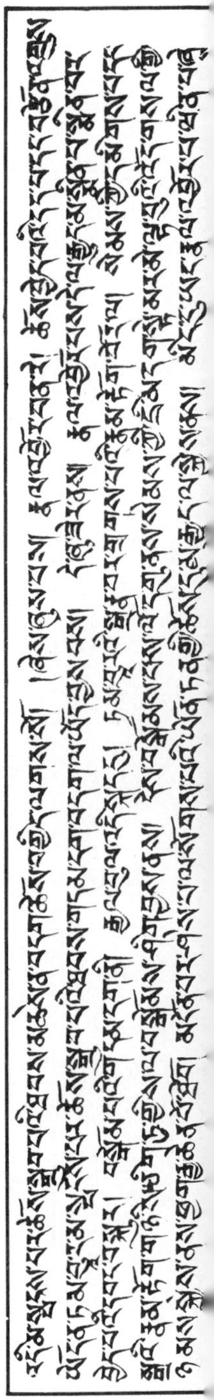

52

53

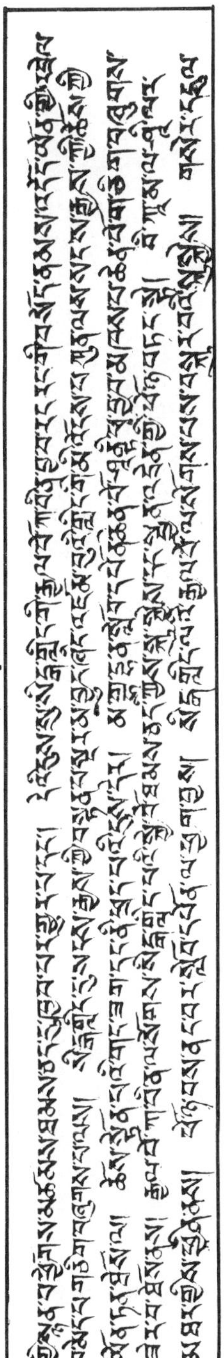

54

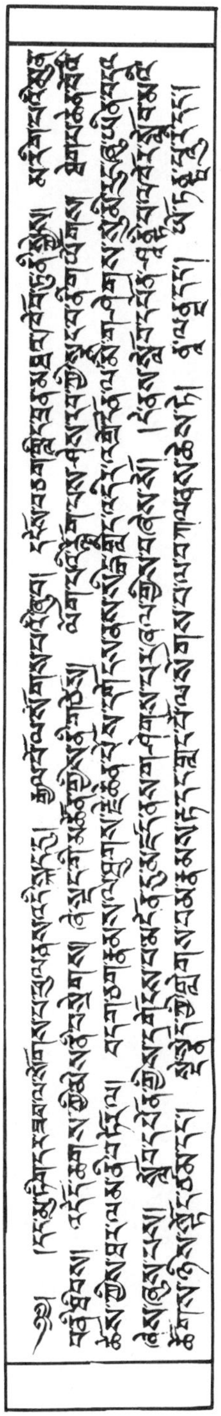

55

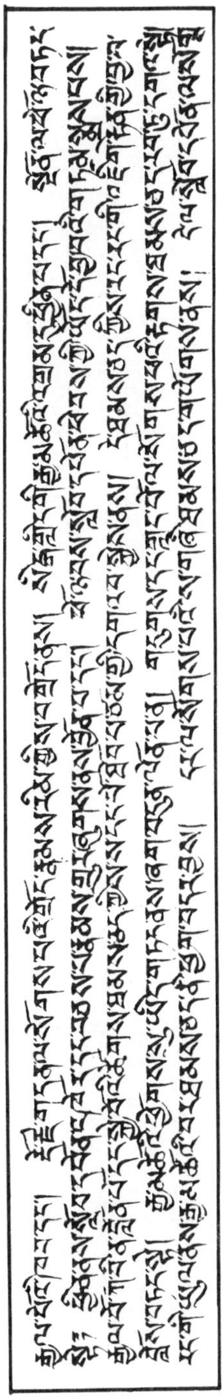

56

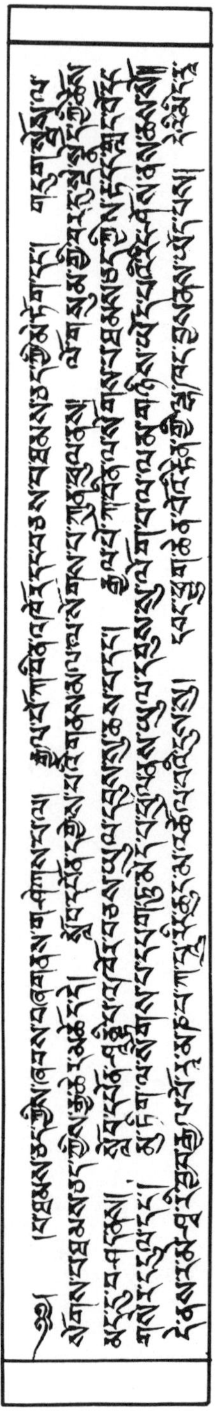

57

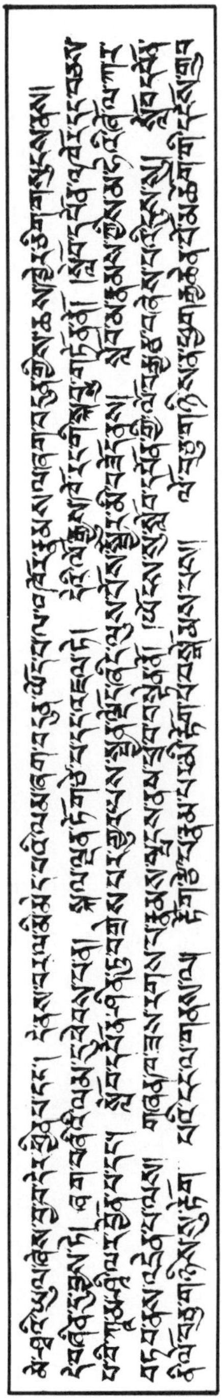

58

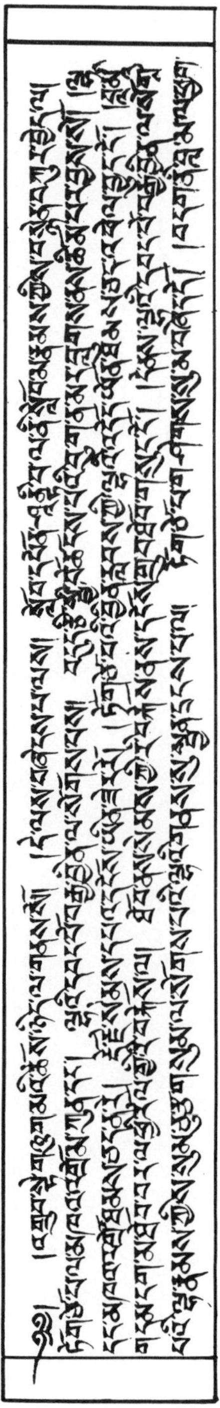

59

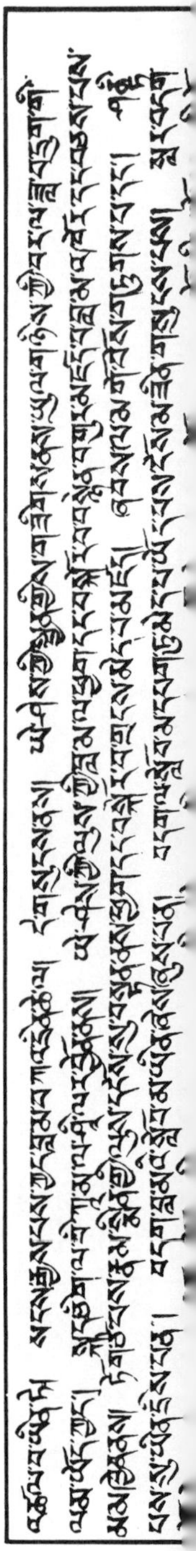

60

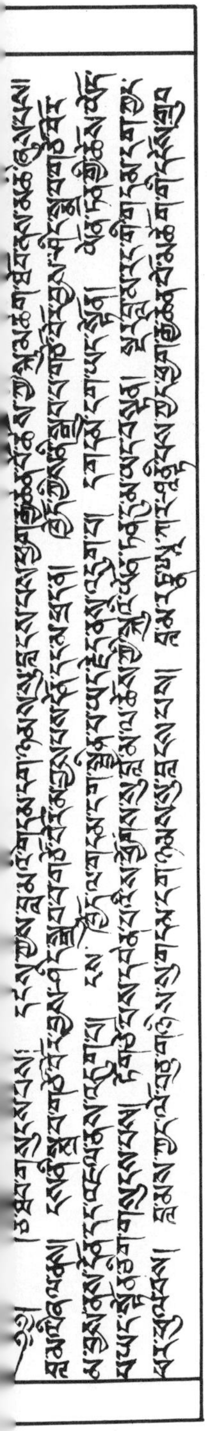

61

62

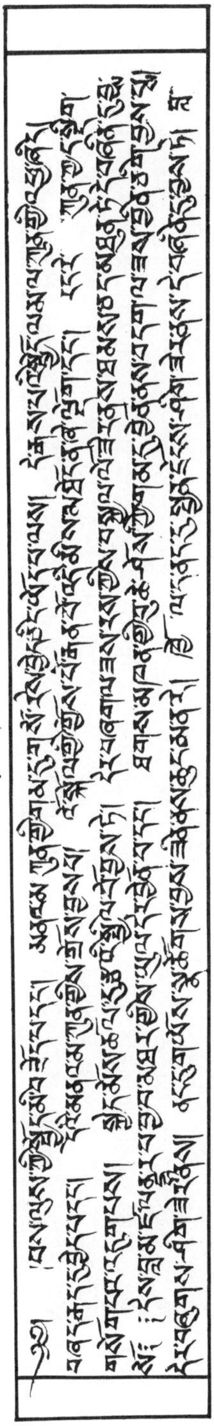

63

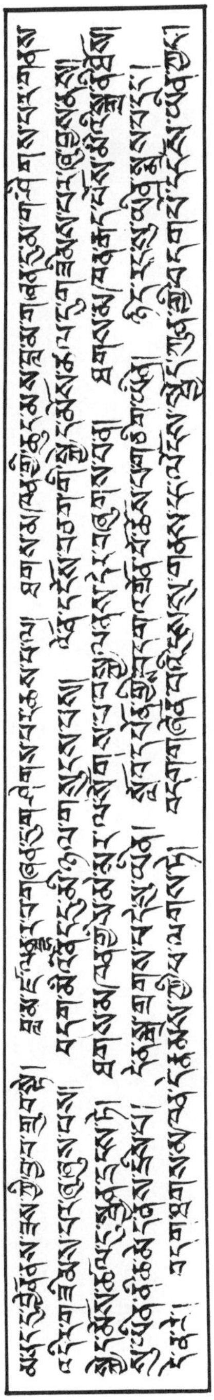

64

65

༄༅། །དེ་ལྟ་བུ་དང་མཐུན་མ་ཀུན་གྱིས་བདག་ལ་འཕྲུལ་སྣང་བྱེད་ཅིང་། གཞན་གྱིས་མཐོང་གི་རྟོགས་ནས་སྐྱེ་དམིགས་ཆ་ལ་འདི་ལྟར་སྒྲུབས་ནས་བཞག་པ་ཡིན་ལགས།
འཁོར་བ་འདི་ཚེས་ལ་སྙིང་པོ་མེད་པ་འདི་འདྲ་བ་ལགས་སོ་ཞེས་སྨྲས་པ་དང་། རྗེ་ལ་ཆུ་ར་པས་ཐུགས་མཁན་ལ་གསུངས་པ། འདུས་བྱས་ཐམས་ཅད་མི་རྟག་པ།
སྡིག་པ་རང་སོང་བ་ཐམས་ཅད་དཀའ་ཐུབ་བསྐུལ་བ། ཆོས་ཐམས་ཅད་བདག་མེད་པ། མྱང་འདས་ལས་འདས་པ་ཞི་ཞིང་བདེ་བ་ཡིན་པས། ཉེ་རྒྱུགས་ཀྱི་ཆོས་མི་གོས་
སམ་ཞེས་གསུངས་པས།། དགོས་ལྡན་ཞེས། རྗེ་ལ་ཆུ་རས་པས་ཐུགས་མཁན་དེ་ར་ཕྱིས་རྗེར་སྐྱེ་དུ་ཀྱི་ཡལ་འཁོར་དུ་དབང་བསྐུར་བ། དམ་དག་བྱིན་ནས་སློམ
དུ་བཅུག་སྟེ་སྨྲམ་གཞན་དུ་ཤེགས་པ། དེས་ཀྱང་རྗེ་མའི་དམ་ངག་ཡིད་ལ་བྱས་ཏེ། སྒྲུབ་བཞིན་མཐར་མ་ལོག་པ་ཀུན་ལ་ཁ་ཡང་མི་ཟེར་བ།

66

དགག་དམ་བྲལ་ནས་ལོ་བཅུ་གཉིས་སྒྲུབ་པ་བྱས་ནས་ཡོན་ཏན་མང་པོ་ཐོབ་པ་མིས་མཚོར་བ་ལ། དུས་གཅིག་ན་བྲུ་ཆེ་བ་དུས་ཟ་འོག་བཟང་པོ་ཞིག་རྟགས་ནས།
བཀྲ་ཤིས་བྱེད་པ་འབྱིབ་ལ་ལག་ཡེད་སྙིང་ལ་ཟན་སྐྱུ་ལ་བ་བརྗེད་པ་དུང་། མཚན་མོ་མནལ་མ་སད་ནས་ཚེ་ལ་སོགས་པ་འི་མིས་མཚོར་བར་ཟས་སྐྱོ་ལ་དབྱིན
པར། ཕྱི་ལ་པོ་འི་ནང་ནས་མི་མ་ར་གྱི་གནང་བ་ཚན་པོ་དང་། བུམ་ལྷ་ཅམ་གྱི་བསྐོར། ཁ་ཟས་ཀྱི་རྣམ་པ་ཅན་མི་པ་མང་པོ་དང་། མི་ཡུལ་དུ་མི་འབྱུང་བའི
གོས་དང་རྒྱན་མང་པོ་ཐོགས་པ་པར་མཐོང་ནས་རང་སར་ཡོག་སྟེ། ཕྱི་ལ་ཉིད་ཀྱི་ཕ་རྒྱན་ལྟར་འདོད་བྱས་པས། ཕྱིས་པ་ཤི་བ་ཡིན་སྐམ་ནས་དངས་པ
ན། མོ་གཞན་ཡང་འོངས་ནས་སྐྱེ་མོ་སཆ་པ་དུ་ལྟར་བྱེད་པས།། སྨམ་པ་ཞིན་དུ་ཐམས་ཅད་ཀྱིས་མཐོང་ནས་ལ་མཚན་སྐྱེས་ཏེ། ཞང་དུ་ཡོག་ཕྱེ་ངས

67

༄༅། །ནས་ལྟར་གྱི་གཏམ་བརྗོད་པ་ནི་བུ་ལགས་པ་འདི་གཅིག་ཀུན་འདི་འདྲ་བ་མི་མ་ཡིན། འདྲེ་གཅིག་འདུག་ཟེར་ནས་སྨྲ་དོ། །ནང་པར་མི་ཀུན་གྱི
མཐོང་ནས། ལ་སྟོན་གཡར་འི་མི་ཐམས་ཅད་ཀྱིས་ལྟར་ཕྱིན་ནས་ཕྲག་བྲས་པ་དང་། དེ་ཡི་ཕྱུར་བན་ལུས་རྗེས་ཏེ་ལོ་བཅུ་དྲུག་ལོན་པའི་ཚོད་དུ་ཆུར
ནས༑ སྐུ་ལས་འོད་ཟེར་དཔག་ཏུ་མེད་པ་འབྱུང་བས་མི་ཀུན་གྱིས་མི་གི་ལྟར་མི་བཟོད་པ་དང་། ལུས་མི་ལོད་གཡའ་དཀའ་པ་ལྟར་སོད་པ་ལ་སྣང་
བ་ཐམས་ཅད་ངོ་དུ་ཤར་ཏེ། མིང་ཡང་ཤཱཀྱ་བཞིན་གྱི་ལ་ཐམས་ཅད་དུ་གྲགས་འགྲོ་དོན་དཔག་མེད་མཛད། མཐར་ལ་ཆེ་ནི་གར་འི
སྐྱོ་བ་འི་ཚོགས་དཔག་ཏུ་མེད་པ་དང་བཅས་ཏེ་ལུས་དེ་ཉིད་ཀྱིས་མཁའ་སྤྱོད་དུ་གཤེགས་སོ། །དེ་ནས་རང་གི་དང་གྲུབ་དང་བླ་མའི

68

གདམས་ངག་ཉམས་སུ་བླངས་ནས། ན་ཆེད་རྒྱན་པ་ཆོ་འདི་ཉིད་
དོ། །གུ་རུ་ཏཀྵི་པའི་ལོ་རྒྱུས་རྫོགས་སོ།།
མ་ཁྱབ་དེ། དེའི་ལོ་རྒྱུས་ནི་ཡུལ་ལྷ་ཀ་ར་ཤ་ར་ཕྱོགས། བི་ཥྞ་
བ་ཡོད་པ་ལས། རིགས་ལྷམ་མཁན། རང་ཉིད་ཀྱང་བི་ཥྞ་
ཏ་ག་ཙུ་འདོད་འབར་བྱེད་པ་ཡིན་པ་ལས། དེའི་གམ་དུ་རྣལ་

འབྱོར་པ་ཆེན་པོ་མཆོག་གི་དངོས་གྲུབ་ཐོབ་པ་དུ་རུ་དབ་ཡིན་གསུང
༄༅། །ཙ་མ་རི་པའི་ལོ་རྒྱུས་བཞུགས་སོ། །གུ་རུ་ཙ་མ་རི་པ་ཞེས་བྱ་བ་ནི་ལྷམ
གར་ཝ་བ་འི་གྲོང་ཁྱེར་ན། བཟོ་རིགས་མི་འདྲ་བ་བཅོ་བརྒྱད་ཚང་
གར་ནི་ལྷམ་གསར་སྙིང་གི་བཟོ་བོ་ལས་བྱེད་ཅིང་། ལས་དེས་
འཚོ་བ་ཞིག་འོང་བ་ལ། དེས་ལྷམ་གྱི་བཟོ་འགྲོ་བོ་རྒྱུས

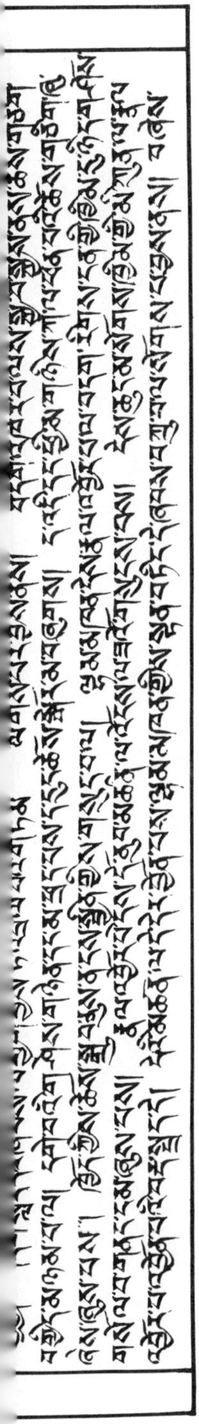

69

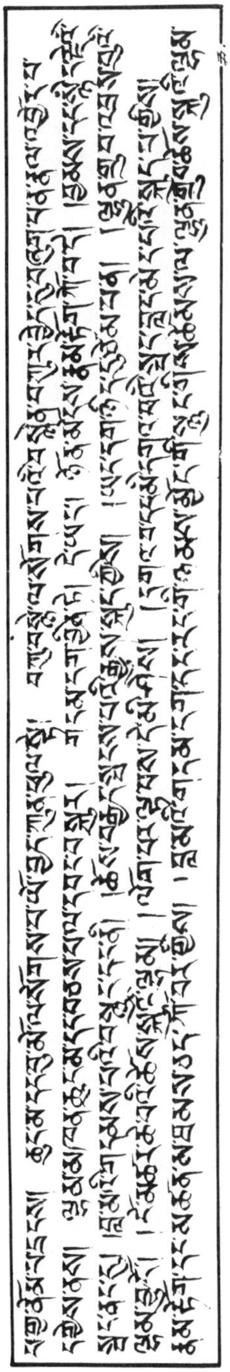

70

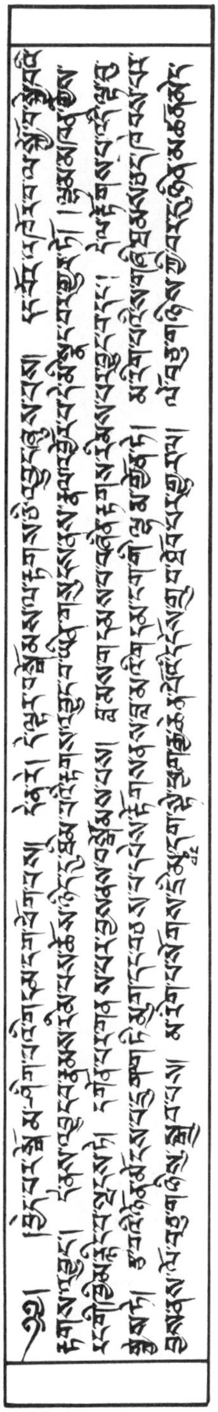

71

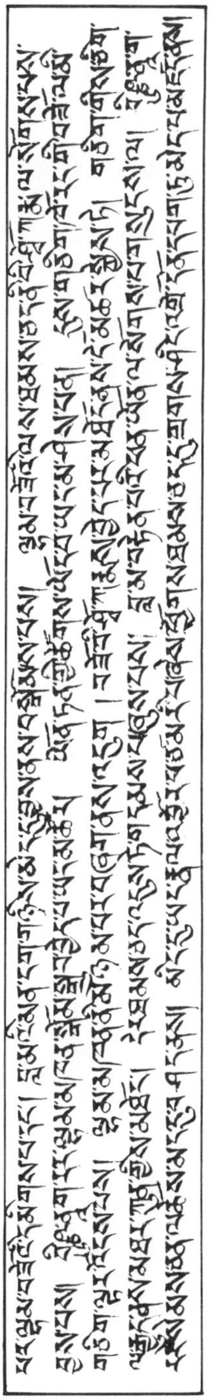

72

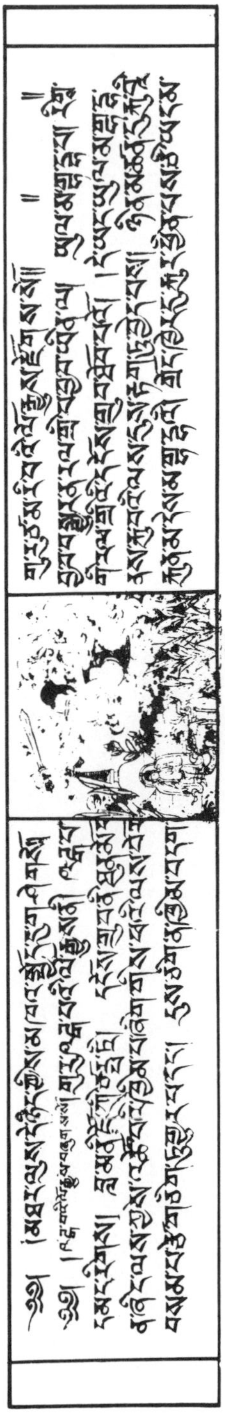

73

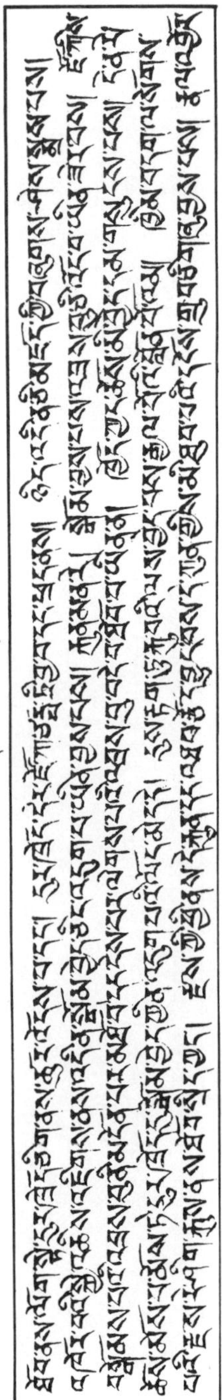

74

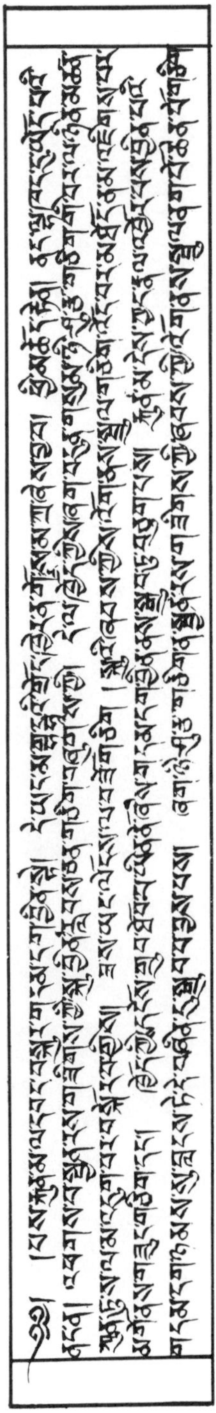

75

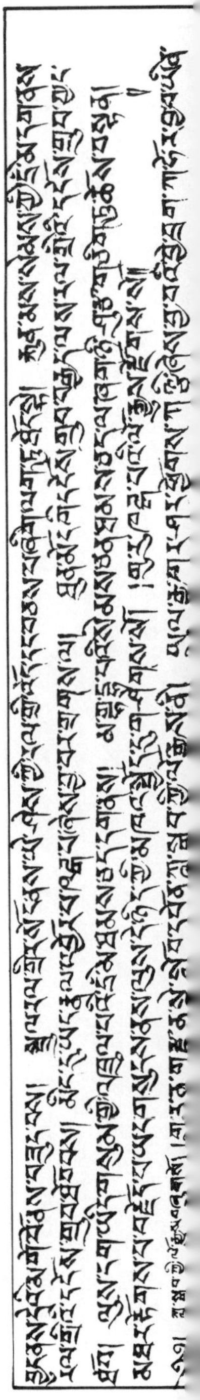

76

77

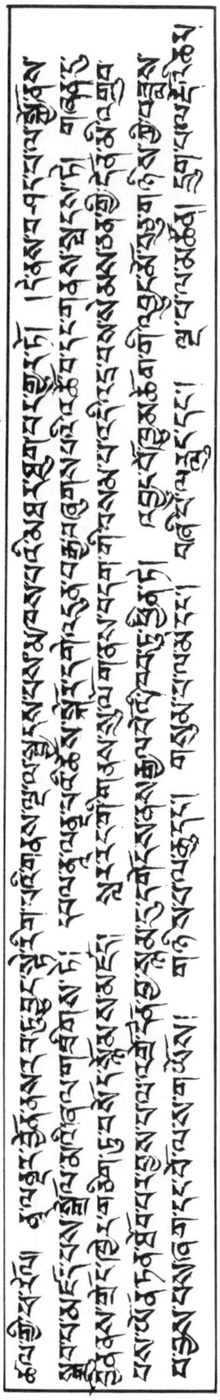

78

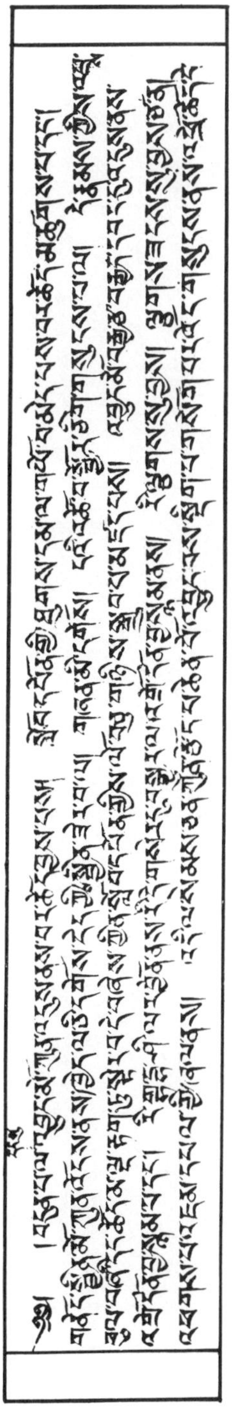

79

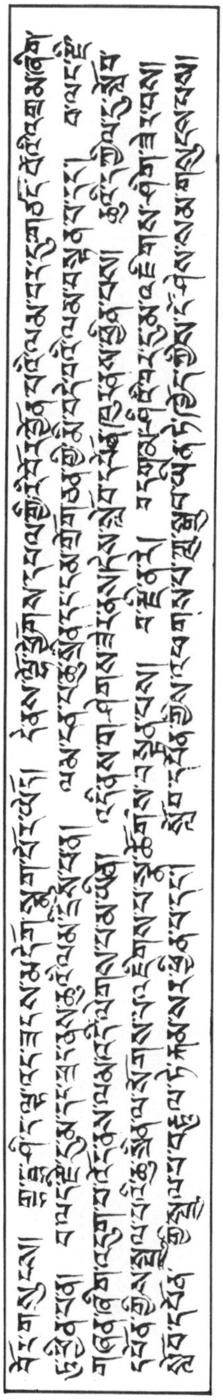

80

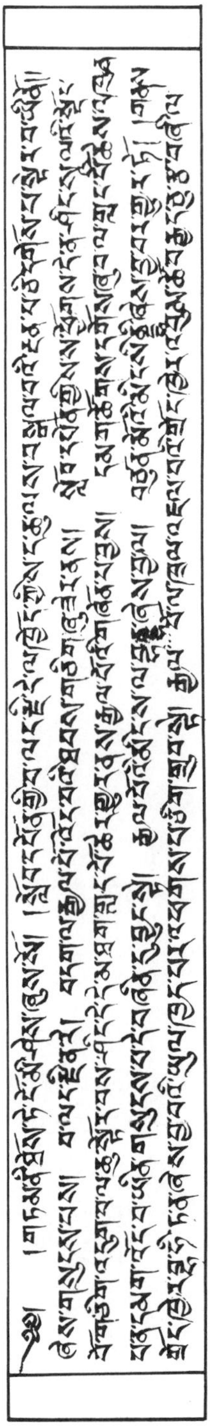

81

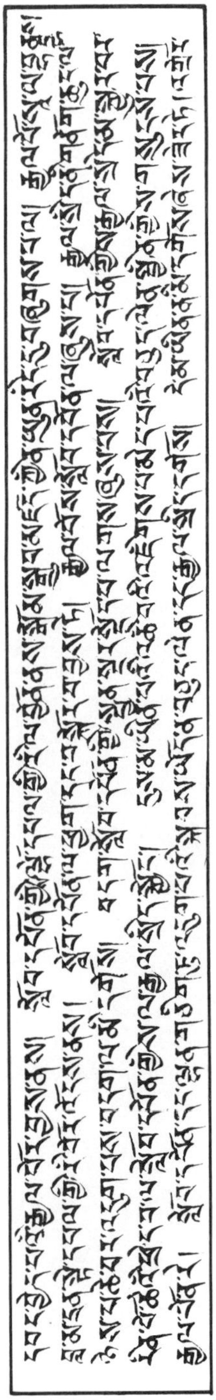

82

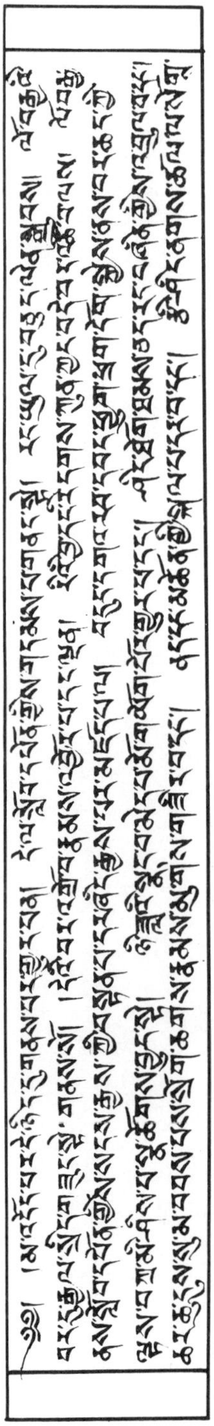

83

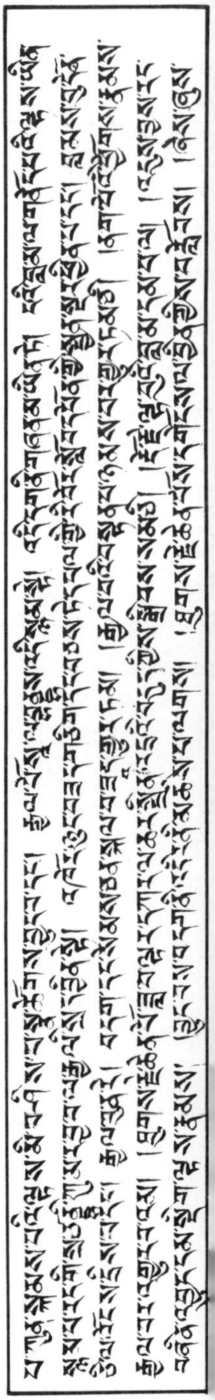

84

85

86

87

88

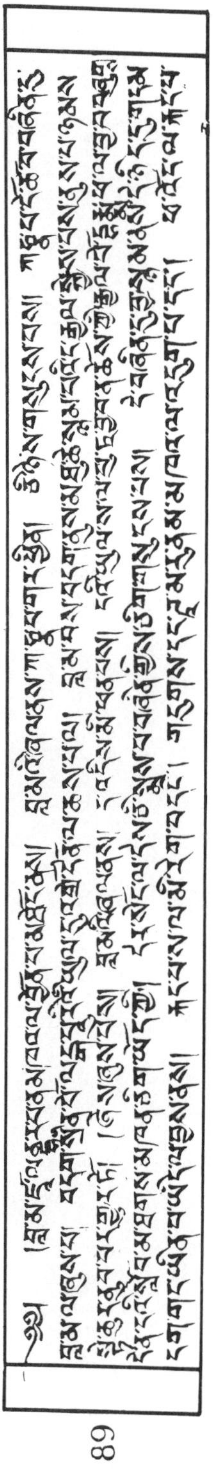

89

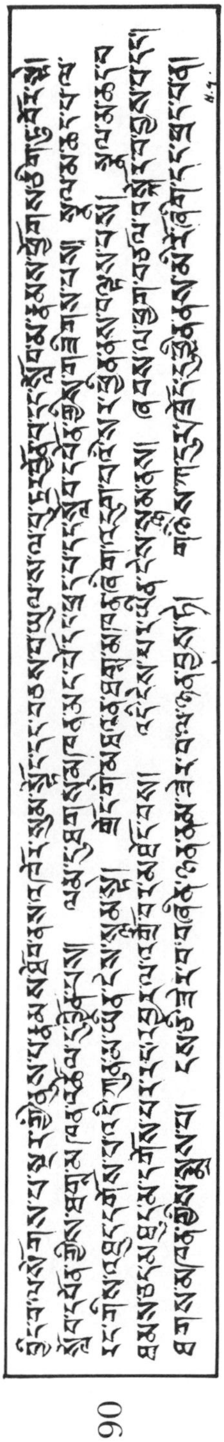

90

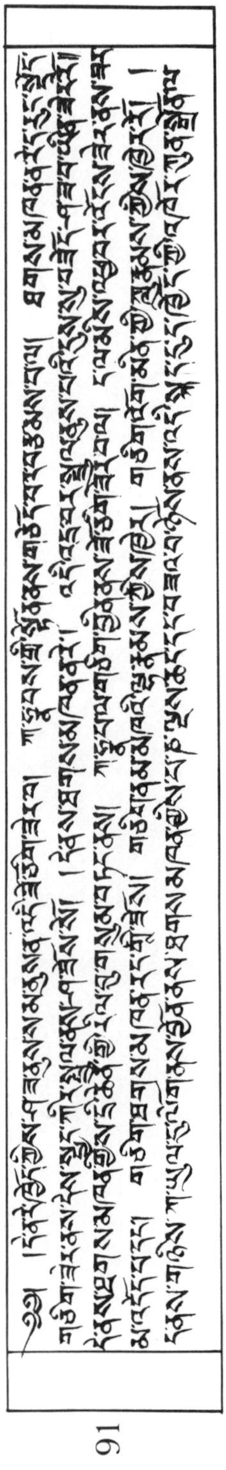

91

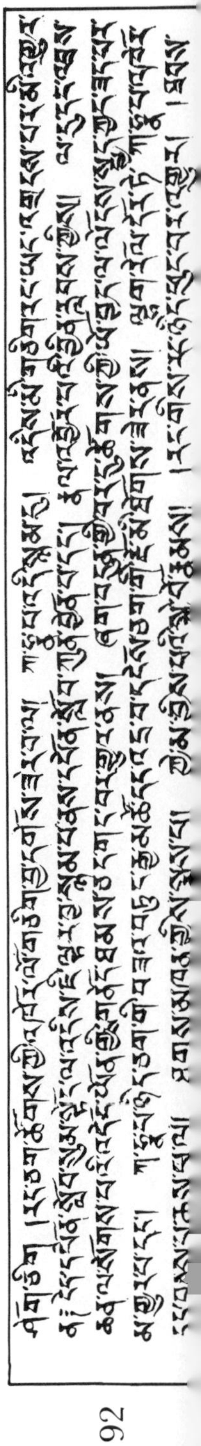

92

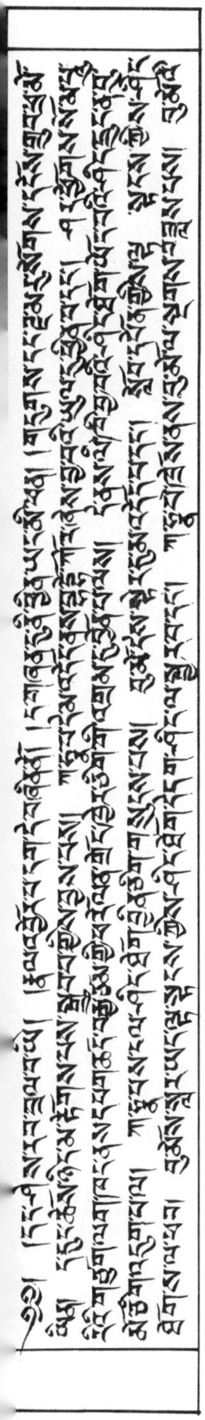

93

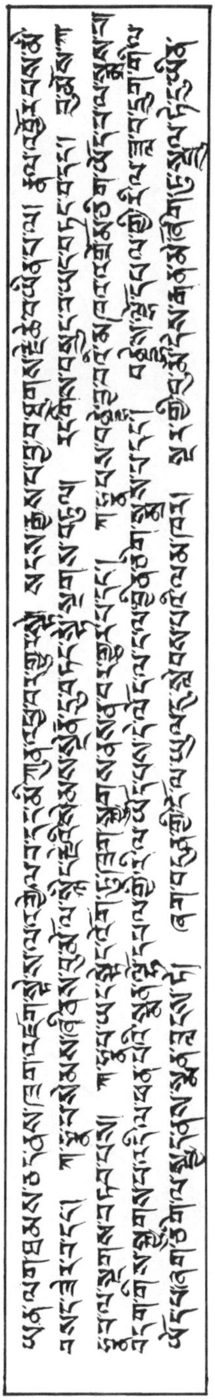

94

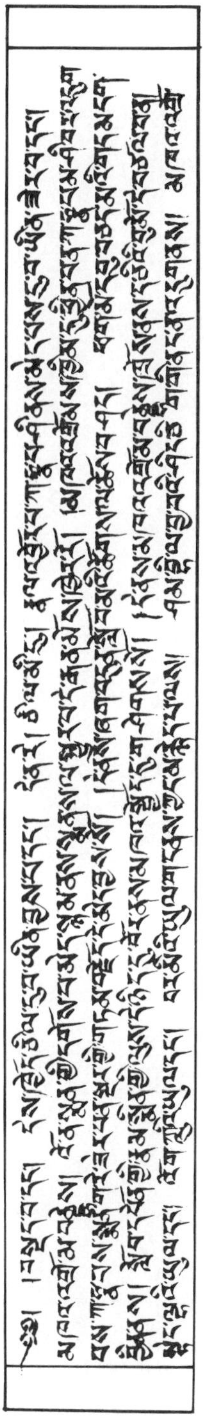

95

96

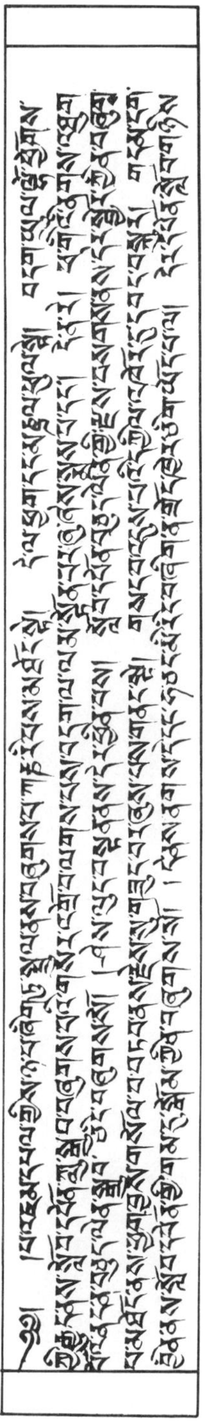

97

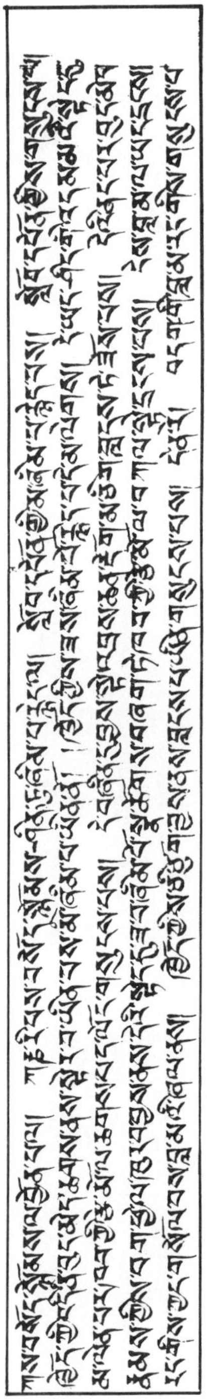

98

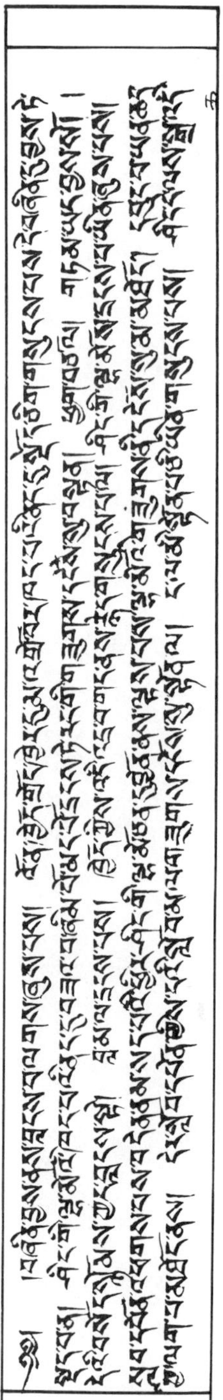

99

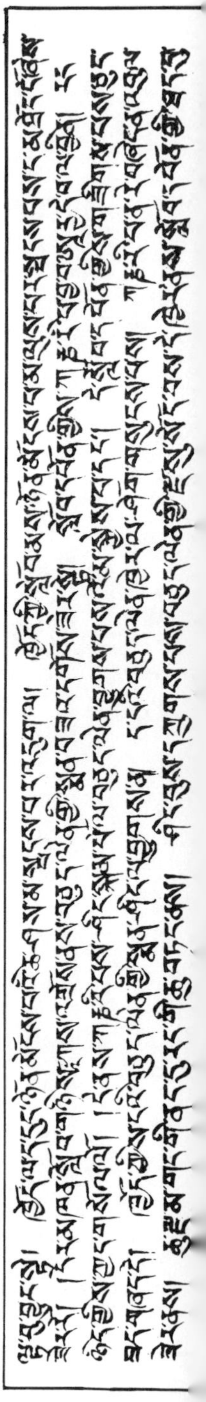

100

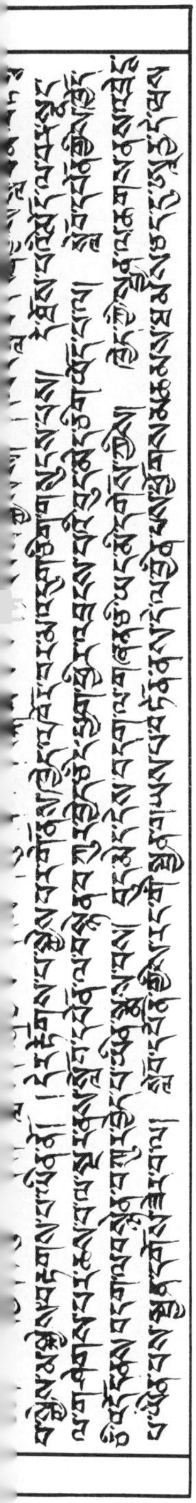

101

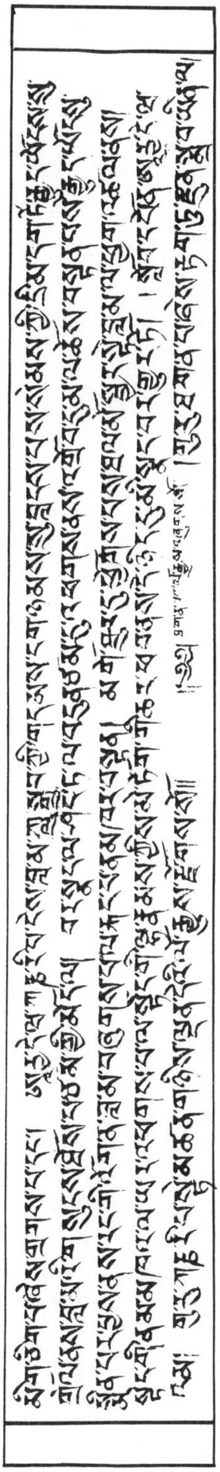

102

103

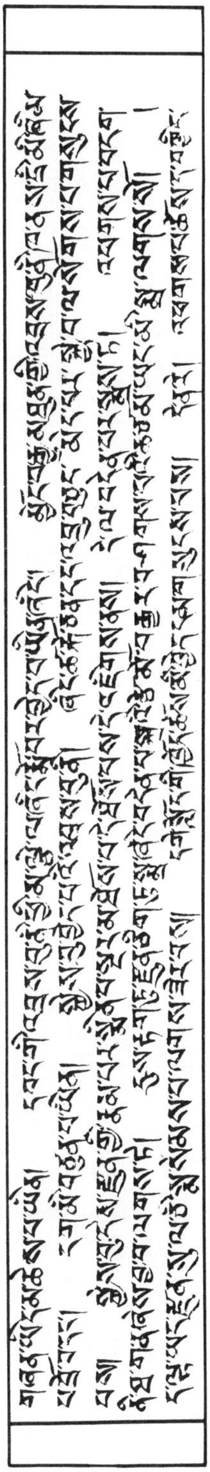

104

105

106

107

108

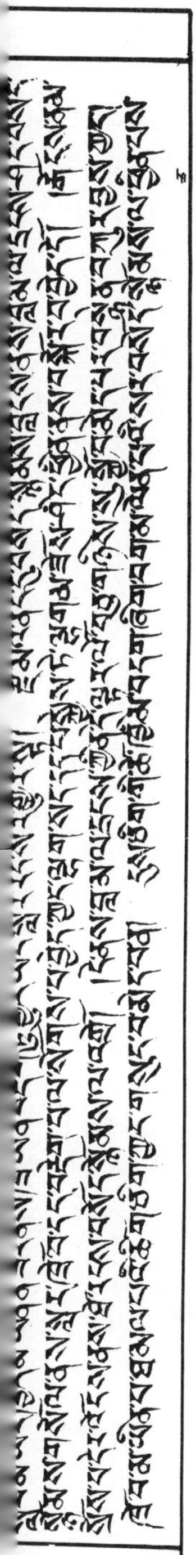

109

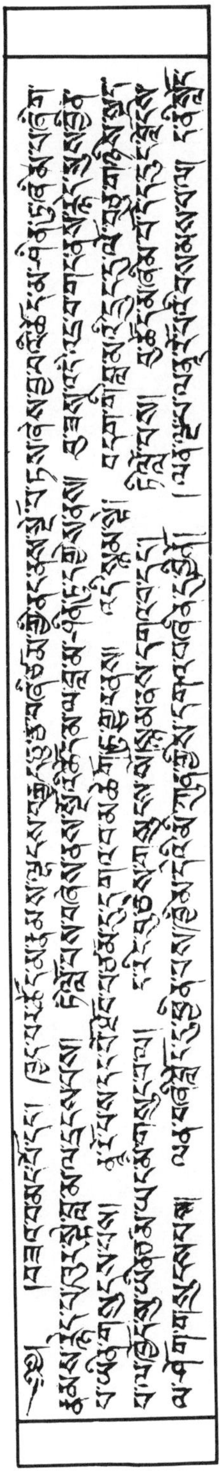

110

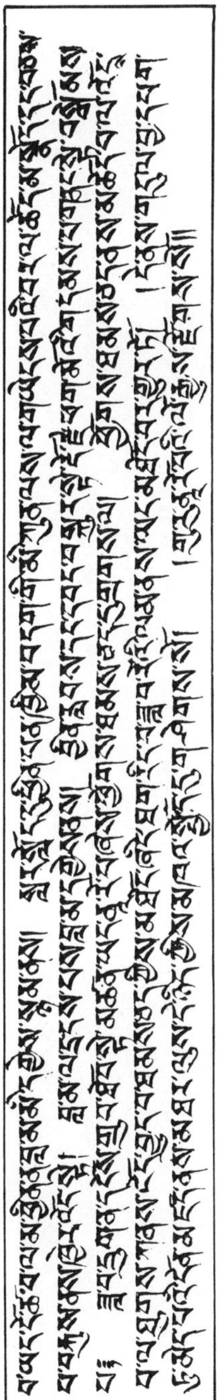

111

112

113

114

115

116

117

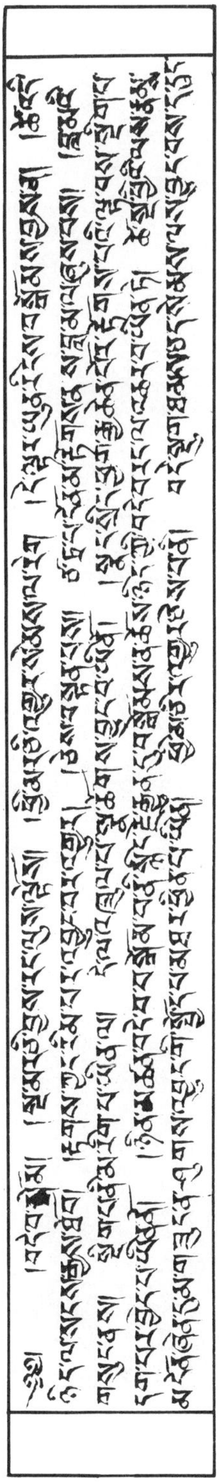

118

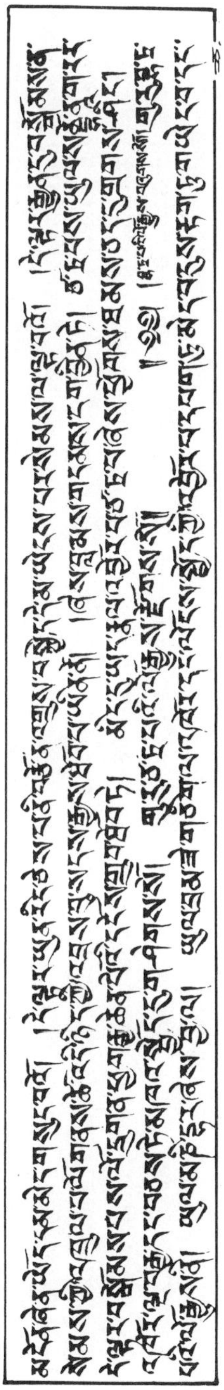

119

120

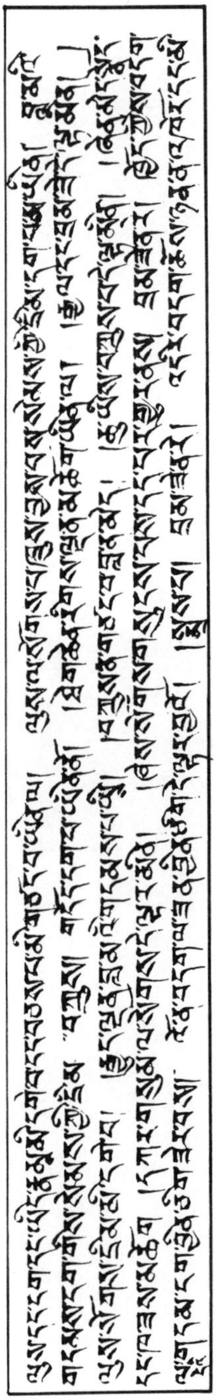

121

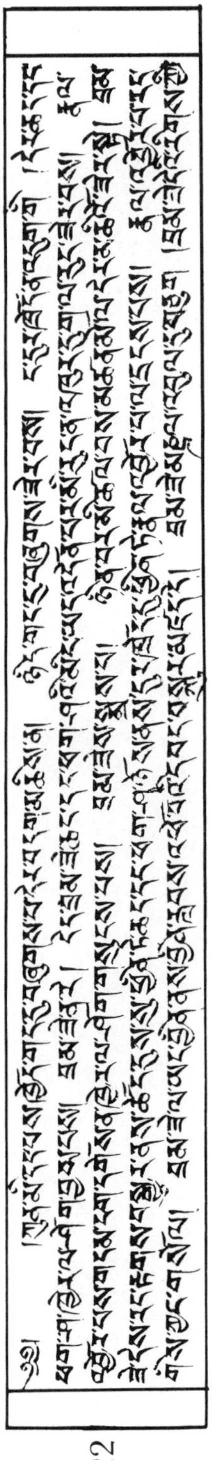

122

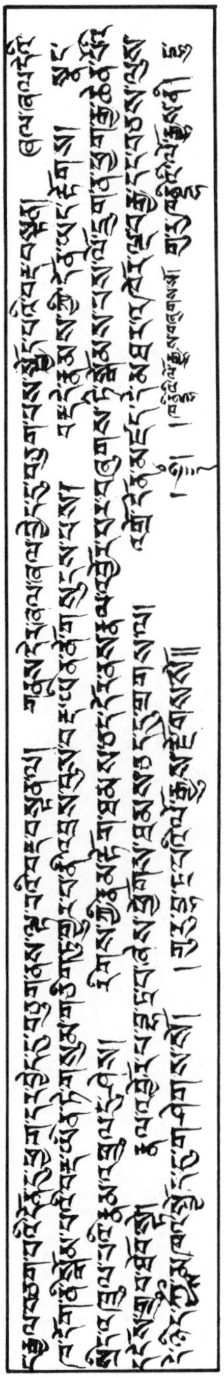

123

124

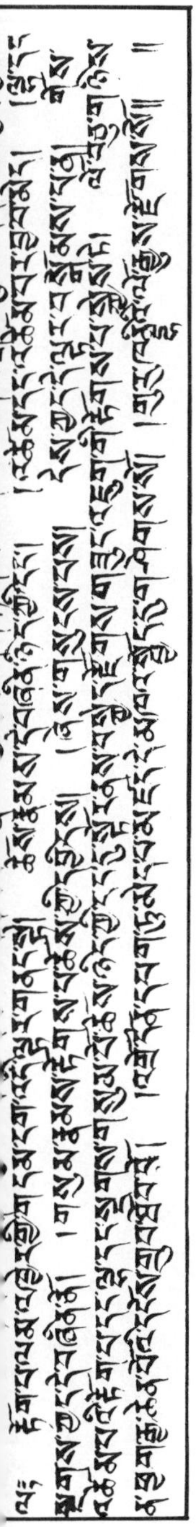

125

126

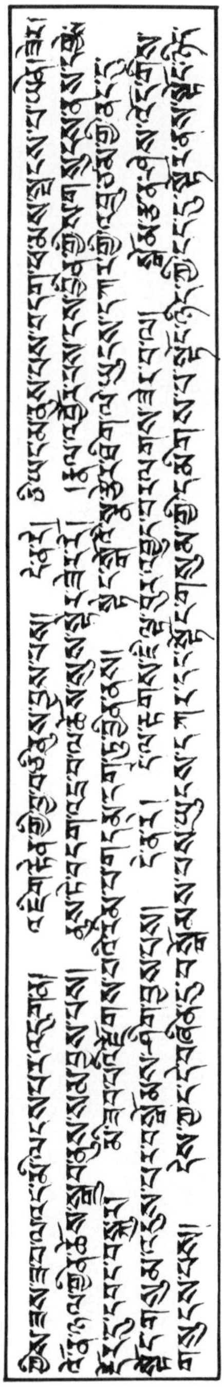

127

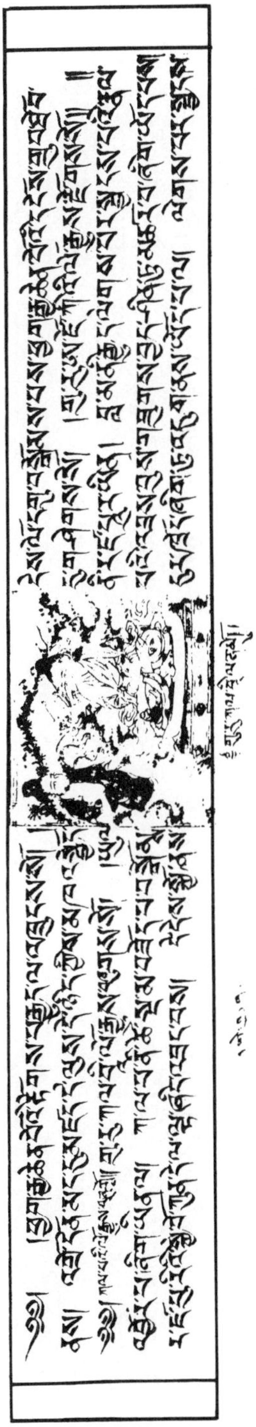

128

129

130

131

132

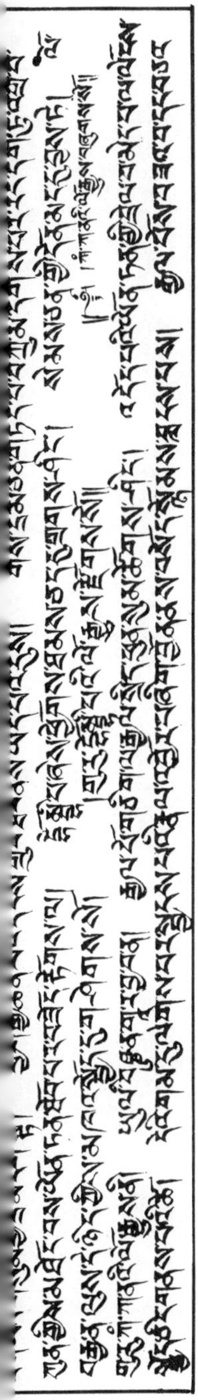

133

134

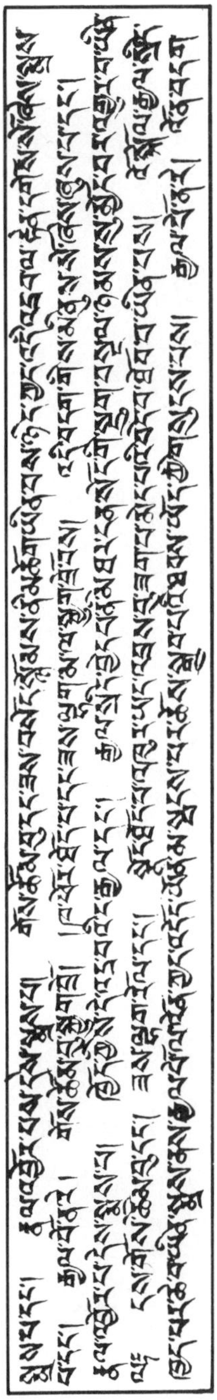

135

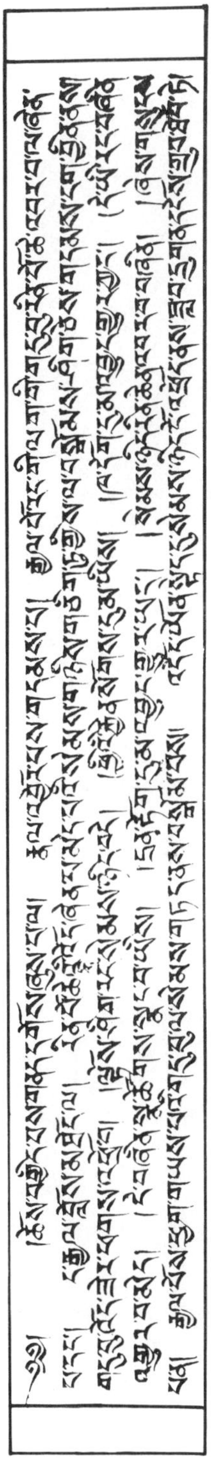

136

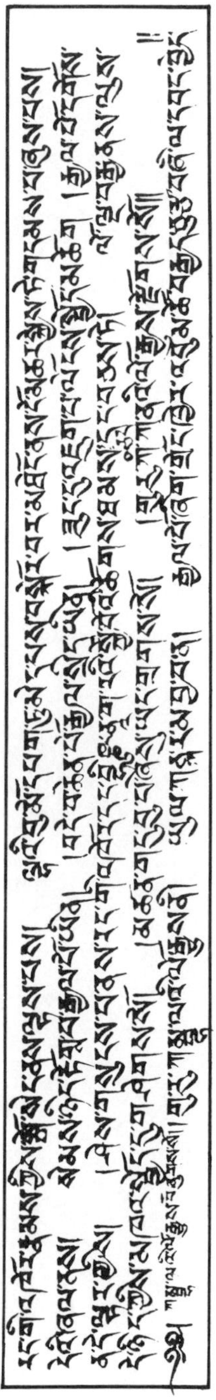

137

138

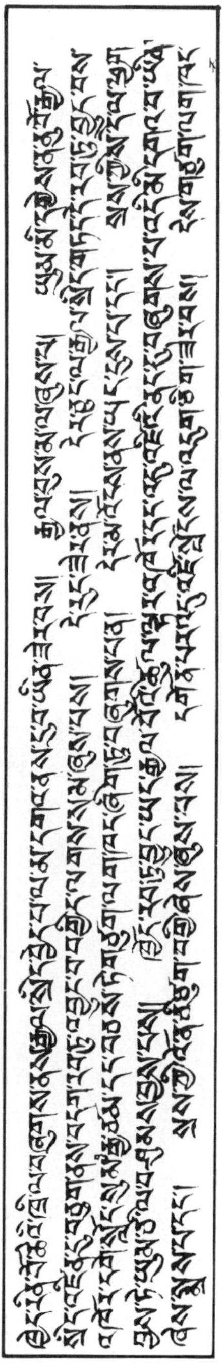

139

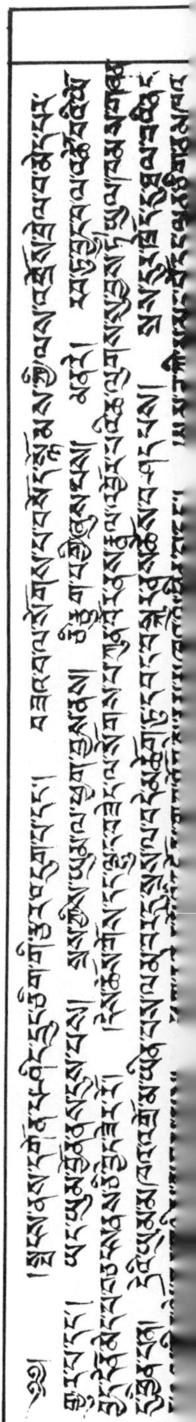

140

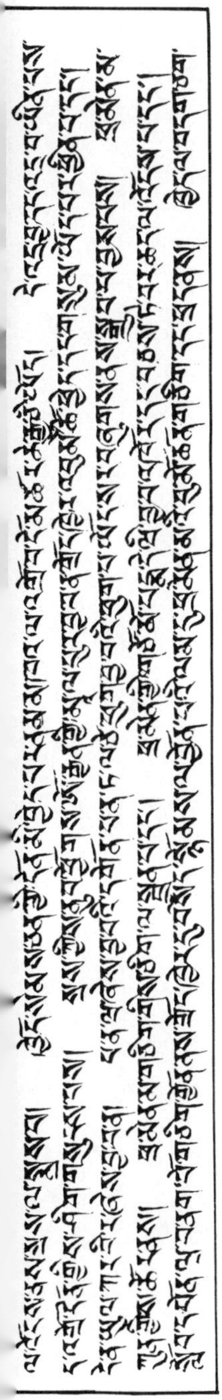

141

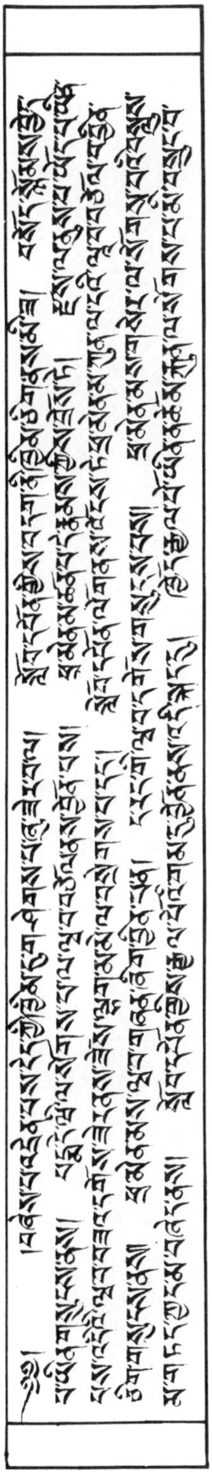

142

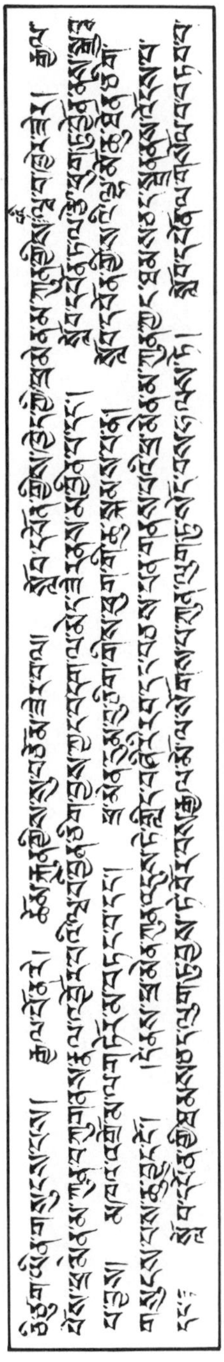

143

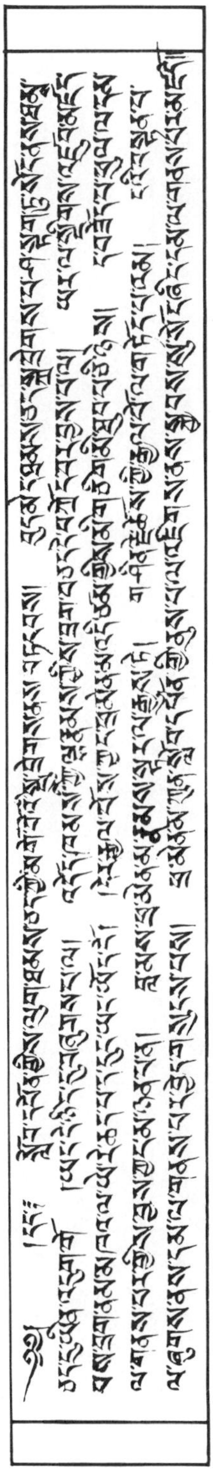

144

145

146

147

148

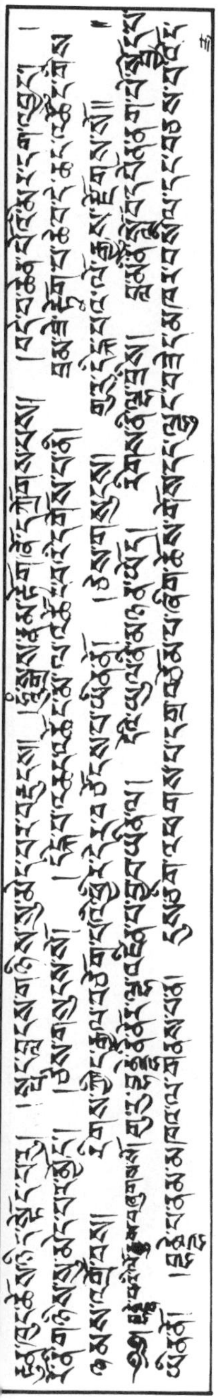

149

150

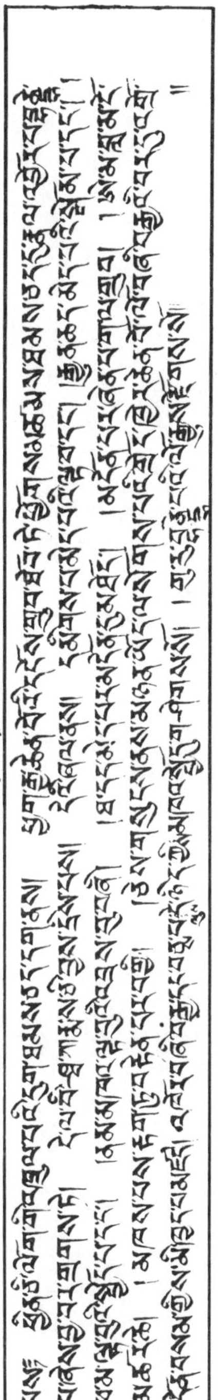

151

152

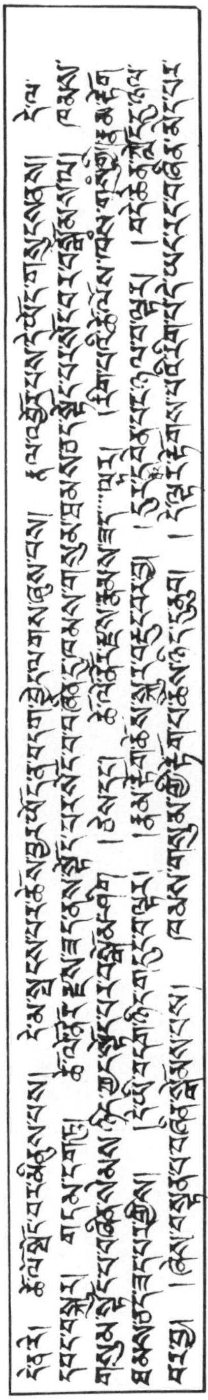

153

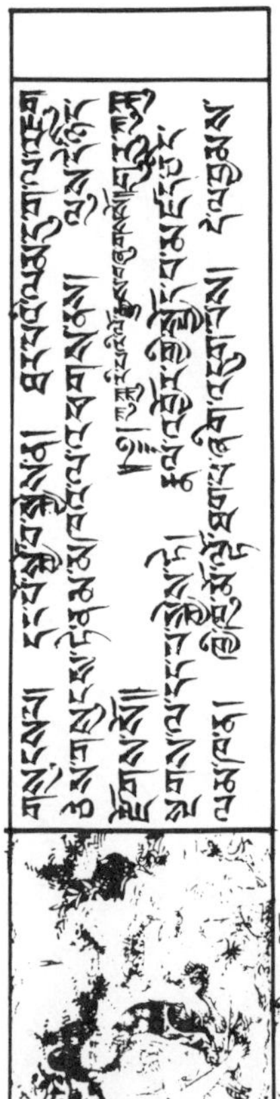

154

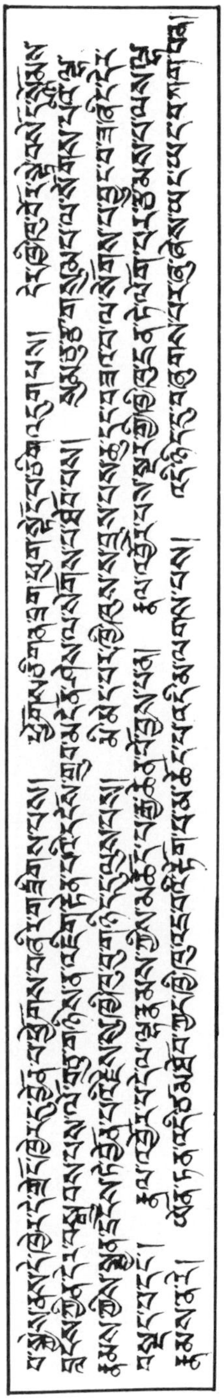

155

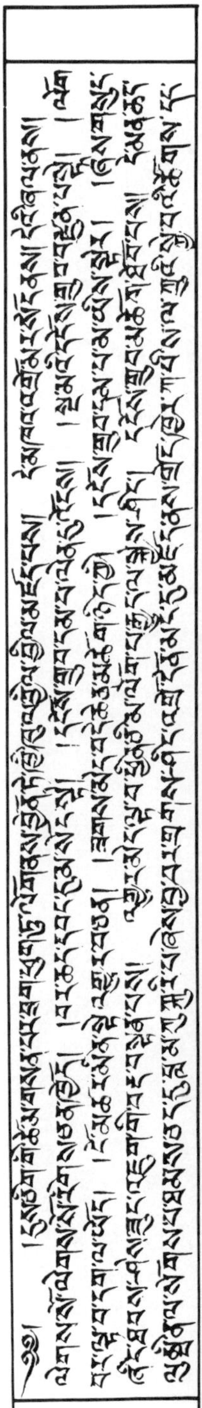

156

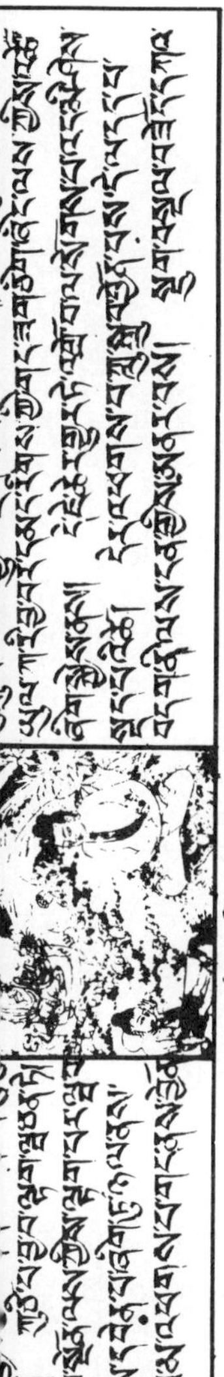

157

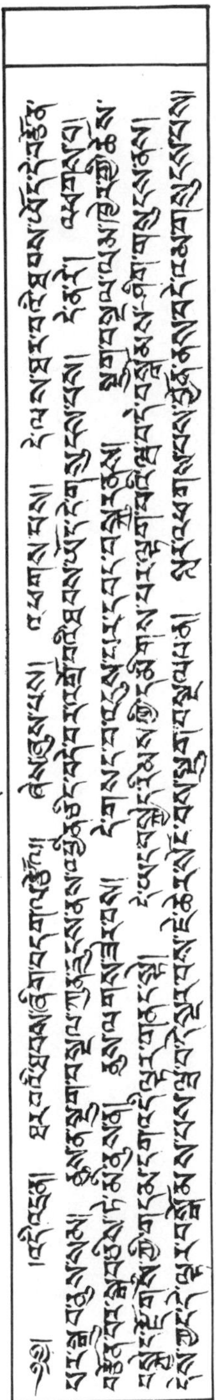

158

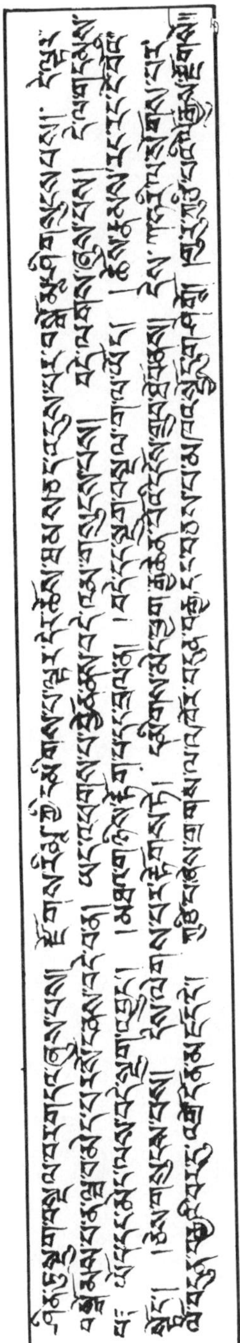

159

160

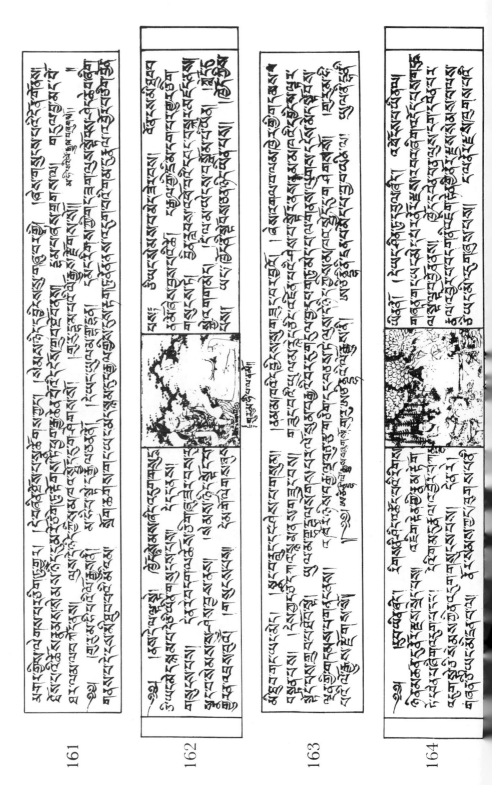

161

162

163

164

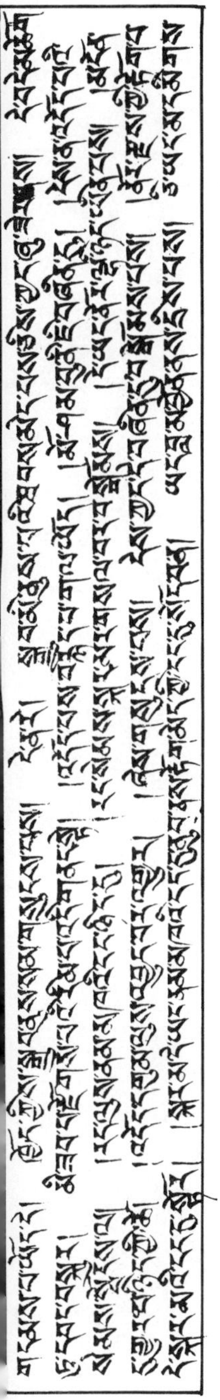

165

166

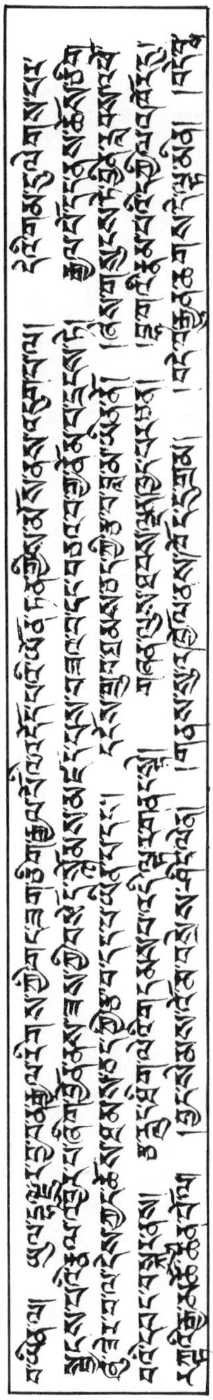

167

168

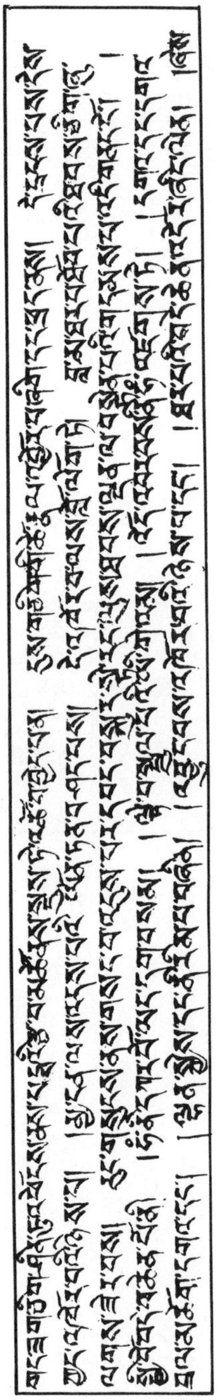

169

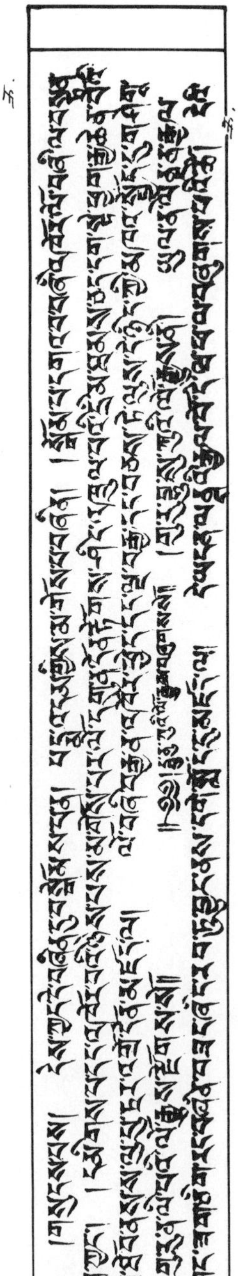

170

171

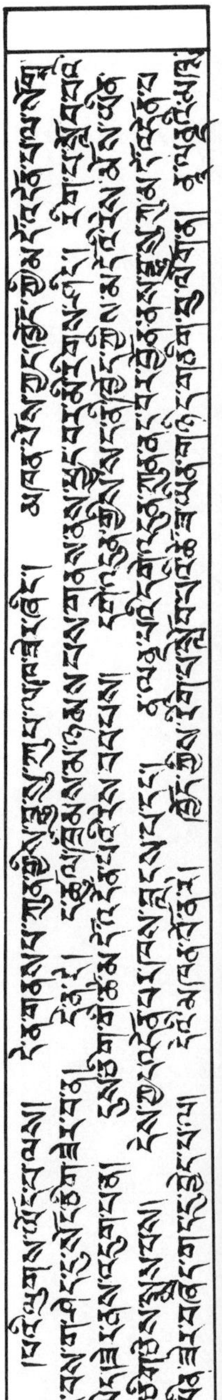

172

173

[illegible]
བསྐོར་བས་དེ་བས་འདུག་ནས་ཞུར་ཞེས་སྨྲས་པས། ངར་ང་ཡང་ཤེས་ཟེར་ནས་མ་ཉན་པར། མི་ཁྱེན་པོས་འཁྲུགས་པ་འཇམ་དཔལ་གྱི
ཕྱག་ནས་ཨ་ར་པ་ཙ་ན་བསྒྲུབས་ཏེ། སྔགས་འདི་མཚན་གཉིད་མ་ལོག་པར་བཟླས་ཤིག་ཟེར་ནས། སྔགས་ཀྱི་དམ་ས་པ་ཕྱིན་ནས་དེས
ཀྱང་མཚན་གཉིད་མ་ལོག་པར་བཟླས་པ་བརྟགས་ནས་སྔགས་བཟླས་པས། འཕགས་པ་འཇམ་དཔལ་དེར་དངོས་སུ་བྱོན་ནས། ཧཱུ་ལུ
ཀུ་པ་ཁྱོད་ཅི་བྱེད་གསུངས་པས། བདག་ལ་ཤར་པར་མཛོད་འདི་ན་པ་རི་རེ་མེས་བབ་ལགས་པས། འཕགས་པ་འཇམ་དཔལ་ལ་བགྲོལ

174

༄༅། །ཁའུ་དེ་བས་བ་ཡིན་ཞུས་པས། འཕགས་པའི་གསུང་ནས། ཁྱོད་ཀྱིས་ང་ངོ་ཤེས་སམ་གསུངས་པས། བདག་གིས་མ་འཚལ་ལགས་
ཞུས་པས། འཇམ་དཔལ་ཡིན་གསུང་བས། ཨོ་ན་བདག་ལ་ཤེས་རབ་ཀྱི་སྒྲུབ་ཆོག་ས་པའི་དངོས་གྲུབ་ཞུ་ཞུས་པས། འཕགས་པའི་ཞལ
ནས། ཁྱོད་ལ་དམ་རིག་པ་འཛིན་གྱིས་ནང་བར་མཛད་ཕྱིན་ཅི་ལོག་གསུང་ས་ནས་མི་སྣང་བར་གྱུར་ཏོ། །དེ་ནས་ནང་པར་མདོ་འདོན་པའི་དུས་སུ།
དགེ་བསྙེན་གྱི་ཀུན་དགའ་ར་བ་ར་རྒྱལ་པོ་ལ་སོགས་པའི་སྐྱེ་བོའི་ཚོགས་ཐམས་ཅད་ཧཱུ་ལུ་ཀུ་པས་མ་ངོ་འཚར་བ་ལ་ལྷ་ཡིས་ཞེས་གཅིག་ལ་ཅིག་སྨྲ་བ་དང་།
མེ་ཏོག་ལ་སོགས་མཆོད་པའི་ཡོ་བྱད་ཀུན་བྱེར་ནས་སྐྱེ་བོའི་ཚོགས་ཐམས་ཅད་བཞད་ཆ་ང་ཀྱི་ཆེ་དང་དུ་དེར་འབྱེན་པ་དང་། ཧཱུ་ལུ་ཀུ་པ་དགེ་བསྙེན་གྱི

175

གདུགས་མཆོད་གསོལ་ནས། ཞུམ་པ་མེད་པར་གཙུག་ལག་ཁང་གི་ཁྲིའི་སྟེང་དུ་བྱོན་ནས་བཞུགས་པའི་ཚིག་ཟིན་བྱིན་ཕྱུང་བར་འཕགས་པར་འདུག
ནས་ཐམས་ཅད་དྲི་ཆགས་པ་སྐྱེས་པ་ལ་མཐུན་ཡོལ་བས་བཅད་དེ། བདག་གིས་མ་དོ་སྟོར་སྒྲུང་བ་གཅིག་བཤད་དམ། མི་བྱུང་བ་ཅིག་བཤད་གསུངས་པས།
བརྗོད་ཀུན་གཅིག་ལ་གཅིག་ལྟ་ཞིང་། སྐྱེ་བོའི་ཚོགས་ཀུན་དང་། རྒྱལ་པོ་ཡང་གཞན་དགར་བྱེད་ལ། རྒྱལ་པོ་ན་རེ། ཁྱོད་ཀྱིས་ཟ་ལུགས་ཀྱང
སྨྲ་མི་འབྱུང་བ་གཅིག་ཤེས་ལ། ཉ་ལ་པ་དང་འཆགས་པའི་སྐྱོད་ལམ་ཀྱང་ལུར་མ་བྱུང་བ་ཞིན་ཕྱིན་པས། ཆོས་ཀྱང་སྨྲ་རམ་བྱུང་བ་གཅིག་ཤོད
ཅིག་ཟེར་བ་ལ། དེས་སྤྱོད་འཇུག་ལེའུ་བཅུའི་བདག་ཉིད་བ་ཤོད་ནས་ཐམས་མཁའ་ལ་འཕུར་བས། ཉ་ལ་ནུ་པའི་བརྗོད་ལྷ་བརྒྱད་དང་། རྒྱལ་པོ་དེ

176

༄༅། །ཞྭ་པ་ལ་ལ་སོགས་པ་སྐྱེ་བོའི་ཚོགས་ཐམས་ཅད་དང་བཅས་མི་རྟོག་སྟོར་བས་དབུས་ནུབ་ཙམ་དུ་ཆགས་ལ། འདི་ནི་ཧཱུ་ལུ་ཀུ་པ་མ་ཡིན་ཏེ་
མཁས་པར་འདུག་གོ་ཟེར་ནས། རྒྱལ་པོ་དང་པཎྜི་ཏ་ཀུན་གྱིས་ཤཱནྟི་དེ་ཝ་བ་ར་བ་ཏ་གསལ་ལ། རྒྱལ་པོ་དང་པཎྜི་ཏ་ཀུན་དང་རྒྱལ་ཞི་བ་ར་གྲགས་པས
ཞི་བ་ལྷ་ཞེས་གྲགས་པ་ཡིན་ནོ། །དེ་ནས་པཎྜི་ཏ་རྣམས་ཀྱིས་དེ་རིང་འདུས་པ་ཀུན་གྱིས་དེའི་འགྲེལ་པ་ཞིག་མཛད་པར་ཞུས་པ་ས་ཕྱིས་མཛད་ལ། དེ་དག
གི་མཁན་པོར་ཞུས་པས་མ་གནང་བར། ཆོས་གོས་དང་ལྷུང་བཟེད་ལ་སོགས་པ་རབ་ཏུ་བྱུང་བའི་ཡོ་བྱད་དཀོན་མཆོག་དང་གཙུག་ལག་ཁང
དུ་ཕུལ་ནས། མཁན་པོ་དང་བང་ལ་འདུན་གྱིས་མཆོར་བར་བྲིས་ཕྱིན་ཏེ། རི་མ་ཀྱིས་ཛེ་ཀ་རི་བྲ་བའི་གྲོང་ཁྱེར་འབུམ་མཚོ་ཕྱིན་ཡོད་པར་ཤིང

177

178

179

180

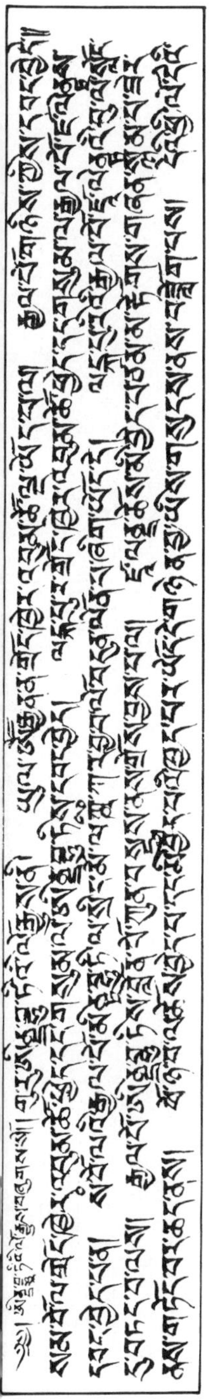

181

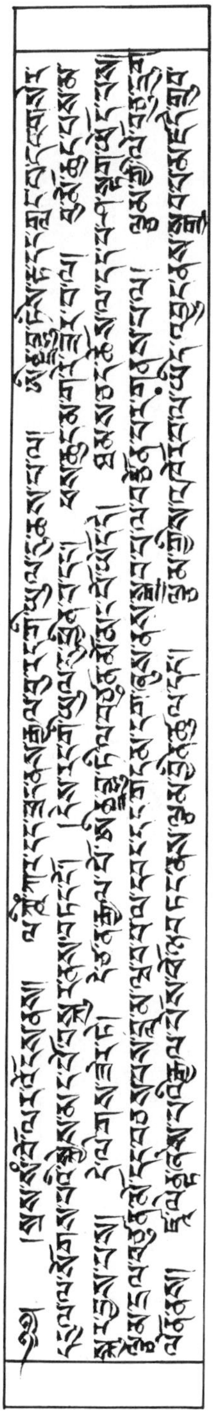

182

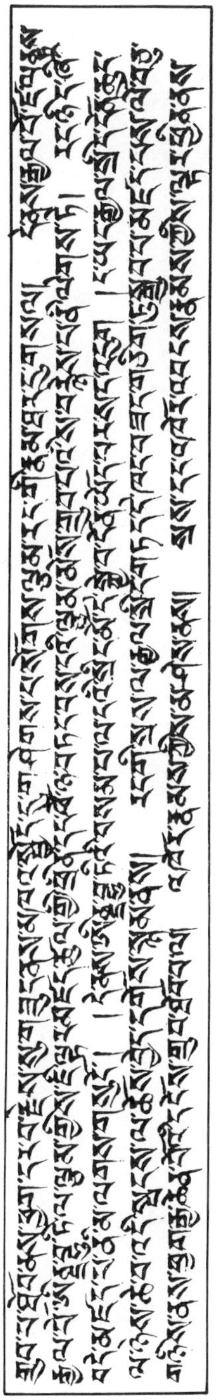

183

184

185 ཀོ་བའི་ལོ་རྒྱུས་ནི། ཡུ་ལེ་རྟོག་ལར་ཁ་ཟས་འཚོང་བའི་རིགས་ཀྱི་གང་ཟག་གཅིག་གིས་རྡུལ་རྡུག་ཙུ་ཏྲ་ལ་འཁོར་བ་ཞིག་ལ་འཚོ་བ་དྲངས་བས། ཞག་གཅིག
རྣལ་འབྱོར་པ་ནར། ཁྱེད་དང་ལ་བསྐོན་པ་ཀུར་བྱེད་པ་ཅི་ཡིན་གསུངས་པས། དེས་ཁྲིམ་པའི་ལ་མཆོག་གས་དགོས་པ་ལ་གས་ཞུས་པས། འོན་ཁྲིམ་པའི
ལམ་རྒྱུ་གས་སྐྱ་བ་ནུས་པ་མ་གསུངས་པས། ཚུལ་ལགས་ཟེར་ནས། དེས་བྱིན་རླབས་འཛོབ་པའི་དབང་བསྐུར་མཛད་དེ། སེམས་ཉིད་དོ་སྤྲོད
བུའི་གདམས་པ་འདི་ལྟར་གནང་ངོ་། །རང་སེམས་ཡིད་བཞིན་ནོར་བུ་ལ། །འཁོར་འདས་བྱེ་བྲག་རྣམ་པར་འཆར། །རྟོགས་དང་མ་རྟོགས་གཉིས
ཡིན་པས། །འགྱུར་མེད་སེམས་ཉིད་ངང་ལ་ལྟོས། །གཉིས་འཛིན་རྣམ་རྟོག་ག་ལ་འཁྱུད། །རང་བཞིན་མེད་ཕྱིར་དེ་ཉིད་དང་། །ཆོས་རྣམས་གང

186 ༄༅། །ཡང་འགྲུབ་པ་མེད། །མ་རྟོགས་འཁྲུལ་པའི་འདོད་པས་བཅིངས། །ཅེས་གསུངས་པས། དེས་ཀྱང་སྒོང་བ་རང་གི་སེམས་སྒྲུ་གོ །
སེམས་རིས་འགྲོ་འོང་མེད་པས་གནས་ལུགས་ཀྱི་ངང་དུ་གོ་ནས། རང་སེམས་འགྱུར་བ་མེད་པའི་དོན་ལ་གནས་པས་ཟླ་བ་དྲུག་ན་འཁྲུལ་པའི་རྟོག
པ་འགགས་ནས་རང་སེམས་གཉུག་མའི་དོན་རྟོགས་ཏེ། གཅན་གཟན་ལྷ་ར་དུ་ར་ཁྲིད་འཁོར་པར་བྱེད་ཅིང་། ཉེས་སྟོན་པའི་སློབ་པས་གྲོང་དང་
གྲོང་ཁྱེར་དུ་འོངས་ནས། མི་ཀ་བགྲང་ནས་འཇིགས་འཇིགས་སུ་བལྟས་པས། སྐྱེ་བོ་དག་ཟླ་མ་འཇིགས་འཇིགས་སུ་ལྟ་བ་ཟེར། ཕྱོགས་ཐམས་ཅད
དུ་མེ་ཀོ་པ་ཞེས་གྲགས་སོ། །དེས་ཟབ་མོའི་ཆོས་ཀྱི་གདམ་འཕྱུ་མང་དུ་བསྟན་ནས། མཐར་རྟོགས་པ་ལ་སློགས་པ་བརྗོད་དེས་ལུས་དེ་ཉིད་ཀྱིས་མཁའ་

187 སྤྱོད་དུག་ཤེགས་སོ། །གྷུ་མི་ཀོ་པའི་ལོ་རྒྱུས་རྫོགས་སོ།།
པའི་ཡུལ་བྲབ་ནས་ཞག་བཞི་རྒྱུན་པ་འི་སོ་ན། གནས་དང་
ཡོད་པའི་ཚོ། སློབ་དཔོན་ཤཱ་ཀྱི་བ་སྒྲོ་ཡིའི་རྒྱལ་པོ་ཡིས་སྨྲ
ཡུལ་ཡང་མེད་པ་འིས་འདིར་བདག་ཉི་འདི་བ་ཤིག་ལ་འདིར
གསུངས་པ། ཉི་བོ་བརྗོད་བའི་སྒྲུབ་གདམས་ངག་ལ་ཡོད

༄༅། །ཀོ་ཏ་ལི་པའི་ལོ་རྒྱུས་བཞུགས་སོ།། གྲུ་རུ་ཀོ་ཏ་ལི་པའི་ལོ་རྒྱུས་ནི། ར་མེ་ཤྭ
ཡུལ་གྱི་ཕྱེད་དུ། ཀོ་ཏ་ལི་པ་རྟོག་ཙེ་པ་རི་བོ་ཞིག་བཀོ་ཞིང་
དྲངས་ནས་སྐྱར་ཡུལ་དབུས་སུ་ལོག་འབྱོན་པ་དང་འཕྲད་དེ།
གནས་དང་ཡུལ་བྱེད་པ་ཡིན་ཞེས་ཞུས་པས། ཤཱནྟི་པས
ན་ཁྱོད་ལ་དགོས་སམ་གསུངས་པ་དང་། དགོས་ཞེས་ཞུས

188 ༄༅ །པས༔ དེའི་ཞལ་ནས། ཁྱོད་ཀྱི་ལས་ནི་འདི་ལྟ་བུས། །ལུས་ནི་ངལ་བ་རབ་ཏུ་འགྱུར་བས་ན། །ལས་ནི་ཤིན་ཏུ་ངན་པ་སྟེ། །ཁྱིམ་ཅི་ལོག་གི
ལས་དྲུག་ཡིན། །སའི་རྐོ་བ་ནི་སྤྱིན་པ་དང་། །གཞན་ལ་མི་གནོད་ཚུལ་ཁྲིམས་རྫོང་། །སྡུག་བསྔལ་བཟོད་པའི་བཟོད་པ་དང་། །དེ་ལ་བརྩོན
པས་བརྩོན་འགྲུས་དང་། །དེ་ལ་མ་ཡེངས་བསམ་གཏན་དང་། །དེ་ཤེས་པ་ཡེ་ཤེས་རབ་ཕྱེ། །ཁྱིམ་ཅི་ལོག་གི་ལས་དྲུག་པོ། །སྙིང་རྗེ་ལ
ཡང་དག་ལུས་དྲུག་གིས། །སྙམ་ལ་གཟུགས་སྦྱིན་པ་དང་། །རང་རྒྱུད་བསྲུང་བའི་ཚུལ་ཁྲིམས་དང་། །སེམས་ཉིད་བཟོད་པའི་བཟོད་པ་དང་། །དུ
[illegible]

189

190

191

192

193

[illegible]

194

[illegible]

[illegible]

195

[illegible]

196

[illegible]

[illegible]

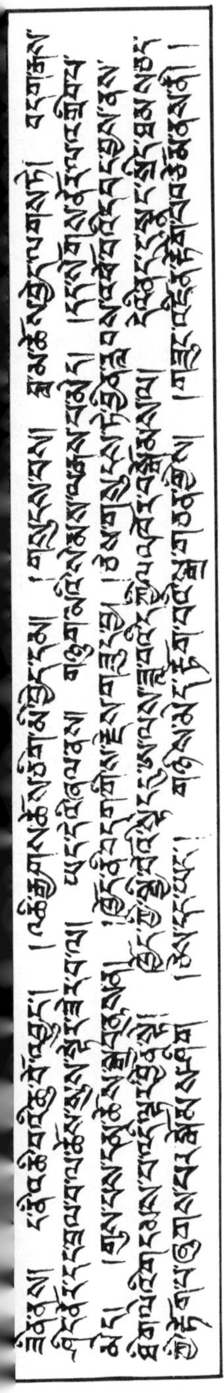

197

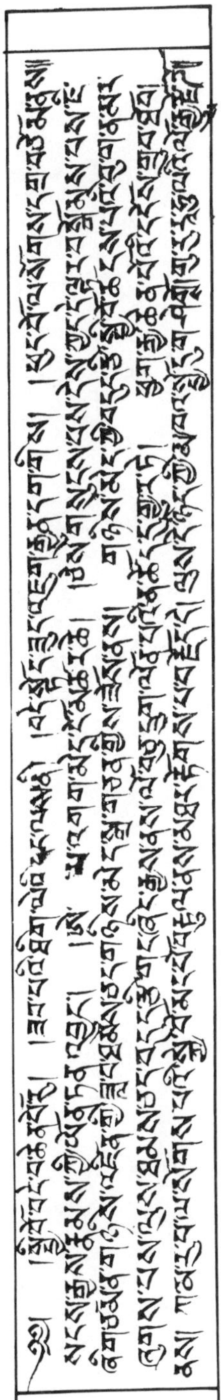

198

199

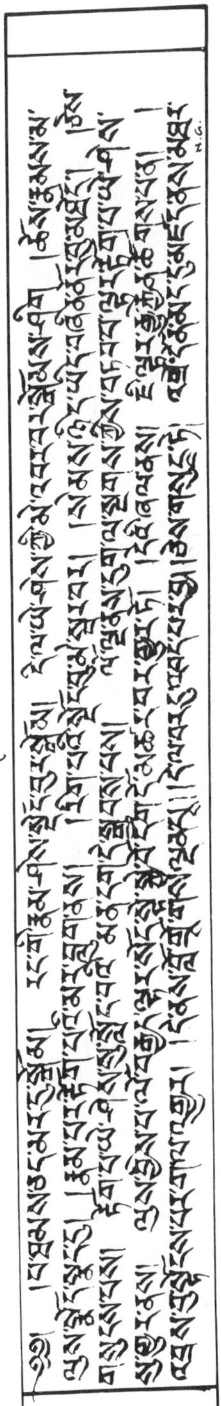

200

201

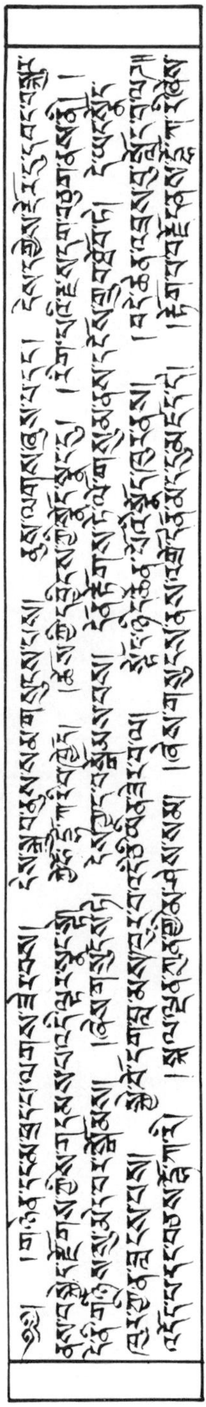

202

203

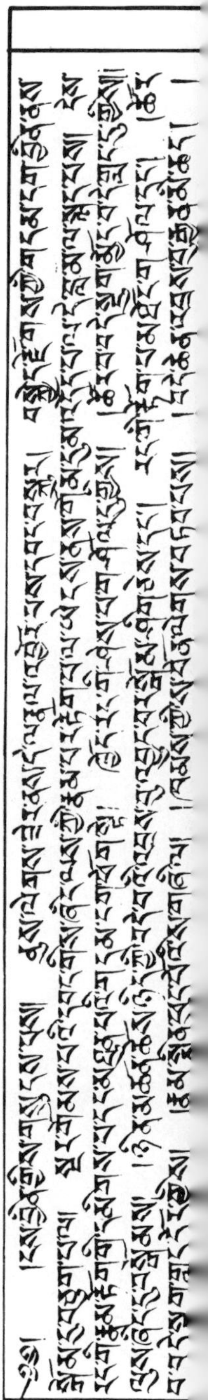

204

205

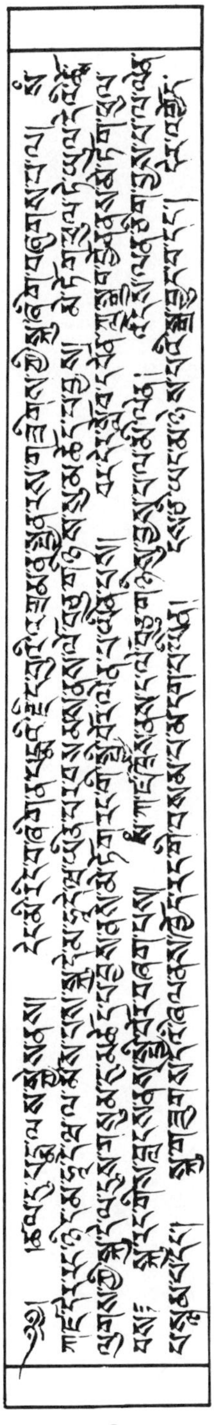

206

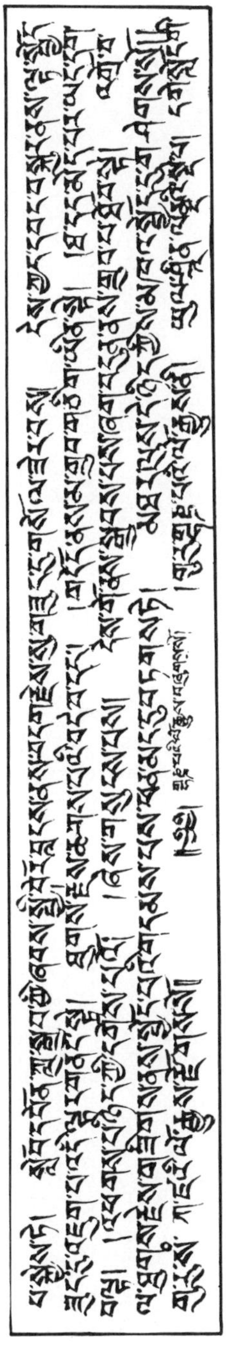

207

208

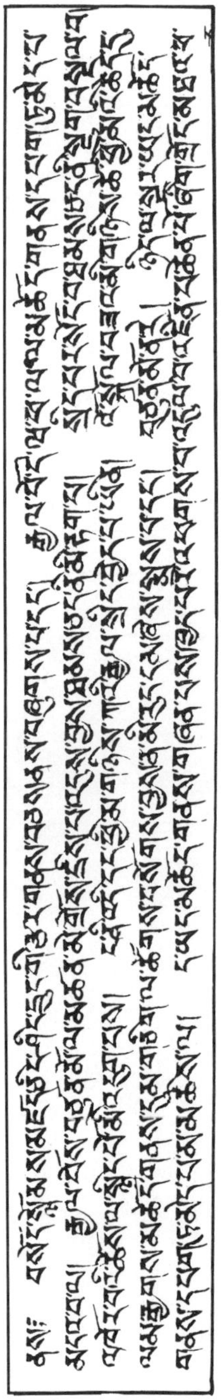

209

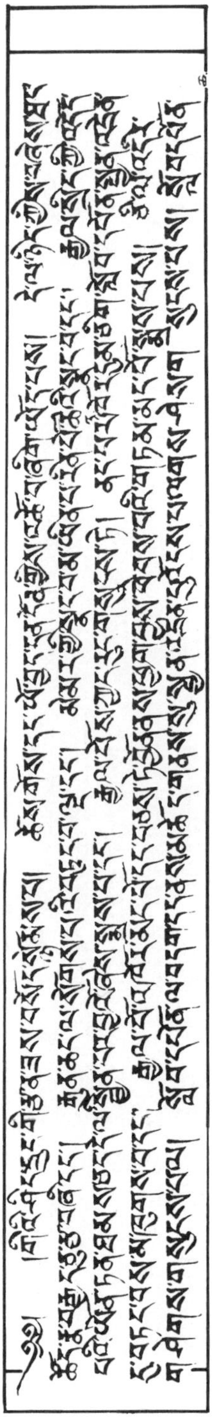

210

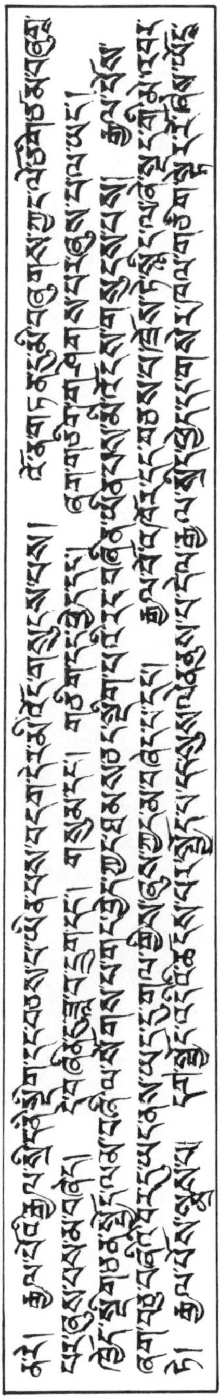

211

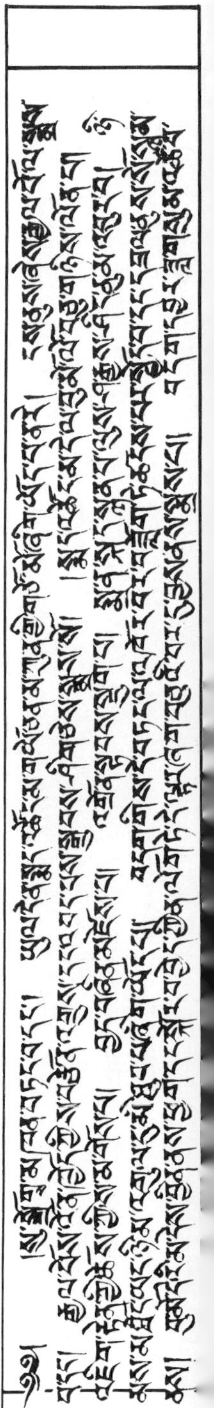

212

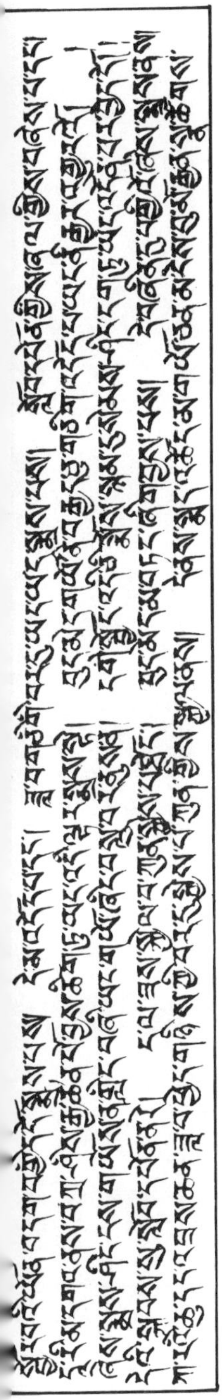

213

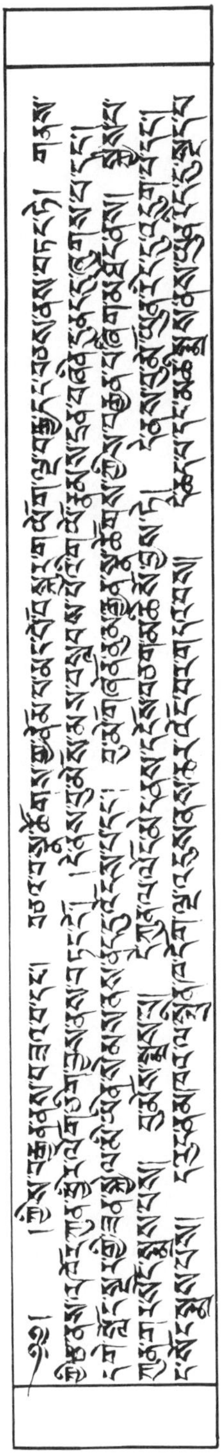

214

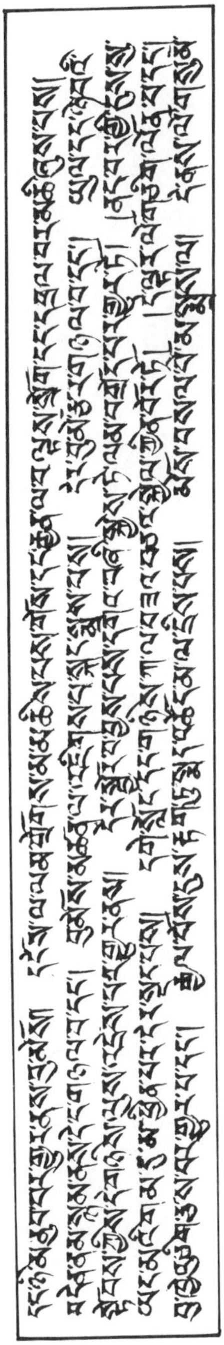

215

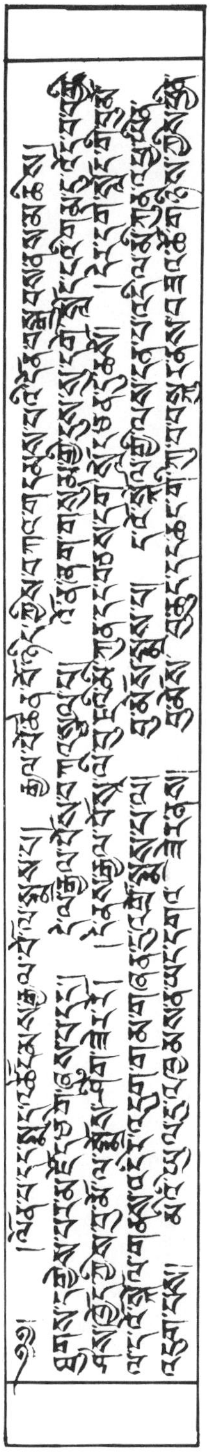

216

217 པ་དང་། ལམ་བར་དུ་རྒྱལ་པོ་དང་ཕྲད་ནས་གླང་པོ་ཆེའི་སྟེང་ནས་བབས་ཏེ་ཞུས་པ། དགེ་སློང་གི་གོས་ཀྱི་ནང་ན་ཅི་ཡོད། བུ་མོ་འདི་ཁྱོད་ཀྱི་ཅི་ཡིན
ཞུས་པ། དགེ་སློང་ནའི་གོས་ཀྱི་ནང་ན་བུ་ཆུང་དང་ཀུ་བ་ཡོད། བུ་མོ་འདི་དེའི་ཆུང་མ་ཡིན་ཞུས་པས། རྒྱལ་པོ་ན་རེ། ངས་སྔོན་དང་པོ་འདི་དུས་སུ་ཁྱོད་
ཀྱི་གཙུག་གི་ནམ་དུ་མི་བོ་དང་ཟེར་བ་ལ། ད་ལྟ་ཁྱེད་རང་རང་བུ་དང་ཆུང་མ་ཅི་བྱ། ཤིག་ཅན་ཅིག་ཁྱེད་རང་འདྲ་ག་སྨྲས་པས། སློབ་དཔོན་གྱིས་ལ་ཉེས་པ
མེད་པ་ལ་སྐུར་པ་མ་འདེབས་ཞིག་གསུངས་པས། སླར་ཡང་སྐུར་བ་བཞིན་དུ་བཏང་བས། སློབ་དཔོན་གྱི་བུ་ཆུང་དང་ཀུ་བ་ལ་ཕྲལ་བས་པས།
ས་འི་ལྷ་མོ་འཇིགས་ཏེ་ས་གས་ནས་ཆུ་རྡོལ་བ་དང་། ཆུ་ལེན་ངས་བུ་ཆུང་དེ་རྡོ་རྗེ་དང་ཀུ་བ་དྲིལ་བུར་སོང་། འོད་ཟེར་བདེ་མཆོག་དང་། བུ་མོ་ཡུམ་རྡོ་རྗེ

218 ༄༅། །ཞག་མོར་སོང་ནས། རྒྱལ་པོ་འཁོར་དང་བཅས་པའི་ཉམས་མ་ཁའི་སྟེང་དུ་བདེ་མཆོག་ཡབ་ཡུམ་རྡོ་རྗེ་དྲིལ་བུ་དང་བཅས་པ་རང་བྱུང་བ་དང་།
རྒྱལ་པོ་ལ་སོགས་པས་མ་གྲིན་གཅིག་ཏུ་ཉམས་མ་ཁ་ལ་བལྟ་སྣང་ནས་སློབ་དཔོན་ལ་སྐྱབས་སུ་མཆི་ཞེས་ཞལ་གསོལ་བ་བ་འདེབས་ཀྱང་རྡོ་རྗེ་ཕྲེང་བའི་ཏིང
ངེ་འཛིན་ལས་མ་བཞེངས་པ་དང་། སྔ་བའི་ཚོགས་ཐམས་ཅད་དབང་གསལ་བའི་རྒྱུ་མཐུ་ཉམས་ཆེན་ལས་གྲུབ་པན། འཕགས་པ་སྤྱན་རས་གཟིགས་སྣང་
ཅིག་དེར་བ་ཞིག་ས་ནས། ས་གས་པའི་རྒྱ་ཁ་ནས་ཀྱིས་བ་ཀ་གནས། རྒྱལ་པོ་ཁྲབ་ལ་འཁོར་དང་བཅས་པ་དབུགས་དབྱུང་བ་བར་མཛད་དོ། །དེ་ནས
སླར་ཡང་བླ་མ་ལ་གསོལ་བ་བཏབ་པས། དེ་ཧཱུྃ་བྱ་གཅིག་བསྒྲགས་པས་རྒྱ་ཐམས་ཅད་མི་སྣང་བར་གྱུར་ཏོ། །དེ་ནས་རྒྱལ་པོ་འཁོར་དང་བཅས་པས

219 བཟོད་པར་གསོལ་བས། འཕགས་པའི་སྐུ་ཡང་དེ་ཉིད་དུ་རྡོ་ཡི་རང་བྱུང་དུ་བོད་སྣེ། ད་དུང་ཡང་ཞབས་འོག་ནས་ཆུ་བྲུ་རེ་ཙམ་འདུག་ཟེར་རོ། །
དེ་ནས། རྒྱལ་པོ་ལ་སོགས་པ་ལ་དེས་གདམས་ངག་གསུངས་པ་ནི། རྗེ་ལྷ་ར་སྣང་དང་དུག་ཉིད་ཁྱང་། རང་གི་ངོ་བོ་ཅིག་ཉིད་ལས། འཕྲུལ་བུ་ཡང
ཉིད་གཉིས་སུ་འབྱུང་། །དེ་བཞིན་སྣང་བྱ་གཉིས་པོ་གཉིས། །ངོ་བོ་ཅིག་ཏུ་ཐ་དད་མེད། །མ་ཁས་པས་རྟོག་ལས་སྐྱོང་མི་བེད། །ཕྱིས་པ་མི་མཁས
པ་དགག་གིས། །མ་རྟོགས་དུག་ལྔས་འཁོར་བར་འཁྱམས། །ཞེས་གསུངས་པས། རྒྱལ་པོ་ལ་སོགས་པའི་སྐྱེ་བོའི་ཚོགས་ཐམས་ཅད་མི
ལོག་པའི་སྨིན་བསྒྱུར་ རིགས་ནས་ཅིག་ཏུ་མཐུན་པར་དང་བར་གྱུར་ནས། འགྲོ་བ་དཔག་ཏུ་མེད་པ་ལམ་ལ་བཀོད་པར་གྱུར་ཏོ། ཆོས་ཏུ་ཡང

220 ༄༅། །དྲིལ་བུ་བ་ཞེས་བརྗོད་དེ་ནས། དེང་བ་ནའང་སློབ་དཔོན་དྲིལ་བུ་བ་ཞེས་གྲགས་པ་ཐམས་ཅད་དུ་གྲགས་སོ། །བུ་མོ་དེས་སློབ་དཔོན་ལ
སྐྱེ་བ་ལྔ་མ་ལ་ལན་དྲུག་གི་བར་དུ་རྒྱལ་ཁྲིམས་ལ་བར་ཆད་བྱས་པ་ཡིན་ལ། ད་རེས་ཀྱང་རྒྱལ་ཁྲིམས་ལ་བར་ཆད་བྱས་པས། སློབ་དཔོན་ཉིད
ཀྱི་དང་བུག་ཉིས་འཛིན་གྱི་རྣམ་རྟོག་ཐམས་ཅད་སྦྱོར་ནས་རྒྱུད་སྨིན་པའི་སློབ་མ་ཀྱིས་ལམ་དུ་སོང་བ་ཡིན་ནོ། །ཐམས་ཅད་བྱུག་རྡོ་རྗེ་བུ་མོ་དེས་ཀྱང
སྟར་ནས་བསྟེན་པ་ཀུ་རུ་ཕྲིས་པའི་ཕན་ཡོན་ཀྱིས་ད་རེས་རྫོགས་དགའ་ཡིན་གསུང་། དེ་ལྟ་བུའི་ཡོན་ཏན་དང་ལྡན་པའི་སློབ་དཔོན་དྲིལ་བུ་པ་ལ་གསུམ
ཉིད་ཀྱིས་གཉིས་ཀ་མ་ཁ་བ་སྤྱོད་དག་ཤིགས་སོ། །གུ་རུ་ཏྲཱི་ཛུ་པ་ སློབ་དཔོན་དྲིལ་བུ་པའི་ལོ་རྒྱུས་རྫོགས་སོ།།

221

222

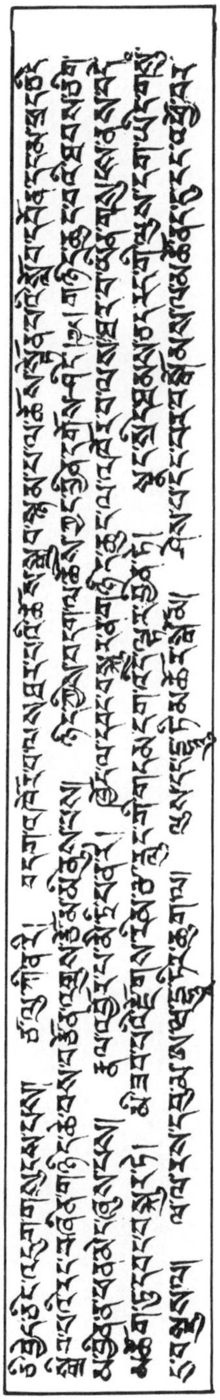

223

224

225

226

227

228

229

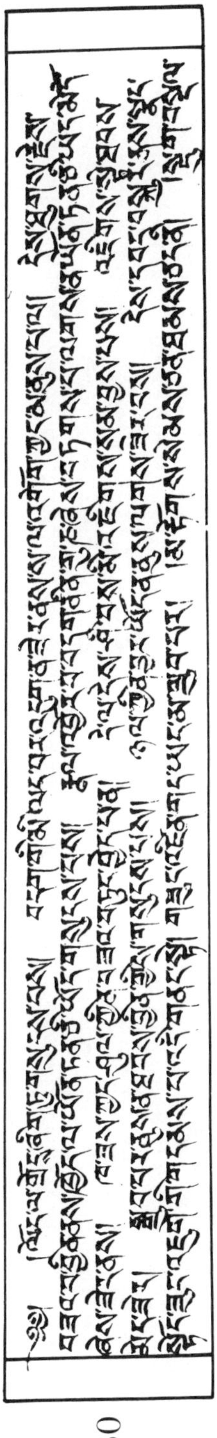

230

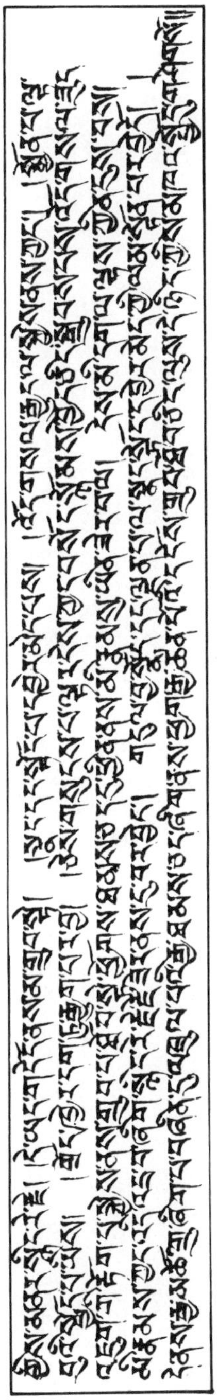

231

232

233

234

235

236

237

[illegible]

བར་དུ་ཚེ་རབས་ཀྱི་རྣམས་གཅིག་ནས་ཀ་རྣ་ལ་ཚེ་རབས་ཐུགས་ཀྱི་སྤྱན་ངས་བསྒྲུབས་ལ་ཆེན་པོ་སྦྱོར་སྒོ་འཕགས་པ་ལ་སྒྲི་ཕྱུགས་ཆེན་པོ་ཡང་བ་དང་ནས།
འཕགས་པ་ལ་ཀྱང་ཞལ་ངར་ངོས་སུ་བསྟན་ཏེ། ཇི་དེ་ཡི་བླ་མ་དང་ཡིད་ཕྱེ་བས། དཔྱེ་རང་དེ་བ་གཉེར་བར་མ་བྱེད་པར་ཕྱིར་ལོག་ལ་བཀའ་ལ་བྲན་མ
དུར་བར་ཕྱེས་ཤིག་གསུངས་པས། དེ་དག་འདུ་བ་ནམ་མ་ཁར་ལ་ཞུགས་དེ་ཙམ་པ་ཀ་ཡ་རེ་རེ་ཕྱིན་པས། ཐམས་ཅད་ཀྱིས་མཐོང
བས་ངོ་མཚར་སྐྱེས་དེ་ག་དམས་པ་ཞུས་པས། སྔར་སྔོན་དཔྱེ་ར་མེ་དཀྱིག་དམ་པ་པ་ཡང་གསུངས་ཏེ། དེ་མན་ཆད་བླ་མ་བཅ་དེ་པ་ཞེས

238

༄༅། །བྲམ་ཟེ་གྲགས་ཅན་དཔལ་ལྡན་དེ་ཉིད་ཀྱིས་མ་ཁ་ལ
༄། ཙམ་པ་ཀ་ཡིའི་ལོ་རྒྱུས་བཞུགས་སོ། །གུ་རུ་ཙམ་པ་ཀ་འི་ལོ་རྒྱུས་ནི། ཡུལ
ཇི་ལ་རྒྱལ་བུ་གཅིག་ལ་རྒྱ་ལ་བསྒྲོད་ཀྱི་འཁོར་བ་ཡོད་ལ་སྨྲ་མ
ཇི་ལ་དུ་ཚོས་བརྩིགས་ཤིང་རྒྱལ་སྲིད་ཀྱི་བདེ་བས་སྨྱོས་ནས
ཚལ་ཀྱི་ནང་དུ་མེ་ཏོག་གི་ཁང་བ་ཡིག་ཀས་པ་རྒྱས་ཏེ་འདུག

རྗེ་གུ་རུ་ཙམ་པ་ཀ་པ་ནམ

ཕྱིར་ཏུག་ཤིག་གསུངས་སོ། །གུ་རུ་པཎ་ཏི་པའི་ལོ་རྒྱུས་རྫོགས་སོ།
ཙམ་པ་ཀ་ཡིས་ཀྱང་། མི་རྟོག་མེད་ལས་བརྟགས་པ་ཡིན་ནོ།
རྩེ་གསུ་ཤིང་ལོ་རྣམས་ཀྱི་བྲི་ལ་རྒྱལ་མེད་བཅིག་ཡོད་ལ།
ཕྱི་མ་མི་ནུས་ལ། རྒྱལ་པོ་དེ་མི་རྟོག་ཙམ་པ་ཀ་ཡི་སྔ་དམ་
པའི་སྐྱུ་དང་སྒྱུ་མ་གུང་མ་རྟོག་ཙམ་པ་ཀ །ཁྱེད་གས་ཙམ།

239

དེ་ཞིམ་པོ་འབྲུས་བདེ་ལྷ་བུ་འདི་ན་གསང་བ་ནང་ལ་འཇོར་བ་གཅིག་གིས་དེ་ལ་བསོད་སྙོམས་བླངས་པས། རྒྱལ་པོས་ཀྱང་ཞབས་བཀུར།
སྟན་བཏིང་བ་ལ་སོགས་པ་བཀུར་ནས་བཞེས་ཚ་བཟང་ལ་ཏེ་དེས་ཆོས་གསུངས་པས། རྒྱལ་པོ་ལ་འཁོར་དང་བཅས་པ་ཐམས་ཅད་ཀྱིས་དེ་མཆོད་
གནས་སུ་ཕུལ་ཏེ་བཞུགས་པ་ན། རྒྱལ་པོ་ན་རེ། ཁྱོད་འཁོར་བས་ཡུལ་མང་པོ་ར་ཕྱིན་ནས། མེ་ཏོག་འདི་འདྲ་བ་དང་བདག་འདྲ་བའི
རྒྱལ་པོ་གཞན་ཅན་གཟིགས་སམ་ཞུས་པས། དེ་ན་རེ། མེ་ཏོག་ཙམ་པ་ཀ་ནི་དྲི་མ་ཆེ་ལྷན་འགྱུར་ཀྱང་། རང་གི་ལུས་ལ་དྲི་མ་སྣ་ཚོགས་དེ་མ
ཡིན། །རྒྱལ་པོ་ཡི་རྒྱལ་སྲིད་གཞན་ལས་ཁྱད་པར་འཕགས་གྱུར་ཀྱང་། །འཆི་བར་གྱུར་བའི་ཚེ་ཡང་མེད་པར་འགྲོ། །ཞེས་གསུངས་པས།
N.G.

240

༄༅། །རྒྱལ་པོས་བརྟགས་པས་ལུས་ལ་ཞེན་པ་དང་ལོག་ཏུ་སོང་ནས། སླར་དེ་ལ་གདམས་ངག་ཞུས་པས། དེས་དང་པོ་ར་ལས
རྒྱུ་འབྲས་བསྟན། དེ་ནས་དབང་བསྐུར་བྱས། གདམས་པ་ལམ་བསྐྱེད་རྫོགས་གནང་བས། དེའི་རྣམ་རྟོག་མེ་ཏོག་ལ་སོང་ནས་སྒོམ
ཚུལ་འདི་ལྟ་བུ། རྟོག་པ་ལས་བྱེ་རྒྱུ་མིང་དམས་པ་འདི་ལྟར་གནང་ངོ་། །སྣང་ཙམ་ཉིད་ནས་སྟོང་པ་ནས། །བློ་མ་ཞེན་དང་མི་རྟོག
ལ། ། ཟང་སེམས་སུ་དབྱེར་མེད་གནས་བསྒྱེད། །ཟག་མེད་བདུད་རྩི་སྦྲང་རྩིའི་གསུམ། །དེ་བཙོག་ཏུ་བསྒོམ་བ་ན། །འབྲས་བུ་བདེ་ཆེན་འགྱུར
བར་འགྱུར། །དུག་བ་རྡོ་རྗེ་འཆང་ཆེན་བཅོ། །བཀའ་ཡིན་ཕྱི་ཚོམས་མེད་པར་བསྒོམས་ཤིས་གསུངས་པས་དེས་ཀྱང་ལོ་བཅུ་གཉིས་བསྒོམས
N.G.

241

242

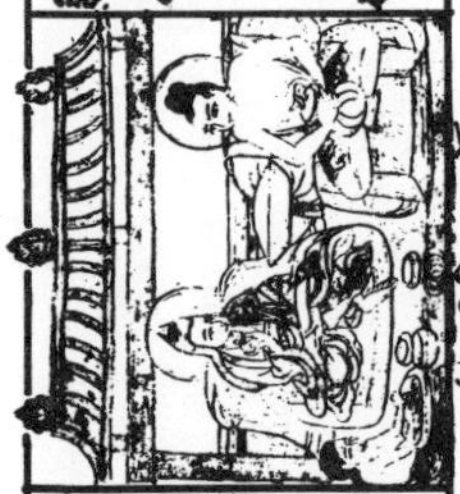

243

244

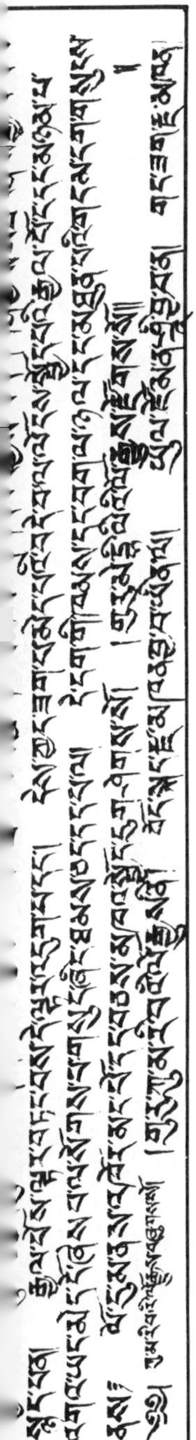

245

246

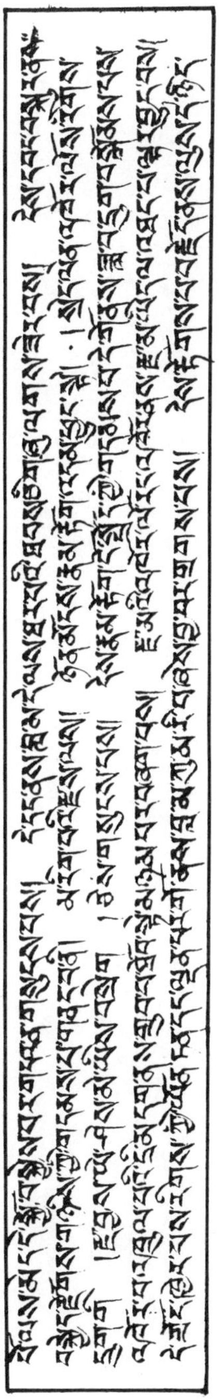

247

248

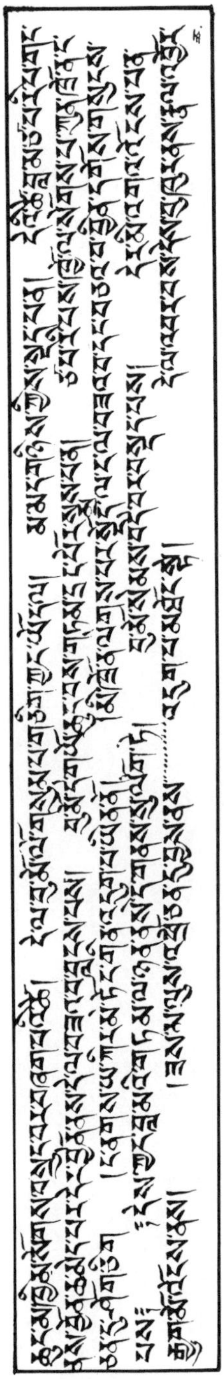

249

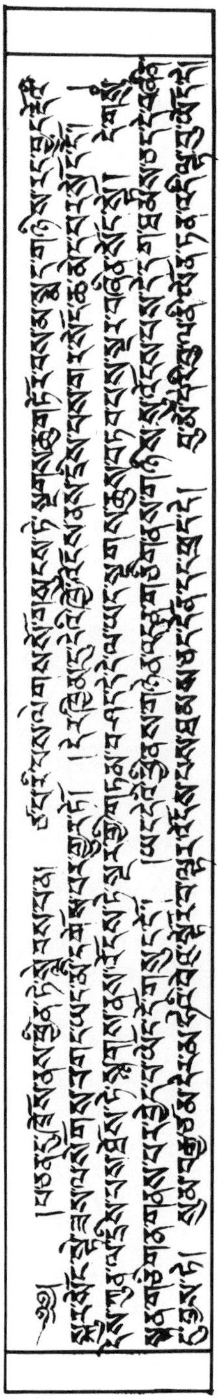

250

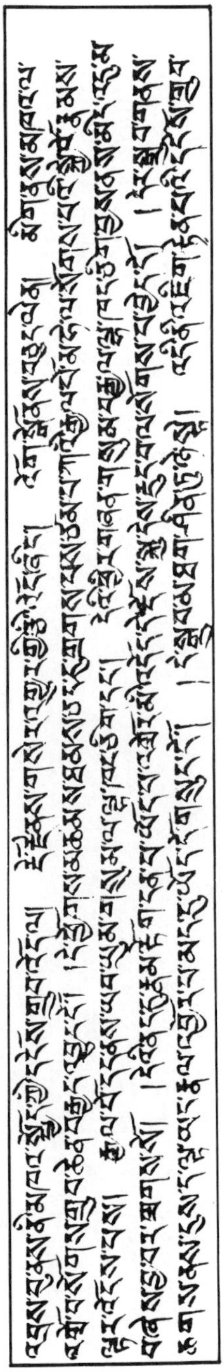

251

252

253 ཞིང༔ གསོལ་ཆེ་མ་བྱས་ཅི་བྱེད། རང་གི་རིགས་དང་མཚམས་པའི་ཁྱིམ་ཐབ་གཅིག་ལེན་མོད་ཟེར་བས། དེའི་ཞུ་ལ་ནས། བདག་ནི་འཁོར་བས་
འཇིགས་ཤིང་སྐྲག་པན། ཐར་པ་བདེ་ཆེན་མཆོག་ནི་སྒྲུབ་པར་བྱེད། དེ་ཡང་རྗེ་བཙུན་བཟང་འདི་ལ་མ་བསླབས་ན། གྲོགས་ཀྱི་འདི་འདྲ་རྟེན་དང་པ་རོག་ལ་འཁྱེར།།
དེས་ན་རྗེ་བཙུན་བཟང་འདི་ནི་རིན་པོ་ཆེན་འདི། །ཁྱིམ་ཐབ་མི་གཅིག་ཅར་ནང་དུ་བཅས་པ་ན། །དགོས་འདོད་ཀྱི་འཛོམས་ས་ཕྱུག་བསྒྱུ་ལ་སྣ་ཚོགས་འབྱུང་། །
དེ་ལྟར་རྗེ་གསན་ནས་བདག་གི་ཁྱིམ་ཐབ་སྤྱོད་རྩ། །ཞེས་གསུངས་པས་དེ་ལ་དང་ནས་བཞིན་སྐྱེམས་དྲངས་ཏེ། ང་ལ་ཐར་པ་ཐོབ་པའི་ཐབས་
ཅིག་ཞུ་ཟེར་བས། དེ་རང་གི་ཁྱིམ་དུ་ཁྲིད་ཡིན་པས་དགོས་འདོད་ར་ཤོག་གསུངས་པས། དེ་བྱ་བ་དང་ལ་དང་མ་དྲན་སྟོང་དགོངས་ཁ་བྲོས་ནས་

254 ༄༅། །དེར་འཛོམས་པ་ལ། བླ་མའི་བུ་མོ་དེའི་རྒྱུད་སྨིན་པར་མཐོང་ནས་བདེ་མཆོག་ཏུ་དབང་བསྐུར། བསྐྱེད་རྫོགས་ཟུང་འཇུག་གི་གདམས་
པ་གནང་བས། ཞག་བདུན་དུ་དགོན་པ་དེ་ཉིད་དུ་སྒྲུབ་པར་བྱས། དེ་ནས་པ་མ་ཐམས་ཅད་དུ་ཕྱིན་པས་དེ་དག་བཙོག་པ་དང་ངན་སྨྲས་ལ་སོགས་པ་བྱེད་
པས༔ བུ་མོས་ཁམས་གསུམ་འཁོར་གནས་པ་མ་རྟོགས་པ་ནི་མི་དུ་ལ། རིགས་དང་རུས་ཆེ་བས་ཀྱང་ལ་ཕོ་རང་འགྱིག དེ་དངས་ལ་བཟློ་ག་པ་མེད་པས་
ན༔ བདག་ནི་བླ་མ་རྗེ་ནས་ཐར་པ་སྒྲུབ་པར་བྱེད་པོས་ཀྱི་བ་གཅིག། །དེས་ལམ་དུ་ཁྱེར་རོ་ཟེར་བས། དེ་རྣམས་བཀའ་གཅིག་དང་ནས་ཙང་མི་
ཟེར་བ་ན། དེས་ཀྱང་བླ་མའི་གདམས་པ་སྒོམ་འདི་ལས་དང་བྱ་བ་ཐམས་ཅད་གློས་བཏང་ནས་ལོ་གཅིག་ཏུ་ལྷུང་བ་ན། ཕྱ་ར་ཀྱི་ཀྱི་འཛིན

255 ནས་ཁྱེར་བས། དེའི་ཁྱིམ་དུ་ཕྱིན་པ་དང་། འཇིག་རྟེན་གྱི་ལས་དང་བྱ་བ་རྗེ་ལྟར་བྱེད་ཅིང་ཁ་དང་ལུས་ཀྱང་ཐུབ་ལ་དཀའ་སྤྱད་པ་ལ་སོགས་
པ་ཟེ་ཕྱིད་ཡོད་པན། བུ་ཆེ་ཡང་རིམ་པར་བུ་དང་བུ་མོ་གཉིས་སྐྱེས་པ། དེ་ཡང་དེ་ཁེ་ཉ་འདྲ་བ་ཡོད་པས་རིགས་ཀྱི་བུ་ཆེ་འདི་འདྲ་བ་ཟེར་
ནས་སྨོན་པར་བྱེད་པའི་ཚེ་བླ་མ་དང་ཕྲད་ནས་ལོ་བདུན་གཉིས་ལོན་པན། རྒྱལ་རྒྱུར་ཕྱིན་ནས་ཁྱིམ་དུ་འོངས་པས་ཤིང་ཞིག་ལ་རྐང་པ་འཕྲོས་
ནས་རྫ་མཆག་པས་དཀར་འདུག་སྟེ་ཁྱིམ་དུ་ཉི་མ་ཕྱིད་ཀྱི་བར་དུ་མ་འོངས་པས། ལྷ་རྒྱིན་བཙན་རྫ་མཆག་པོ་ལ་ལྷ་ཤེས་འདུག་པས།
དེ་ལ་གཏམ་ཅི་སྨྲ་ས་ཀྱང་མི་ཉན་པར་ལྟ་བན། ཐམས་ཅད་འཇིགས་གཟུང་དམ་ཅི་ཟེར་ཅིང་ཉི་མ་རྒྱས་ལ་བང་པན། ཐོག་མ་མེད་པའི་སེམས་

256 ༄༅། །ཅན་རྣམས། །ལུས་ཀྱི་རྫ་མཆག་པ་ལ། །ཁྱིམ་  དུ་ལོག་པ་ག་ལ་ཡོད། །བདག་གི་རྫ་མ་དེ་རིང་ཆག །ད་ནི
འཁོར་བའི་ཁྱིམ་དུ་ནི། །མི་ལྡོག་བདེ་བ་ཆེན་པོར་འགྲོ། ། ཨོ་མ་བླ་མ་རྗེ་མཆོག་ཆེ། །བདེ་བ་ཐོབ་འདོད་དེ་ལ་བསྟེན།
ཞེས་གསུངས་ནས་ནམ་མཁའ་ལ་འཕགས་ཏེ་ཞུགས་ཉི་ཤུ་རྩ་གཅིག་ན་ཨ་ཀ་ཙི་ར་བ་ལ་གདམས་པ་གསུངས་ནས་མཁའ་
སྤྱོད་དུ་གཤེགས་སོ། །གུ་རུ་མ་ཎི་བྷ་དྲ་པའི་ལོ་རྒྱུས་རྫོགས་སོ།། ཏི། མེ་ཁ་ལའི་ལོ་རྒྱུས་བརྒྱུད་པས་སོ། །གུ་རུ་མེ་ཁ་ལའི་ལོ་རྒྱུས་ནི།
ཡུལ་དེ་ཝཱི་ཀོ་ཊ་ན་ཁྱིམ་བདག་གཅིག་ལ་བུ་མོ་གཉིས་ཡོད་པ། དེ་དང་པོ་ཞིག་ལ་བུ་གཉིས་ཡོད་པ་ག་ཅེར་དུ་བྲམས་པ

༈ གུ་རུ་མེ་ཁ་ལ་ཀཱ་ན་མོ།།

257

དང༔ བུ་མོ་དེ་གཉིས་ལ་ཐམས་ཅད་ཁ་ཟེར་རེ་བར་བྱེད་ལ། དེ་གཉིས་ཀྱི་ངོ་བུ་བ་ཅི་ཡང་བྲུས་པ་མེད་དོ། །དེའི་ཚེ་བུ་མོ་ན་རེ། རྒྱ་མཚོ་ནང་ན་
ཟེར་བ་འདི་འདྲ་ལ་གཞན་དུ་འགྲོ་མ་དགོས་ཟེར། བུ་མོ་ན་རེ་ཀ་དང་དུ་བྱིན་ཀྱང་ཚིག་སྨྲ་བས་གསལ་བས་འདི་དང་བྲེད་མི་འོང་བས།། འདི་ཉིད་དང་རང་
དུ་སྤྱད་དགོས་ཟེར་བ་ལ་ཚོ། བླ་མ་ཀུ་ཏུ་བ་བྲུ་བ་དེ་ལ་བྱིན་སྟེ། དེ་ནི་རྒྱལ་འགྱུར་ཐོ་མོ་བདུན་བརྒྱ་ལ་བ་སྐོར་བ། མ་རིག་པུ་ཏི་གཏུགས་དབུ
ལ་བཞེ་རེ་བ། ཧ་མ་རུ་རི་སྐྲ་མ་བཀྲོལ་བ་རབ་འབྲེལ་བ་ལ་སོགས་པ་རི་ཡོན་ཏན་དང་པ་གཅུ་མི་དང་བ་སྐྲོ་གསུམ། དཔུང་གཉིས་ཀྱིས་ཚ་སྐྲོལ
གཉིས་ལ་ཡུལ་མི་དང་ཀྱི་ཡང་ཁ་ཟེར་བས། བླ་མ་འདི་ལ་གདམས་པ་ཞུས་ནས་བསྒྲུབ་པ་བྱེད་དགོས་ཟེར་དེ་ཐན་དུ་ཤིན་ཏུ་སྐུ་རིགས་པོ་རྒྱས་

258

༄༅། །ཀྱང་བསྐྱང་དུ་ངོ་གདམས་པ་ཞུས་པས། དེས་ཀྱང་གཞང་སྐྱེ་དབང་བསྐུར་ནས། ལྷ་བ་སྒོམ་པ་སྤྱོད་པ་འབྲས་བུ་ཟུང་འཇུག་
པག་མེ་འཇིག་དམས་པ་གནང་ངོ་། །དེ་གཉིས་ཀྱིས་བརྩོན་པས་བསྒྲུབས་པས་ལོ་བཅུ་གཉིས་ན་གྲུབ་པ་ཐོབ་སྟེ། བླ་མ་ཅན་དུ་བྱོན་ནས་ཕྱག་
དང་མཆོད་བཅུས། བཀའ་དྲིན་ཆེས་ཁྲབ་པའི་གཏམ་བཏང་བས། ཁྱེད་གདང་པ་ཡིན་དེས་མ་ཤེས་གསུངས་པས་ཕྱ་རགྱི་ལོ་རྒྱུས་སྨྲད་དོ།།
འོ་ན་ད་ལ་ཡོན་འབུལ་དགོས་གསུངས་པས། བླ་མ་ཅི་བཞེད་པ་འབུལ་ལགས་ཞུས་པས། ངོ་ན་ད་ལ་ཁྱེད་གཉིས་ཀྱི་མ་མོ་བོ་བྱིན་ཅིག་
གསུངས་པས། དེས་ཀྱང་བླ་མ་པ་ཞེད་ན་འབུལ་ཟེར། དེ་གཉིས་ཀྱི་རང་རང་གི་བཞེས་ཡེ་ཤེས་ཀྱིར་ལ་གྲི་ཧཱུཾ་དང་དང་ལྡན་པ་རེ་བྱུང་ནས་

259

རང་རང་གི་ཡན་ལག་གི་དང་པོ་མགོ་བོ་བཅད་ནས་ཕུལ་ལོ། བདག་གཉིས་པོ་བླ་མ་འདི་བཀའ་དྲིན་གྱི། །བསྐྱེད་རྫོགས་ཟུང་འཇུག་པ་བོར
འདས་སྤྲོས་པ་བཅད། །ལྟ་སྤྱོད་ཟུང་འཇུག་སྤྱོད་སྒང་ཕྱིས་པ་བཅད། །འཕྲེང་བ་རིགས་ཟུང་འཇུག་བདག་གཞན་སྤྲོས་པ་བཅད། །སྤྲོས་མེད་བརྡ
ཡི་རྩལ་ཕྱུང་འདི་འབུལ་ལོ། །ཅེས་གསུངས་བཞིན་དབུ་བཅད་དེ་གཏེར་མ་ཛད་པས། ཀ་དྷུ་པ་ཞལ་ནས། ཨོ་མ་རྣལ་འབྱོར་ཆེན་མོ་གཉིས། །ཡོན་
ཏན་མཆོག་ཐོབ་དགེ་བ་སྟེ། །རང་ཉིད་ཞི་བདེ་དམན་པས་ན། །འགྲོ་བའི་དོན་ཕྱིར་བཞུགས་པར་མཛོད། །ཅེས་གསུངས་པས་མགོ་བོ་སླར་སོས
ཏེ༔ རྣམ་མེད་པར་གྱུར་པས་ཐམས་ཅད་ངོ་མཚར་སྐྱེས་ནས་དབུ་བཅད་མ་དཔུང་གཉིས་སུ་གྲགས་ཏེ་ཀ་དྷུ་པ་རིན་བས་འབྲིང་བྱས་ནས།

260

༄༅། །ཕྱག་རྒྱ་ཆེན་པོའི་དོན་གྲུབ་ཐོབ་སྟེ་ལོ་མང་
མཛད་དེ་མཁའ་སྤྱོད་དུ་གཤེགས་སོ། །བུ་མོ་སྤྱུ་བུ་མོ
ཏི། །ཀུ་རུ་ཀ་མ་བ་ལའི་ལོ་རྒྱུས་སོ། གྲུབ་ཆེན་ཀ་དྷུ
མ་ཐག་པའི་དབུ་བཅད་མ་དཔུང་གཉིས་ཀྱི་བུ་མོ་དེ་ཡིན་ལ

དུ་འགྲོ་དོན་མཛད་ནས་རྫོགས་པ་བརྗོད་པ་ལ་སོགས་པ
ཁ་ལི་པའི་ལོ་རྒྱུས་རྫོགས་སོ།། ।། ཀ་ན་ཁ་ལ་རི་ལོ་རྒྱུས་བཞུགས་སོ།།
བ་སྐྱེ་ན་ཀ་པོ་སྤྱོད་པ་རི་ཞབས་ཀྱིས་རྗེས་སུ་གཟུང་བ་བརྗོད་
རྣམ་ཐར་གོང་གསུམ་རྫོགས་ཤིང་། མཚན་རྣལ་འབྱོར་མ
ཅན་རྗོགས་སོ།། ।། ཀ་ལ་ཀ་པའི་ལོ་རྒྱུས་བཞུགས་སོ།།

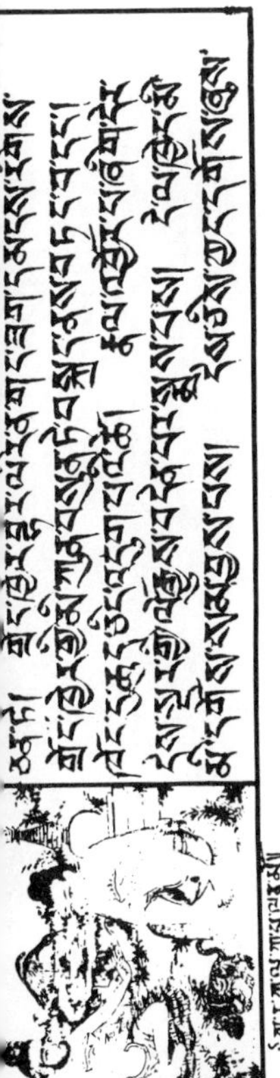

261

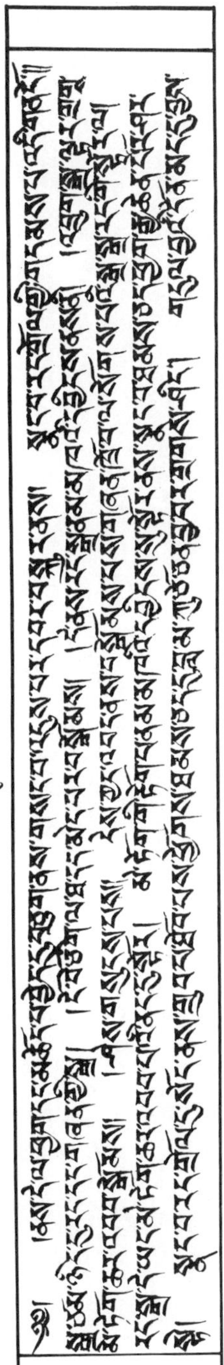

262

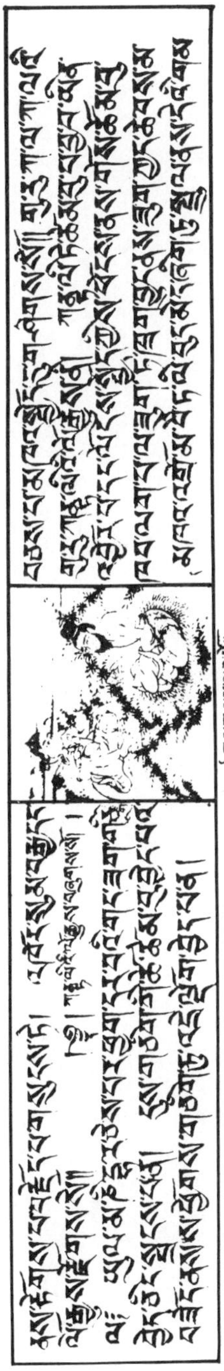

263

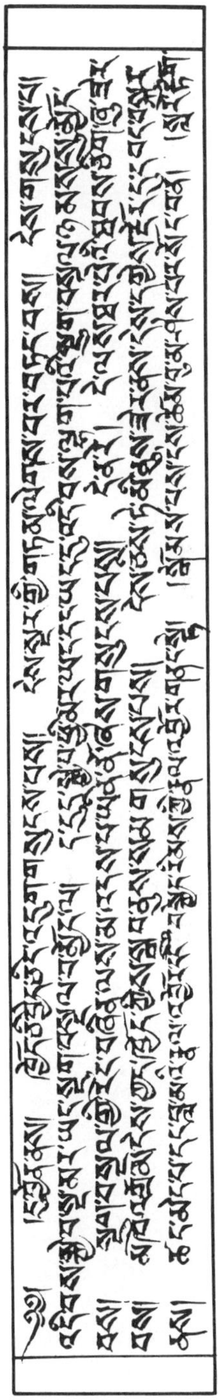

264

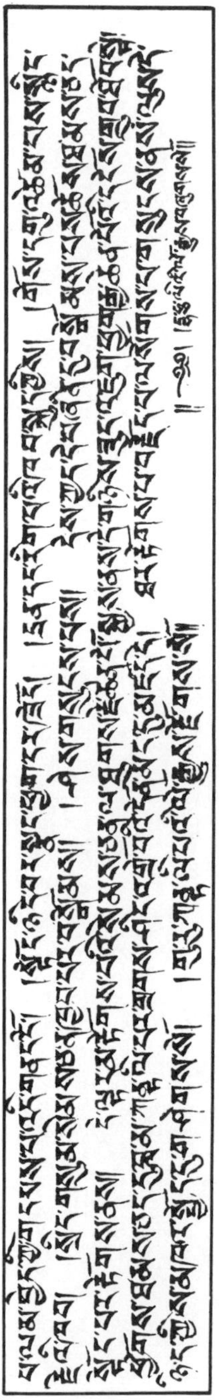

265

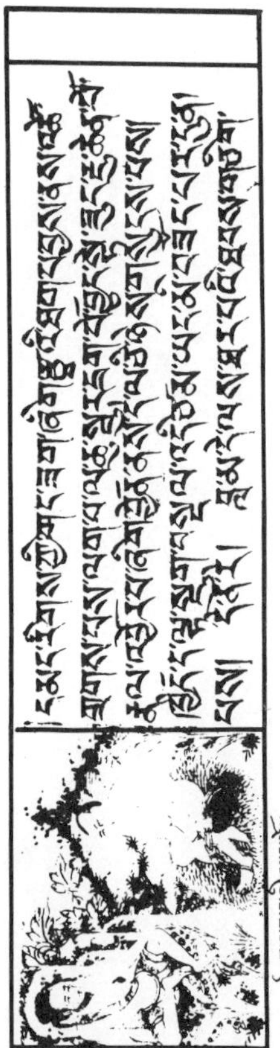

266

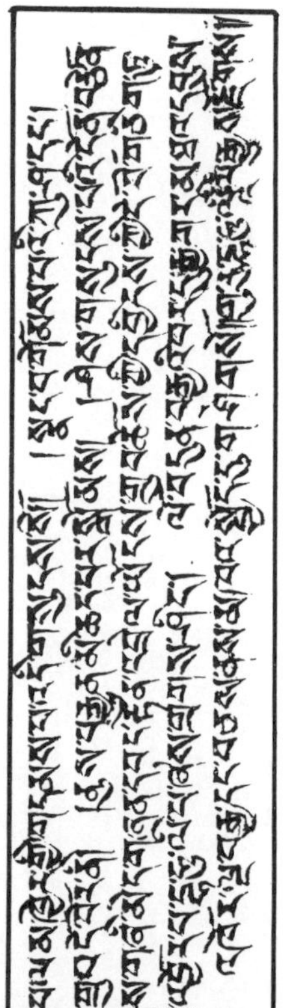

267

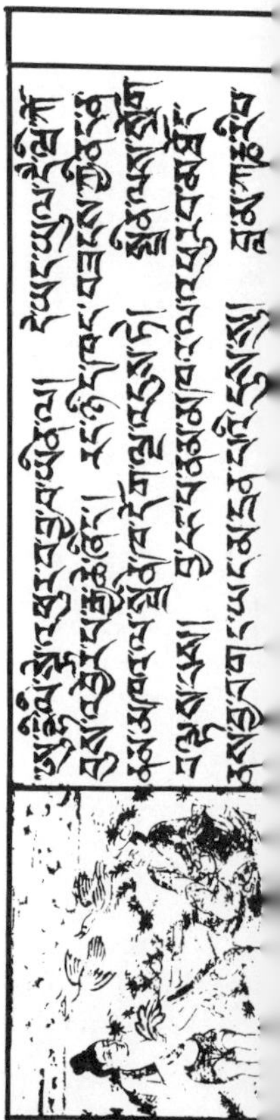

268

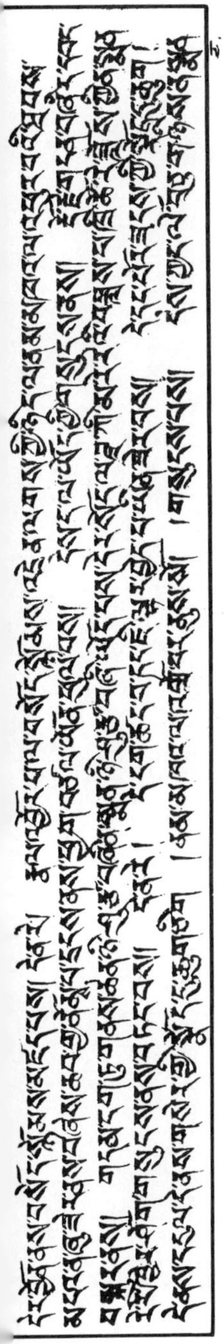

269

270

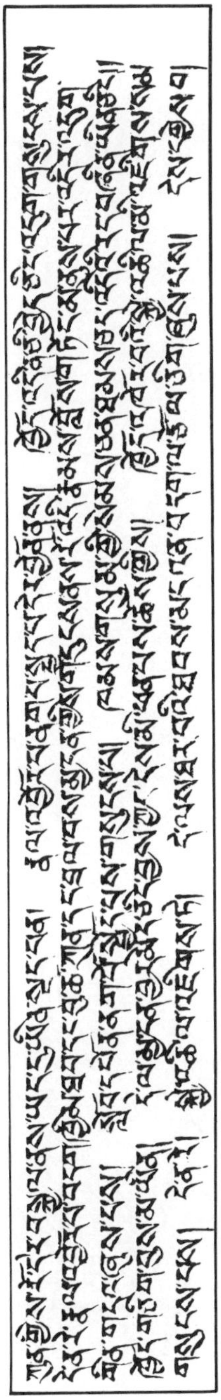

271

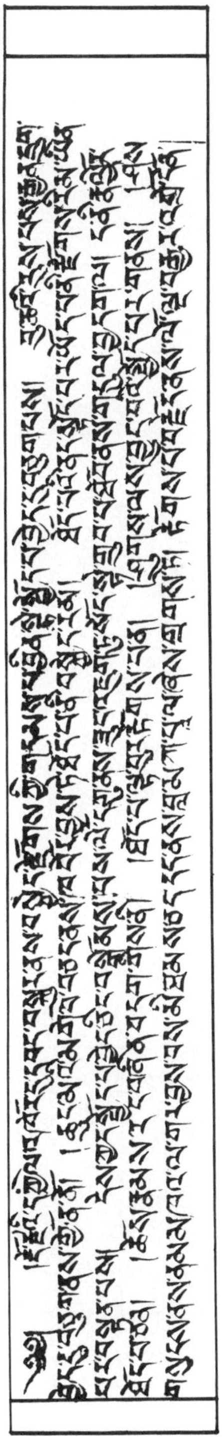

272

273

[illegible]

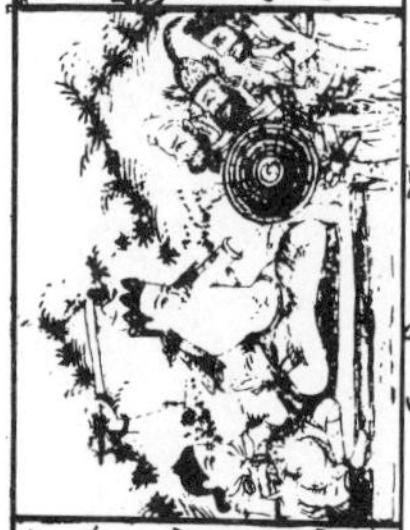

[illegible]

274

[illegible]

275

[illegible]

276

[illegible]

[illegible]

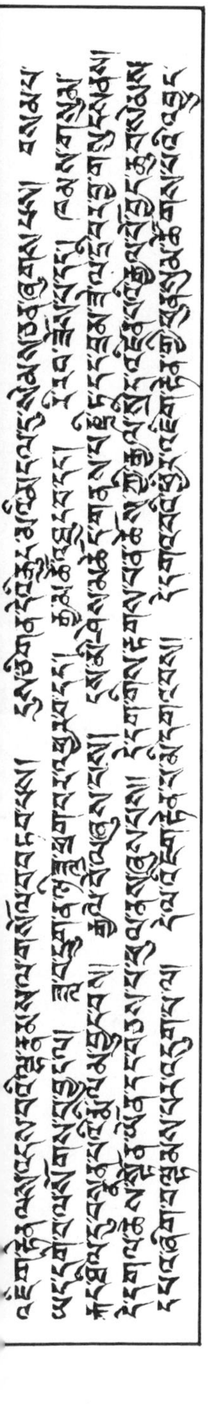

277

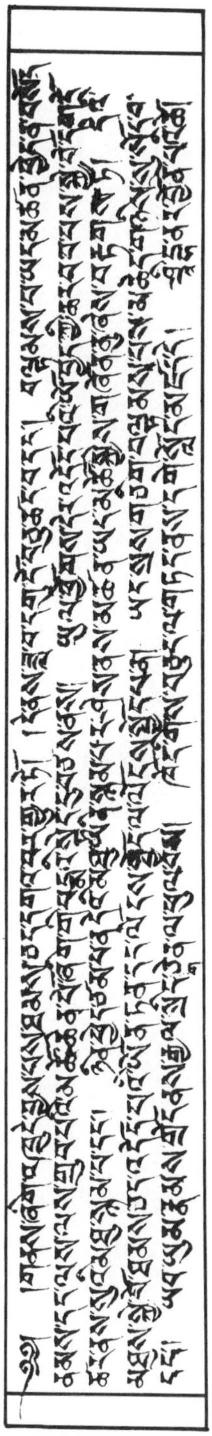

278

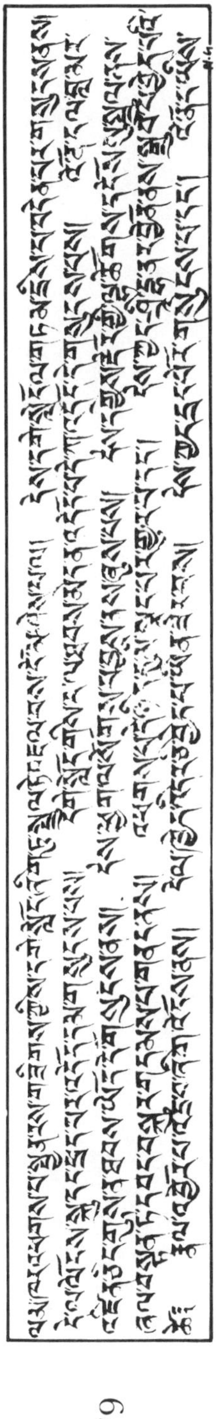

279

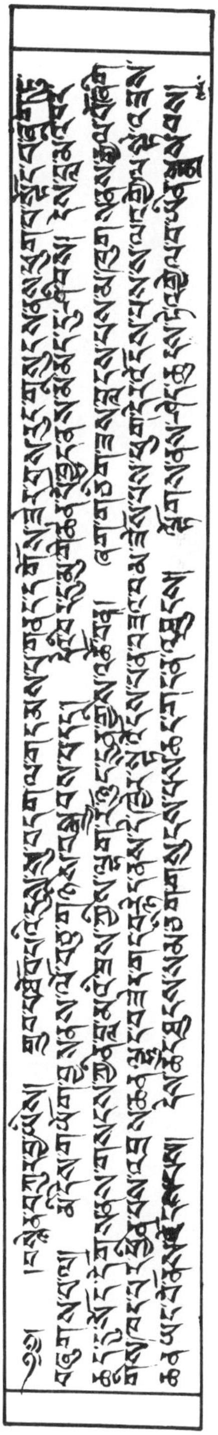

280

281

282

283

284

285

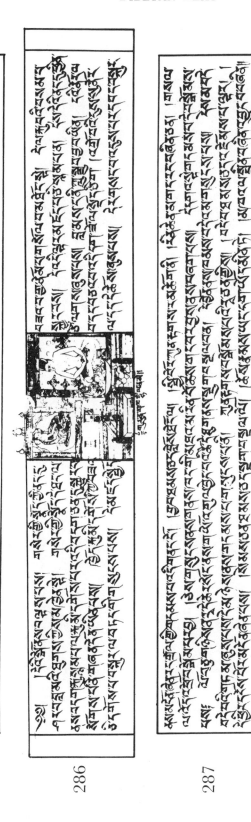

286

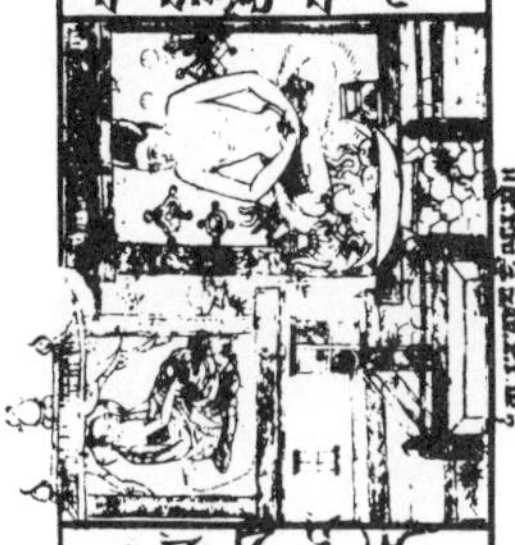

287

288

289

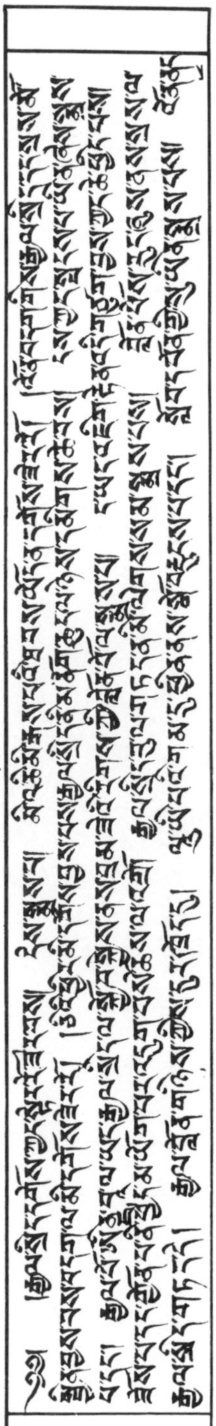

290

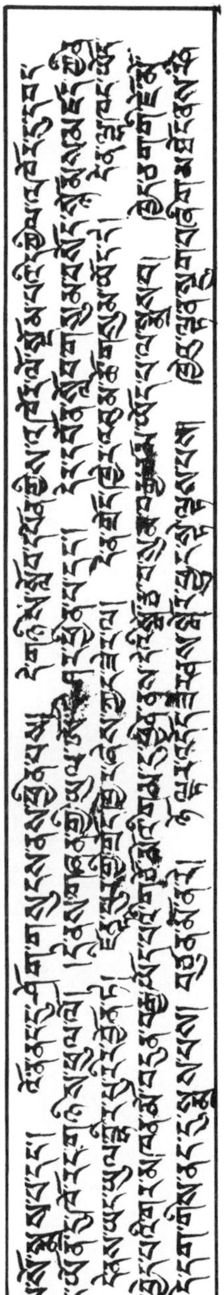

291

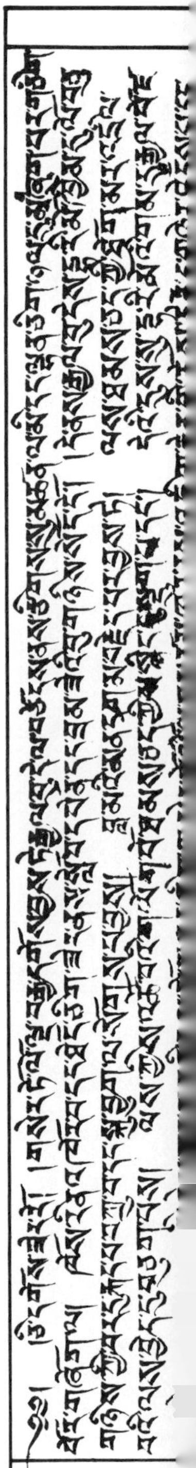

292

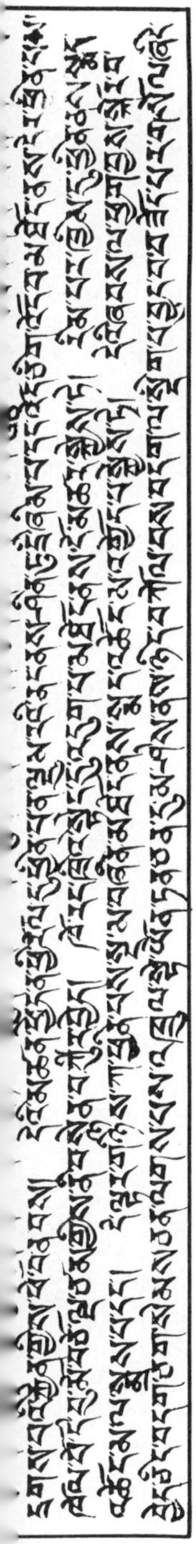
293

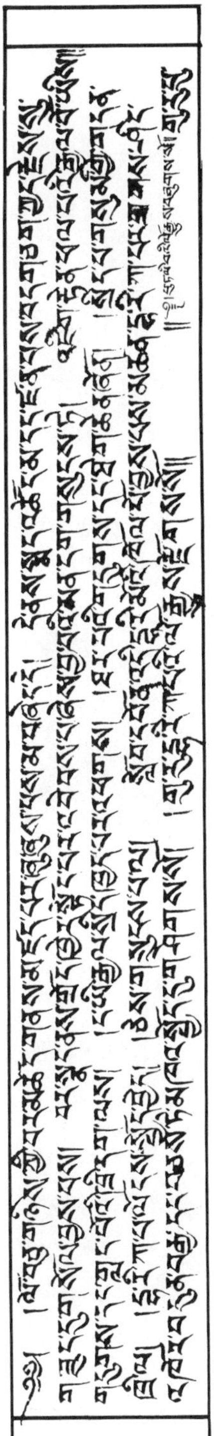
294

295

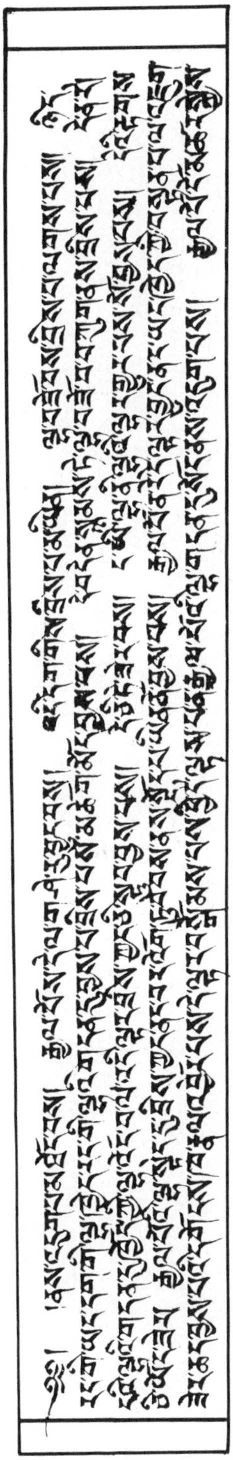
296

297

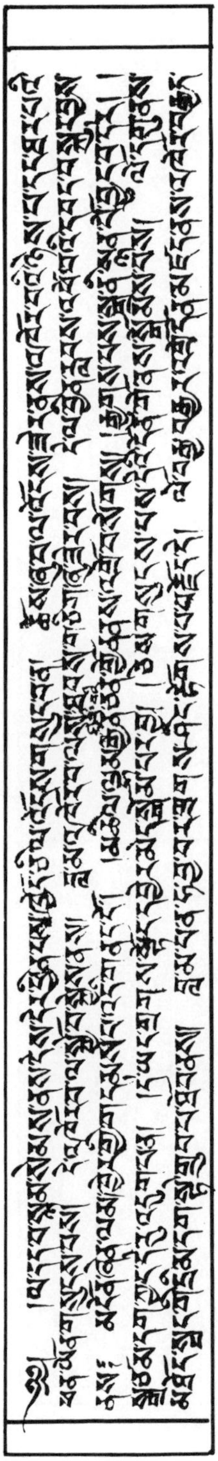

298

299

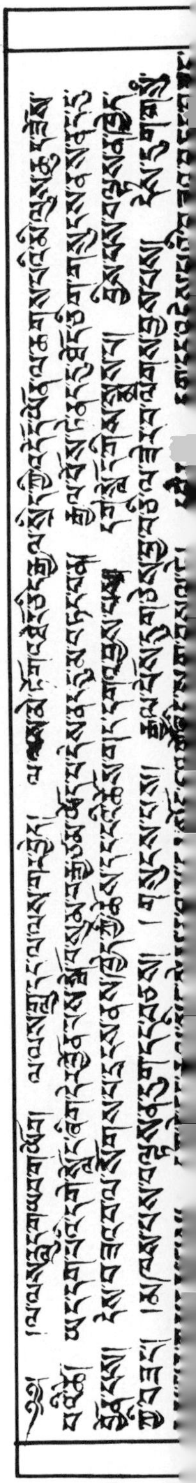

300

301 ལམ་བསྟན་ནོ། །དེས་རྒྱལ་སྲིད་བུ་ལ་བཀོད་དེ་རྩ་བ་ནས་སྤྲ་ད་ཙུ་ས་ཀྱི་ད་ཨ་སྨྲའི་ཚོ་ལ་ཏྲི་བྲ་ཀོ་ཀ་ཡི་འི་སྦྲ་ལ་ཚགས་ནས་ལམ་སྒོམ་མ་དུམ་སྟུ་བ་པ་ལ།
དེར་རྟོག་པ་གར་སྐྱེས་ཐིག་ཆ་རྒྱོལ་བའི་གདམས་པ་འདི་ལྟར་གནང་ངོ་། །དཔེར་ན་ནམ་མཁའ་སྟོང་པ་ལས། །འབྲུག་སྒྲ་སྤྲིན་རྣམས་འདུ་བར་བྱེད། །དེ་ལ
ཆར་རྒྱུན་འབྱུང་བ་ཡིས། །རྩི་ཤིང་ལོ་ཏོག་རྒྱས་པར་ལྟར། །དེ་བཞིན་རྣ་བ་སྒྲོང་པ་རན་ནོ། །ཀོ་ཀ་ལ་ཡི་འབྲུག་སྒྲ་ཡིས། །ནམ་ཤེས་རྟོག་བྱེད་སྤྲིན
བྲང་ནས། །ཉོན་མོངས་དུག་གི་ཆར་རྒྱུན་གྱིས། །ཚགས་སྒྱུད་ལོ་འདབ་བརྒྱ་པར་བྱེད། །མི་མཁས་བསམ་གྱིས་བཞི་པོ་ཐེང་བཞིན་ཅན། །སེམས་ཉིད་སྟོང

302 ༄༅། །པའི་ངང་ལ་སཞི། །གྲགས་སྟོང་རྩེ་རྩེ་མེད་འབྲུག་སྒྲ་ཡིས། །བདེ་ཆེན་ཟག་མེད་སྤྲིན་བཞིན་བསྡུས། །གནས་ལུགས་རང་གསལ་ཆར་
རྒྱུན་ལས། །ཡེ་ཤེས་ལྷ་ཡིས་ལོ་ཐོག་རྒྱས། །ཨ་མ་སྤྲི་ལྷན་རོ་མི་ཆར་ཆེ། །ཅེ་སུ་གསུངས་པས་དེས་ཀྱང་བསྒོམས་པས་ཟླ་བ་དྲུག་ན་གྲུབ་པ་ཐོབ་
སྟེ་མཚན་ཡང་ཀོ་ཀི་ལི་པ་ཞེས་གྲགས་ནས་འགྲོ་དོན་མང་དུ་མཛད་དེ་ལུས་དེ་ཉིད་ཀྱིས་མཁའ་སྤྱོད་དུ་གཤེགས་སོ། །གུ་རུ་ཀོ་ཀི་ལི་པའི་ལོ་རྒྱུས་
རྫོགས་སོ།། ||༄༅། ཨ་ནཾ་གོ་ལའི་ལོ་རྒྱུས་བཞུགས་སོ། །གུ་རུ་ཨ་ནཾ་གོ་ལའི་ལོ་རྒྱུས་ནི། ཡུལ་ སྦྲུཏྟུ་རབྲ་བ་ན་དམ་དར་ཀར་གས་ཀྱི་གང་ཟག་ཞིག་སྤྱི་
བསྟུམ་ལ་བཟེད་པ་བསྒོམས་པས་གཟུགས་བཟང་ཞིང་ཙམ་ངེས་པའི་ཡོ་ངང་པ་ངེས་གཞན་ལ་བལྟམས་པས་རྒྱལ་སྐྱེས་པས། ·དེའི་ཀ་མདུ་དགེ་

303 སྤྱོད་ཞིབ་ཏུ་ལྦ། སྤྱོད་ལམ་མཛེས་པ་ཞིག་བྱོན་ནས་བསོད་སྙོམས་
འཚོ་བ་འདྲེན་པ་ཡིན་ཟེར་ནས་སྤྱན་དྲངས་ཏེ་ཞབས་བཀྲུས་སྟན་
ཏེ༔ དེ་ནས་རེ། ཉིད་འཕགས་པ་ཟས་བསོད་སྙོམས་དང་དཀའ
དགེ་སྦྱོང་གིས་དེ་ལ་བདག་ལ་ཕོར་བ་ལ་འཛེགས་ནས་ཐར་པ་ཐོབ་
པའི་སྒྲོ་ལམ་ཉེས་ཀྱི་རྡོ་ལ་ཕྱང་པ་རིཙི་ཙམ་བདོག་བྱས་པ་ས

ༀ་གུ་རུ་ཨ་ནཾ་གོ་ལ་ནམོ།།

མཛད་པས། དེ་ནས་རེ། ནང་དུ་ཤེགས་པ་དགའ་གིས་ཉིན་ཞག་གི
ལྷབ་བ་ལ་སོགས་པ་ཏྲུས་ནས་བཞེས་ཆ་བཅུ་འོམས་པ་དྲས
ཐུབ་འདི་ལྟར་མཛད་པ་ཅི་འི་ཆེ་དགྲ་བཅུ་ལགས་ཟེར་བས།
པར་འདོད་པའི་ཕྱིར་ཡིན་གསུངས་པས། ཡང་དེ་སུ་འཕགས
དེས་ཁྲར་ཆེ་སྣོ་ཕྱོད་ཀྱི་རྟེན་དང་རྒྱལ་ལ་ཡོན་ཏན་གྱི་ཆེས་མི་འབྱུང་

304 ༄༅། །ལ༔ བདག་གིས་དད་པའི་རྟེན་ལ་ཡོན་ཏན་དཔག་ཏུ་མེད་པ་འབྱུང་ངོ་གསུངས་པས། ཡང་དེས་འཕགས་སུ་པ་ཡོན་ཏན་བྱ་བ་ཅི་ལ་ཟེར་
ཞུས་པས། རྣམས་ཆོ་འདིར་ཆོས་བྱེད་པའི་རྟེན་ལ་མི་རང་མི་མ་ཡིན་བའི་བར་ཆད་མི་འབྱུང་ཞིང་། མཐར་ཐུག་བ་སངས་རྒྱས་ཀྱི་སྐུ་ཐོབ་པ་ལ་སོགས་པ་འདིག
རྟེན་དང་འབྲེལ་རྟེན་ལས་འདས་པའི་ཡོན་ཏན་བ་ཤད་པས། དེ་འདྲ་བ་ཐོབ་པ་འི་ཐབས་གཅིག་ཞུ་ཟེར་བས། དེས་དེ་ལ་སཛྫ་བ་དང་འཚོད་པ་ལ་སོགས་པའི་
འཇིག་རྟེན་པའི་ལས་ནུས་ལས་མ་གསུངས་པས། དེ་འདྲ་བ་གང་ཡང་མི་ནུས་ཟེར་བས། འོ་ན་སྣང་ཐོག་གཅིག་ཏུ་བསྡད་ནས་སྒོམ་ནུས་སམ་གསུངས་པས
ནུས་ཟེར་བས། དེ་བ་དེ་མ་ཆོག་ཅུ་ཁང་བསྒྲུར་ནས་ཆོགས་དྲུག་རང་གསལ་གྱི་གདམས་པ་འདི་གནང་ངོ་། །སྣང་ཚོགས་སྣང་བ་སེམས་ཀྱི་རང་བཞིན་ལས།

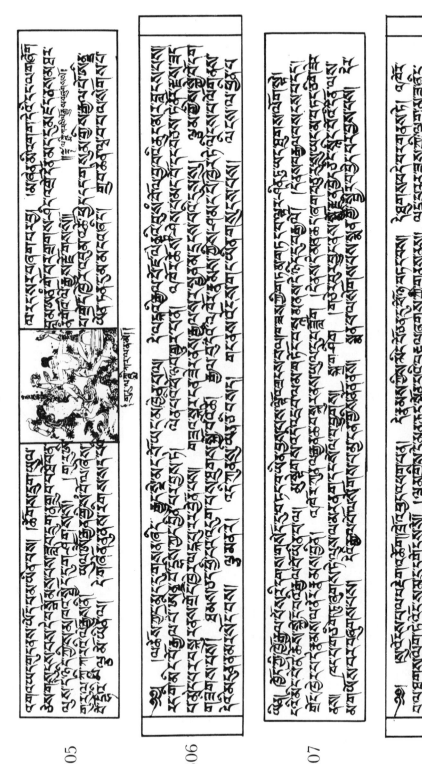

305

[illegible]

[illegible]

306

[illegible]

307

[illegible]

308

[illegible]

309

310

311

312

313

314

315

316

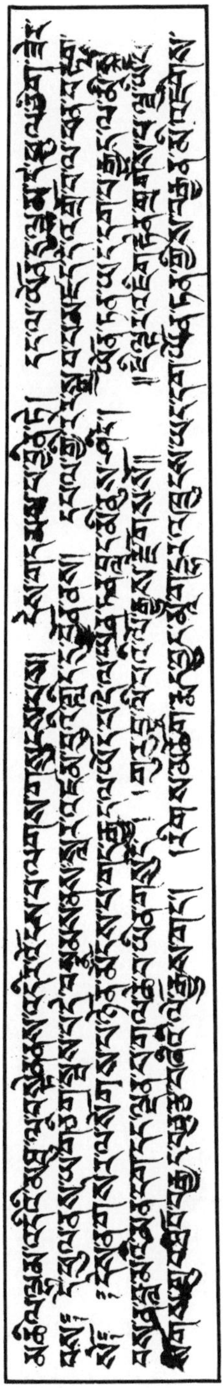

317

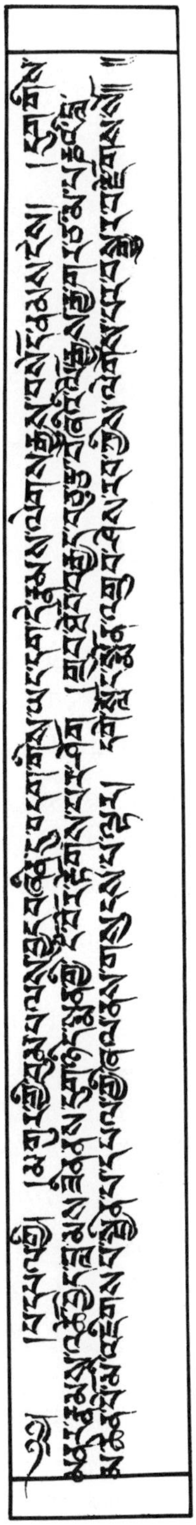

318

# Notes

1. The *Caturaśīti-siddha-pravṛtti* was translated into Tibetan by the monk sMon-grup Shes-rab as the *Grub thob brgyad cu rtsa bzhi'i lo rgyus* and is found as text #5091 in the Peking edition of the bsTan-'gyur (Tokyo: Suzuki Research Foundation, 1961).

2. Bodhisattvas are the Enlightenment Beings who, out of compassion, have chosen to delay their final enlightenment in order to work for the liberation of all sentient beings.

3. The Mahāmudrā's roots lie in the *Samādhirāja-sūtra*, which is concerned with the meaning of the Prajñāpāramitā. The highest realization of the Mahāmudrā is the experience of the Indivisible Unity (Sanskrit *yuganaddha*, Tibetan *zung 'jug*) of the Developing Stage (Sanskrit *utpanna-krama*, Tibetan *bskyed rim*) and the Perfecting Stage (Sanskrit *sampanna-krama*, Tibetan *rdzogs rim*).

4. The siddha-to-be may be instructed in the practice of alchemy, which, in Tantric practice, is considered a spiritual discipline. Alchemy, in whatever tradition—Indian, Chinese, or Western—is concerned with two activities: the transmutation of base metals into gold, and the production of the elixir of life. There are many parallels between alchemical thought and the aims of yoga, since both disciplines are ultimately directed toward transformation and 'divinization'.

Yogins have always been reputed to change the elements into one another, as in changing water into earth so that one might walk upon it, or changing earth to air so that one might walk through solid objects. But these transformations are not alchemical in nature, for the changes are temporary and lack the sense of producing the noble from the base, which is at the center of the alchemical enterprise.

It is the Ārya Nāgārjuna who has the greatest fame in the art of alchemy. In the story of Nāgabodhi, the master, unconcerned with the value of the metal, changes his iron bowl into gold, and simply gives the gold bowl to Nāgabodhi, who had intended to steal it. In the story of Karṇaripa, Nāgārjuna is concerned with the elixir of life, the other aspect of the alchemical quest. In another story, Nāgārjuna contemplates changing a mountain into gold for the benefit of living beings. This incident serves as an object lesson, underlining the need to fully consider the consequences of every action—and the need for a clear head to accompany the willing hand and the compassionate heart.

5. Kāṇhapa, one of the siddhas, struggles with this problem throughout much of his career, and lives out the adage, "Pride cometh before a fall." Kukkuripa, on the other hand, is able to break away from the lesser powers to care for his dog, a ḍākinī in disguise.

6. *Sāmañña-phala-sutta*, p. 88, section 87.

7. Why eighty-four? The text itself does not give us much clue. In the introduction it simply states that these eighty-four have "well come together." By the fact that the list of the specific siddhas constituting eighty-four varies in the Tibetan tradition, it would seem that this number has more than historical significance.

It is interesting that there are supposedly 84,000 positions of yoga known to Śiva of which men are said to know only eighty-four. In the story of the Cakravartin Sudassana in the Pali canon, the number eighty-four or 84,000 occurs quite frequently. The emperor Aśoka is said to have built 84,000 stūpas. This is clearly a number of considerable religious significance.

8. Cemeteries are often portrayed on mandalas as a symbol of the world of samsara. Tantric ceremonies were celebrated in cemeteries, where the various implements associated with the practices—the skull-cup, the thigh-bone trumpet, and the bone beads—were all readily available. Several Buddhist meditations call for contemplating the various stages of a corpse decomposing. If the yogin wants to experience the unpleasantness of life and its inevitable end in the most vivid way, there is probably no better place to go than to a cemetery. Several of the siddhas, Lūyipa among others, actually lived in cemeteries so as to be out of the flow of ordinary human life. Since people customarily avoid cemeteries, the yogin could count on being left in peace to do his meditations.

9. The word *ḍākinī* probably comes from a Sanskrit root meaning 'to fly'. The Tibetans render ḍākinī as *mkha' 'gro ma*, 'the sky-walking woman'. But the idea of 'sky' was interpreted as standing for 'emptiness', and 'walking' is equivalent to 'understanding', so that the ḍākinī is 'the woman who understands emptiness', that is to say, the feminine embodiment of wisdom.

Ḍākinīs occupy an ambiguous place in the human/superhuman classification. Perhaps because of the emphasis on practice, the Tantric tradition frequently gives a very vivid form and embodiment to what many Westerners consider metaphysical abstractions; it is important to remember that while the ḍākinīs are personifications of wisdom and emptiness, they are also real beings. There is precedence for this in the figure of Prajñāpāramitā, the 'Perfection of Wisdom', who is simultaneously the consummation of enlightenment, a class of Mahāyāna Sūtras, and a goddess with a specific iconographic representation about whom hymns are written.

10. Four of the siddhas in this text are women, not a large proportion, but significant in that, as we are told in the introduction, "These four were objects of reverence for an entire dynasty." None of the four were connected with the monastic

order; one was a princess, one a housewife, and two were merchant's daughters. There are many other women in the stories who appear as Tantric consorts of the siddhas. Ḍombipa's consort, originally a girl of low caste, has magical powers in her own right. Saraha has a serving girl who helps him round out his experience, and the entire story of Ghaṇḍhapa centers on the acquisition of his Tantric consort and the scandal it caused the community and its supercilious king.

11. Saliputra is a corrupted form of Pataliputra, the modern Patna, and is a frequently cited locale for the stories.

12. In Tibetan *dran pa cig pa'i ting nge 'dzin.* The samadhi of a single point is a basic meditational discipline in many Buddhist schools, designed to quiet the mind and lead to transcendent insight.

13. The Developing Stage (Sanskrit *utpanna-krama*, Tibetan *bskyed rim*) deals with the processes of visualizations, the generation of deities, the mental production of mandalas, etc. The Perfecting Stage (Sanskrit *sampanna-krama*, Tibetan *rdzogs rim*) deals with practices concerning breath-control, the cakras or 'psychic centers', the *nāḍis* or 'mystic veins', etc.

14. At the end of most of the stories it states that the siddha goes to the realm of the Ḍākas (Tibetan *mkha' spyod*) in "this very body"—in other words, without dying. The term *ḍāka* is the masculine form of ḍākinī, and like ḍākinī, refers to a class of sky-traveling beings. Here 'the realm of the Ḍākas' indicates a type of 'heaven'.

15. King Devapāla ruled from 810-840 A.D. and was one of the most famous of the late Buddhist kings; his reign marked the height of the Pāla dynasty.

16. Somapurī was one of the major Buddhist monastic centers. It was established during the reign of Dharmapāla (770–810 A.D.) at the present Ompur in Bengal.

17. Vajravārāhī (Tibetan rDorje phagmo) is a prominent Tantric deity; she is the consort of Cakrasamvara.

18. A word that occurs frequently in the text is *slob dpon* (Sanskrit *ācārya*). After some deliberation, I have rendered this

term as 'master'. The word *acārya* often denotes a scholastic mastery, but only in a few cases is this what is being emphasized in the stories. The scholastic training of the siddhas is not a predominant motif, indeed the stories of Śāntipa and Dharmapa point to the limitations of stressing 'book learning' to the exclusion of practice. Several of the siddhas however, were prolific authors. See the bibliography of works by the siddhas.

19. The siddhas have sometimes to deal with various superhuman and antagonistic beings. The witches (Sanskrit *veṭali*, Tibetan *phra men ma*) are beings who not only cast spells, but also partake somewhat of the ghoul and the vampire. The siddhas at times battle other types of demons as well, the *gnyan* and *bdud*.

20. The ten virtuous actions are: refraining from killing, stealing, sexual misconduct, lying, slandering, speaking abusively, vain and idle chatter, coveting the property of others, bearing ill-will, and holding wrong views.

21. According to the siddha tradition there are three cycles of *dohas* or songs: the King-dohas, the Queen-dohas, and the People-dohas. Many of the songs of Saraha have been translated into Western languages. The most extensive treatment and analysis of the King-doha is found in Dr. H. V. Guenther's *The Royal Song of Saraha* (Berkeley: Shambhala, 1973).

21. Kāmarūpa is the present day Assam. According to Professor Dhirendra Vajpeyi of the Political Science Department of the University of Northern Iowa, Assam still has a reputation among Indians for weird happenings.

23. The *vina* or *pivang* is a large stringed instrument, still popular in India today. The text also calls it a *tambura*, though this is a slightly different instrument.

24. The eight 'worldly dharmas' are: profit, pleasure, praise, a good reputation, and their opposites: loss, pain, blame, and defamation of character.

25. Viśvakarma (Tibetan *Bi shva karma*) is the 'divine artificer', similar to Vulcan or Haephestos.

26. Śriparvata, 'the Blessed Mountain', is probably located in South India and was Nāgārjuna's 'base of operation'.

27. The four modes of birth are: from water, from egg, from womb, and in a miraculous fashion.

28. Leaves were customarily used as plates from which to eat in India.

29. The *nāḍis* (Tibetan *rtsa*) are the three columns or 'veins' visualized in Tantric practices, which run through the length of the head and torso: the right vein (Sanskrit *lalanā*, Tibetan *ro ma*), the left vein (Sanskrit *rasanā*, Tibetan *rkyang-ma*), and the middle vein (Sanskrit *avadhūti*, Tibetan *dbu ma*).

Through these three veins move the 'breath' (Sanskrit *prāṇa*, Tibetan *rlung*) and the 'energy flow' (Sanskrit *bindu*, Tibetan *thig le*). Sexual imagery is often used to indicate a process of unification and purification. As the right and left veins merge into the middle vein, which is the main channel for the 'breath' (*rlung gi las*), that which has started as desire/attachment then rises into the great joy of Buddhahood.

30. The *Bodhicaryāvatāra* (Tibetan *spyod 'jug*), is a famous Mahāyāna work by Śāntideva. It was translated into English by Marion L. Matics as *Entering the Path to Enlightenment* (New York: Macmillan, 1970).

31. See note No. 29 on the *nāḍis*.

32. A circle of the moon is a white circle as contrasted with a circle of the sun which is a red circle. This is a standard beginning for certain types of Tantric visualizations and practices.

33. The *skandhas* (Tibetan *phung po*) are the five constituents which make up the human experience: the body in the physical world, the feelings, the sensations, the will and active mental dispositions, and the consciousness.

34. A torma is an elaborately constructed offering, often made of butter and embellished with symbols and designs.

35. The famous mantra OM MĀṆI PADME HŪṀ associated with Avalokiteśvara.

# Index


Abhara, 231
Abhayadatta, 2, 259
*abhijñā*, 7
Acinta, 12, 49, 52, 53, 55, 138–140, 254, 275, 285, 286, 288, 301
Agartse, 210
Ajokipa, 12, 108–109, 272, 286, 299
alchemy, 26, 78, 79, 87–89, 142, 256–258, 392
Anaṅga, 247–249, 283, 288, 306
Apatrara, 256
Āryadeva, *see* Karṇaripa
Asaṅga, 4, 5
*avadhūtī*, 159, 162, 183, 397
Avalokiteśvara, 38ff, 73, 172–173, 179, 194, 228, 285, 397

Babhahi, 141–142, 275, 286, 301
Bahana, 202, 287
Bahuri, 208
Bengal, 153, 186, 191
Bhadrapa, 11, 103–105, 271, 286, 299
Bhandhepa, 13, 124–125, 273, 286, 300
Bhandokora, 84
Bhigunagara, 98
Bhikṣana 199–200, 279, 287, 304
Bhilira, 214
Bhusuku, 145–149, 275, 287, 301
*bindu*, 142
*Bodhicaryāvatāra*, 147, 232, 397
Bodhgaya, 23, 61
Bodhinagara, 166
Bodhisattva, 4, 38ff, 228, 392
  first stage of, 94, 152
Brahman, 11, 30, 41ff, 60, 79, 103–105, 122, 228
  heaven of, 8
Buddhapa, 57, 285

*cakras*, 144, 255, 395
Cakrasamvara, 107, 111, 113,

Cakrasamvara (*continued*) 118, 122, 139, 178, 183, 187, 209, 225, 237, 245, 248
Caluki, 182–183, 278, 287, 303
Camaripa, 10, 17, 69–71, 269, 285, 293
Campaka, 196–198, 279, 287, 304
Campaka, city of, 193, 196, 198, 207
Candhikumara, 79
Caparipa, 205–207, 280, 287, 304
Carpati, 73, 285
caste, 10, 11, 104–105, 123, 159, 170, 218
Catrapa, 100–102, 271, 286, 299
Caurāṅgi, 52, 54–56, 268, 285, 292
cause and effect, 91, 197
cemeteries, 13ff, 73, 83, 97, 109, 111, 118, 127, 154, 164, 209, 222, 327, 252, 254, 394
compassion, 39, 84, 173, 185, 217, 225
consciousness, 92

ḍākinī, 14ff, 23, 28, 41, 82, 85, 120, 129, 162, 167, 200, 217, 288, 394, 395
  Bandhe, 15, 85
  Veṭalī, 15, 217, 288
Dārika, 24, 122, 236–239, 282, 288, 305
death, 13, 26, 45, 67, 73, 164, 186, 189, 222, 237, 258
Devapāla, King, 50, 60, 82, 145, 146, 175ff, 395
Developing Stage, 26, 107, 111, 113, 132, 169, 171, 181, 187, 197, 202, 204, 209, 212, 217, 223, 225, 230, 253, 392, 395
Devīkoṭa, 31, 32, 211, 220
Dhahuli, 218–219, 281, 288, 304
Dhanjura, 141
Dharma, 12, 18, 34, 41, 45, 48, 67, 70, 91, 115, 135, 147, 159, 183, 245
  -circle, 27, 146–147
Dharmadhatu, 107
Dharmapa (first), 134–135, 274, 286, 300, 395
Dharmapa (second), 166–167, 277, 287, 302
Dharma-protectors, 31
Dhokaripa, 168–169, 277, 287, 302
Dhombipa, 112–113, 286, 299
Dhukhandi, *see* Khandipa
Dodanti, Mt., 39
*doha*, 18, 43, 396
Ḍombipa, 33–36, 267, 285, 290, 395

emptiness, 15, 97, 137, 169, 189, 197, 202, 246, 263

falsity, 92
fear, 97
five sciences, 76
Four Immeasurables, 17, 125, 225, 226, 255

Ghadhaśīla, Mt., 77
Ghahuri, 57, 58, 59

Ghaṇḍhapa, 174–179, 277, 287, 303, 395
Goraksa, 50–53, 268, 285, 292
Gorisamakra, 73
Gorura, 184–185, 278, 287, 303
Grahara, 224
Great Bliss, 116, 157, 169, 171, 197, 202, 210, 246, 255
Guhyasamāja, 87, 125, 132, 144, 215, 234
guru, 6, 9, 13ff, 16, 17

Hevajra, 26, 33, 35, 57, 82, 101, 109, 162, 169, 180, 217, 223, 228, 230, 240
Hīnayāna, 4, 5
Hindus, 10, 42

icon-painter, 124, 241
impermanence, 14, 45, 66, 149
Indrabhūti, 150–152, 227, 250, 275, 287, 301
Indrapāla, King, 121, 236ff
initiation, 9, 16, 53, 97, 105, 137, 154, 159, 164, 173, 200, 202, 212, 219, 237, 243
inherent nature, 116, 132, 219

Jālandharapa, 66, 67, 81, 82, 161–162, 276, 285, 287, 302
Jalendra, King, 150, 151, 251, 252
Jayānanda, 191–192, 279, 287, 304
Jintapura, 122, 237
Jomanaśrī, 203

Kabina, King, 61–62
Kahora, 75, 76
Kalakala, 214–215, 280, 288, 304
Kalapa, 110–111, 272, 286, 299
*kalyāṇa-mitra*, 16
Kāmarūpa, 163, 165, 396
Kambala, 15, 117–120, 139, 273, 286, 287, 288, 300
Kaṃparipa, 10, 16, 158–160, 276, 287, 302
Kanakalā, 21, 211–213, 288, 304
Kanasati, 29
Kañci, 75, 99, 227
Kāṇhapa (Kṛṣṇācāri), 81–85, 212–213, 270, 285, 288, 295, 393
Kaṅkana, 14, 114–116, 273, 286, 299
Kankarāma, 117
Kankaripa, 12, 44–46, 268, 285, 292
Kantali, 15, 216–217, 280, 288, 304
Kapalapa, 12, 222–223, 281, 288, 305
Kapilaśakru, 128
karma, 10, 26, 31, 48, 49, 53, 85, 90, 131–132, 164, 185, 197, 210, 212
Karṇaripa (Āryadeva), 86–89, 221, 263, 270, 285, 288, 297, 393
Kausāmbī, 126
Khaḍgapa, 72–74, 269, 285, 293
Khandipa (Dhukhandi), 106–107, 272, 286, 299
killing, 28, 37ff, 148–149, 185

Kirava, 224–226, 281, 288, 305
Kokalipa, 244–246, 282, 288, 306
Koṭali (Togcepa), 155–157, 276, 287, 302
Kṛṣṇācāri (Kāṇhapa), 81, 124–125, 223, 286, 288
Kṣatriya, 104, 141, 145
Kucipa, 12, 17, 131–133, 274, 286, 300
Kukkuripa, 128–130, 209, 274, 286, 288, 300, 393
Kumaripa, 203–204, 279, 287, 304
Kunci, King, 21, 238

Lakṣmīnkarā, 151, 250–253, 283, 288, 306
*lalanā*, 159, 183, 297
Laṅkāpura, 150, 251
Līlapa, 14, 25–26, 265, 285, 289
Lucika, 186–187, 278, 287, 303
Lumbinī, 129
Lūyipa, 15, 21, 22–24, 121–123, 237–239, 265, 285, 286, 288, 289
Lvapa, *see* Kambala
lying, 91

Mādhyamika, 4, 17
Magadha, 33ff, 61, 72–74, 136, 137, 205
Maghahura, 44, 46
magical powers, 6ff, 38ff, 84
Mahādeva, 47, 48, 173
Mahāmudrā, 6, 26, 39, 43, 53, 58, 63, 64, 71, 97, 99, 101, 105, 107, 109, 113, 118, 125, 127, 133, 135, 140, 144, 149, 152, 160, 162, 165, 181, 183, 185, 190, 213, 215, 217, 392
Mahāyāna, 4, 5, 15, 16, 61, 104, 239
Mahipa, 136–137, 274, 286, 300
Maitreya, 40, 80, 207, 287
Malakimkarā, 21
Malapura, 119
mandala, 38, 39, 105
Maṇibhadrā, 21, 208–210, 280, 288, 304
Maṇidharā, 216
Mañjuśrī, 77, 87, 146–147, 286, 287
mantras, 30, 146, 229, 397
Medhina, 170–171, 277, 287, 302
meditation, 5, 8, 31, 38, 43, 45, 53, 58, 70, 91, 107, 109, 127, 137, 144, 156, 164, 171, 215, 225, 234, 248
Mekhalā, 21, 211–213, 280, 288, 304
Mekopa, 153–154, 276, 287, 302
Meru, Mt., 120, 228, 232
Mīnapa, 45–49, 268, 285, 292
mind, nature of the, 154, 167, 202, 235, 246, 248
monks, 28, 81, 118, 146, 174, 394

*nāḍis*, 142, 395, 397
Nāgabodhi, 80, 233–235, 282, 288, 305, 393
Nāgārjuna, 4, 5, 9, 14, 17, 75–80, 87–89, 132–133, 173, 233–235, 258, 263, 269, 270, 285, 286, 287, 288, 293, 393, 397
Nālandā, 61, 76, 86, 145–146, 149, 174

Nalina, 143–144, 275, 286, 301
Nāropa, 93–95, 99, 264, 270, 286, 298
Niguṇa, 188–189, 278, 287, 303
nirvana, 40, 66, 143, 154
non-duality, 45, 123, 154, 159, 164

Odantapurī, 61, 180
Odissa, 122
old age, 66–67, 164, 166, 237
oral transmission, 3

Pacari, 193–195, 279, 287, 304
*padmaṇi*, 34
pain, 132, 218–219
Pāla dynasty, 2
Panaha, 242–243, 282, 288, 306
Paṅkaja, 172–173, 277, 287, 303
Perfecting Stage, 26, 107, 111, 113, 132, 139, 162, 169, 171, 181, 187, 197, 202, 204, 209, 212, 217, 223, 225, 230, 253, 392, 395
*prāṇa*, 142
pride, 82, 85, 115
Pūrvadeśa, 188
Putali, 240–241, 282, 288, 306

Rāhula, 12, 163–165, 276, 287, 302
Rājagṛha, 61, 76
Rājapuri, 110, 222
Rāmanapolaka, King, 62
Rāmaneśvara, 23, 62, 155
*rasanā*, 159, 183, 397
Ratnākaraśānti, *see* Śāntipa
*ṛddi*, 7, 8

Sakara, 227–230, 281, 288, 305
Śalabhaṇḍa, King, 78–79
Saliputra, 23, 93, 121, 143, 158, 159, 168, 170, 175, 178, 199, 201, 236
*samādhi*, 26, 113
*Sāmañña-phala-sutta*, 8
Sambola, 150, 151, 250
samsara, 13, 31, 45, 73, 88, 92, 97, 115, 143, 154, 179, 183, 243, 248
Samudra, 254–255, 283, 288, 306
Sandhonāgara, 65, 101, 242
Śāntideva, 5, 145–149, 232, 275
Śāntipa, 60–64, 155–156, 263, 269, 285, 287, 292, 396
Saraha, 41–43, 232, 267, 285, 288, 291, 395
Śariputra, 15
Saroruha (Sakara), 229–230
Sarvabhakṣa, 231–232, 281, 288, 305
Sarvatira, 254
Śavaripa, 37–40, 180, 267, 285, 287, 290
Shalipa, 96–99, 271, 286, 299
Siṇhāla, 155
Śītavana, 76
Śiva, 29, 30, 31, 32, 62, 285, 393
Six Perfections, 17
sleep, 182–183
Somapurī, 27, 29, 31, 81, 84
Śravasti, 124
Śrīdhana, 228, 229
Śrīparvata, 77, 78, 85, 230, 235, 397
suffering, 13, 45, 189, 217, 252
Sūtras, 146–147
Suvarna, 233

Tandhepa, 12, 126–127, 274, 286, 300
Tantipa, 12, 65–68, 269, 285, 293
Tārā, 75, 285
Telopa, 201–202, 279, 287, 304
Ṭeṅgipa, 24, 121–123, 273, 286, 300
Thaganapa, 90–92, 270, 285, 298
Tilopa, 94–95, 98–99, 271, 286, 299
Togcepa (Koṭali), 62–64, 155–157, 276, 285
*torma*, 192, 229
Tṛipura, 27
truth, 55

Uḍḍiyāna, 119, 150, 250
Udheli, 220–221, 281, 288, 305
Umā, 48, 148

Vajradhara, 16, 198
Vajrapāda, 49
Vajravārāhi, 28, 95, 178, 212, 253, 285, 395
Vajrayāna, 3, 5, 9, 15, 16, 18
Vedas, 123
Vighāsura, 96
Vikrama, 37
Vikramasīla, 60ff
*Vimalakīrti-nirdeśa-sūtra*, 15
Vīnapa, 57–59, 269, 285, 292
Vinaya, 31
Virūpa, 8, 27–32, 33, 265, 285, 289
Viṣṇunagara, 69–71, 93, 94, 114
visualization, 159
Viśvakarman, 71, 125, 396
Vyali, 256–258, 283, 288, 306

wisdom (*prajñā*), 3, 4, 5
witches, 30–31, 119–120, 396
women, 15

yoga, 8, 262
Yogācāra, 4, 17
Yogipa, 180–181, 278, 287, 303